My Royal Navy Letters

My Royal Navy Letters

Through Calm and Troubled Waters

John Nixon

First edition, published in 2013

Pinewood Hill

York
www.pinewoodhill.co.uk

© Copyright John Nixon, 2013

Edited by Carol Nixon

ISBN 978-0-9926788-0-7

Printed in the United Kingdom by

Charlesworth Press

Flanshaw Way, Flanshaw Lane, Wakefield, WF2 9LP.

Images front cover: John Nixon as a boy entrant, HMS *Ganges*, 1968; Lieutenant John Nixon, HMS *Collingwood*, 1989; two combined images of HMS *Bulwark* in 1970.

Image for back cover: 320 and 321 classes as Drake Division guard, HMS *Ganges*, 1968.

Contents

FOREWORD 6

PHOTOS AND IMAGES 7

I - JOINING THE ROYAL NAVY [1968] 9

II - HMS *GANGES* [1968-69] 16

III - HMS *COLLINGWOOD* [1969-70] 33

IV - HMS *BULWARK* [1970-72] 42

V - HMS *COLLINGWOOD* & HMS *MAURITIUS* [1972-75] 95

VI - HMS *COLLINGWOOD* & HMS *FALMOUTH* [1975-1979] 130

VII - HMS *KENT* & HMS *FALMOUTH* [1979-82] 155

VIII - COMMISSIONED OFFICER [1983-92] 177

IX - LESSONS AND REFLECTIONS 198

BIBLIOGRAPHY 206

ABBREVIATIONS OF RN LETTERS 208

Foreword

It is probably true that those who choose to write an autobiography do so in order to offer some enlightenment and lessons to others, as well as recollecting major events in their lives. The principal driving force behind this desire is likely to be a burning desire to 'tell their story' regarding some particular aspects of their lives that continue to attract so much of their inner thoughts. Writing one's life story down for posterity can be therapeutic as the writer can attempt to analyse and make sense of his/her life with the wisdom of hindsight, and without the frantic 'stimulus-response' pressures they were previously under.

The motivation for writing this book involves many complex reasons and influences, which include the social aspects of my childhood in colonial Africa and a disrupted education on returning to England. These contributed to the decision for me to join the Royal Navy at the vulnerable age of 15 at HMS *Ganges*. This was the springboard to a 24-year career that contained many opportunities and challenges, not only within the Royal Navy itself but within my family.

My choice of title stems from two influences. Much of the material I have used is based on the letters I wrote home to my parents, and the term 'letters' is associated with academic achievement and status. In this regard I have my parents to thank for keeping safe the scores of letters I wrote home as they have ensured the accuracy of my recollections, and for encouraging me to make progress throughout my career. As the sub-title suggests, however, it was not all plain sailing. Because of the large number of acronyms associated with the Royal Navy, I have compiled a list of abbreviations at the end to assist the reader.

In compiling this book I have naturally mentioned many people who have shared phases of my life, or remain part of it. As such I have been aware of the possibility of mentioning issues or events that have a degree of sensitivity attached to them. To address this point I have either preserved the anonymity of individuals when describing such situations, or expressed issues raised by them in a general (but sufficiently clear) way for the reader to appreciate the point being addressed. In each chapter I have also mentioned or quoted from some of the music that influenced me emotionally or philosophically. This will assist the reader in identifying particular periods and artists between 1968 and 1992. I have done this because music has always been an important aspect of my life from an early age and inspired me to learn to play the guitar. Both listening to music and playing the guitar were sources of entertainment and comfort throughout my career. Music has also been a means of bringing me into contact with many highly talented and like-minded people.

Finally, I have attempted to illustrate that the lessons of my story are relevant to people in other walks of life as many of the challenges human beings face have common manifestations. However, there are clearly some pressures that are exclusive to people who serve their country in the military. I am sure many serving and former members of the Royal Navy will find some commonality with their own experiences in the chapters of this this book. In the final chapter, however, I address some of the sociological and psychological aspects of my experiences in order to learn lessons and broaden interest to people in other walks of life.

Joining the Royal Navy with no educational qualifications inspired me to advance myself both professionally and academically. Although many people encouraged and inspired me along this journey, I particularly acknowledge my class instructor at HMS *Ganges*, Chief Petty Officer Gordon Jones. I also acknowledge and thank family members who gave their personal help and time in the writing of this book, and those who both helped and served with me: Malcolm Allard, Kevin Calvert, Roy Brooks, Gerald Taylor, Michael Ross, Terry Rice, Peter Slynn, Paul Hankins and Michael Rose.

Photos and Images

Photo 1 - Willowgarth High School Rugby Team, 1966...11
Photo 2 - Willowgarth High School Netball Team, 1968...12
Photo 3 - Travel Warrant from Barnsley to Ipswich 13
Photo 4 - The early days at *Ganges* rowing on the river..20
Photo 5 - Letter heading on HMS *Ganges* writing paper 23
Photo 6 - 17 Mess after inspection with PO Allard and CPO Jones 24
Photo 7 - Captain Napper inspecting 320/321 classes on parade 25
Photo 8 - Stuart Ostler in our famous *Ganges* sports rig 26
Photo 9 - A seven-legged race on one of our 'fun days'...26
Photo 10 - Roy Brooks, JN & Pete Kerley (No.1 uniform explained) 27
Photo 11 - *Ganges* 48-strong ceremonial guard march past.......................................30
Photo 12 - Drake Guard performing the General Salute 31
Photo 13 - HMS *Ganges* soccer colours with motto 'wisdom is strength' 31
Photo 14 - *Temeraire* Division Cock Trophy winners, HMS *Collingwood*....................35
Photo 15 - Temeraire Division football team, HMS Collingwood................................36
Photo 16 - My family during a visit to *Collingwood* in 1969..37
Photo 17 - HMS *Bulwark* (22,000 tonnes) in 1970 43
Photo 18 - *Bulwark* alongside in Gibraltar, 1970 49
Photo 19 - Hands to bathe en route to Cape Town 52
Photo 20 - Arrival in Cape Town..53
Photo 21 - JN and Roy ashore..53
Photo 22 - Barbara, John, Valerie with dogs Trixie and Penny in Rhodesia 55
Photo 23 - *Bulwark* in rough seas after Cape Town 55
Photo 24 - *Bulwark's* 1st XI football team at HMS *Terror*, Singapore........................58
Photo 25 - Photograph of Carol I received in Singapore...60
Photo 26 - Royal Navy Far East Radio Electrical Branch badge.................................62
Photo 27 - My 'enhanced' portrait taken in Singapore for Carol 62
Photo 28 - *Bulwark's* Weapons Electrical branch in tropical uniform..........................66
Photo 29 - Post card of Hong Kong Harbour, 1970...66
Photo 30 - HMS *Bulwark's* grand arrival in Kobe, Japan..67
Photo 31 - Tower at Expo 70..68
Photo 32 - Japanese visitors, Kobe..68
Photo 33 - *Bulwark* in the setting sun of the South China Sea 70
Photo 34 - *Bulwark* arriving in Freemantle, Australia 74
Photo 35 - *Bulwark's* procedure alpha and sad departure from Freemantle................75
Photo 36 - Family photo with Carol after returning from the Far East........................77
Photo 37 - The civic hall in Stockholm..79
Photo 38 - Carol and John at their wedding 80
Photo 39 - The family photo at the wedding of John and Carol 81
Photo 40 - Catalan Bay, Gibraltar in July, 1971...84
Photo 41 - The first photo I received of my daughter, Lisa...86
Photo 42 - With daughter, Lisa, Christmas 1971..89
Photo 43 - *Bulwark* in Grand Harbour, Malta during Operation Exit 91
Photo 44 - *Bulwark* departing Malta for our final voyage back to the UK 93
Photo 45 - Carol and Lisa at Stokes Bay after moving south.......................................97
Photo 46 - Lisa and new puppy in the front garden 102
Photo 47 - The victorious Bigara swimming team..105

Photo 48 - The spirit of Mauritius, November 1973...107
Photo 49 - Carol, Lisa and Philip at Chaland...109
Photo 50 - Philip outside on a sunny Mauritius day 109
Photo 51 - HMS *Mauritius* first XI football team..111
Photo 52 - HMS *Mauritius* first XV rugby team 111
Photo 53 - Sister Barbara (left) recovering in hospital, 1974...........................113
Photo 54 - POREL Tony Lewis and JN ready for divisions................................114
Photo 55 - Admiral Lewin visiting the Comcen 115
Photo 56 - Meeting the Secretary of State for Defence, Roy Mason..................116
Photo 57 - the Day Watch Team and the Dalek they built 116
Photo 58 - Lisa and Philip welcoming home their new baby brother 122
Photo 59 - The R.M.S. *Windsor Castle* alongside in Durban..........................124
Photo 60 - Lisa, John and Philip at the southern tip of Africa 125
Photo 61 - The sea voyage in R.M.S. *Windsor Castle* 126
Photo 62 - Czech and Czech Mate 127
Photo 63 - Little Red Riding Hood and a reluctant Robin Hood 128
Photo 64 - Our arrival in Southampton docks in late July, 1975.....................129
Photo 65 - Fred with Christopher 129
Photo 66 - Peg with Christopher 129
Photo 67 - Carol, children and our Hillman Imp in the Forest of Bere............133
Photo 68 - Lisa, Christopher and Philip in Elsfred Road, Hill Head................136
Photo 69 - The Type 12 Frigate, HMS *Falmouth* 138
Photo 70 - Family portrait taken while at Elsfred Road in 1979 149
Photo 71 - Ward life at RNH Haslar..151
Photo 72 - Guided Missile Destroyer HMS *Kent* leaving Singapore 156
Photo 73 - The Radar and Radio Section, HMS *Kent,* 1980 159
Photo 74 - Meeting the Duchess of Kent in HMS *Kent*, 1980 166
Photo 75 - HMS *Kent* passing under London Bridge, 1980..............................166
Photo 76 - HMS *Hermes* returning from the Falklands on 21st July 1982.......174
Photo 77 - London Marathon completion & medal...180
Photo 78 - Royal Naval College Greenwich as a Sub Lieutenant, 1983...........182
Photo 79 - Carol and John (Instructor Lieutenant) 189
Photo 80 - Teaching microprocessors to artificer apprentices..........................192
Photo 81 - Teaching staff at Parsons Block, HMS *Sultan*, 1988 193
Photo 82 - With Carol, Lisa & Lt. John Cockcroft, HMS *Collingwood*, 1991............195
Photo 83 - Graduation of Christopher from Bath University, 1994....................197

Figure 1 - Career path possibilities and issues/timings 82

I - Joining the Royal Navy [1968]

It was 8.00 am on the 21st May, 1968, as I walked out of the back door of our terraced family home in Brierley, South Yorkshire, and onto the back street in the early morning sunshine to meet Uncle Bernard. He had agreed to drive me to the railway station at Barnsley, from where I would commence my train journey that day. Through the open door of our home I could hear my favourite song of that Hippie era in the voice and words of Scott McKenzie (Phillips, 1967) playing on the radio:

If you're going to San Francisco/ Be sure to wear some flowers in your hair
If you're going to San Francisco/ You're gonna meet some gentle people there

My father, Alan, paced around next to the car looking pensive and a little serious as he perhaps now grasped the fact that his 15 year-old son, dressed in a suit and tie, was leaving home to join the Royal Navy. We wouldn't get to see our local football team, Rotherham United, play as often as we did while I was going to school and living at home, or play tennis, cricket and football together in the village park as we often did. My mother, Veronica, in her normal motherly and caring manner, brought out some other items for the journey that would take me to Ipswich in Suffolk by the end of the afternoon. She fussed around a little, as she often did, which was perhaps her way of dealing with the fact that I was leaving home at such a young age to face the world and a career in the armed services. She was naturally concerned for my welfare and a little apprehensive. My parents and I had made the decision for me to join the Navy rather than staying on at school to complete my formal qualifications, but the full implications of that decision now became more apparent to all of us.

The sense of departure and potential 'severance' increased as my 17-year old sister, Valerie, and younger 10-year old sister, Barbara, came out to say good-bye. Valerie was carrying our younger brother, David, who was only eight months old. With a mixture of excitement about the uncertainty and challenges that lay ahead, and the wrenching feeling people experience when saying farewell to a close-knit family, as we were, Uncle Bernard drove the car to the end of the street amid hand waves and farewells, turned left, and headed for Barnsley station some eight miles away. At the end of the street at the opposite side I got a brief glimpse of Mr Nun's farm where I had worked as his assistant for six enjoyable months between me leaving school and joining the Navy. Life in the village would go on in its familiar manner even though I would only visit it infrequently from now on. As we drove through the mining villages of South Yorkshire towards our destination, with me receiving encouragement and advice from Uncle Bernard, who had been a Merchant seaman, I reflected on the reasons I had decided to join the Navy and leave the area.

I had been born in the village of Hemsworth, only a few miles from our home in Brierley but my parents had emigrated to Southern Rhodesia in the 1950s when I was three years old. This was a period of British colonialism and although only modestly wealthy there we had enjoyed a healthy outdoor lifestyle, employed a maid and a gardener so that my parents could both work, and lived in a comfortable white-washed bungalow in the pleasant suburb of Braeside in the capital city, Salisbury (as it was then). We returned to England in 1963 and resumed our life, rather traumatically for most of the family, in the industrial north. I say *traumatically* because we spent more than six months living with various relatives in sometimes trying circumstances, separated from my father who remained in Rhodesia for some months before joining us. Once I had reached school-leaving age it became clear to me and my parents that my opportunities were limited in the local area, and also relevant was the fact that I had probably inherited my parents' adventuring tendencies.

With four children and a two-bedroomed home, there were also 'crowding' issues for my parents to deal with, although this was not a reason to leave home as we managed the situation as many other larger families did in that area. More importantly, at the meeting I had with the school careers advisor, I had been told that I could either become a miner or perhaps work on a fishing trawler at Hull or Grimsby. A job in engineering was also another option, but none of these had appealed to me and like some people born into that environment, there was a strong drive inside me to get away and do something 'different' with my life, as my father and quite a number of his relatives had done in their lives. Although I finished school at Willowgarth High in the top academic form, I had been disadvantaged somewhat in my educational development by the move from Rhodesia to England, and my elder sister, Valerie, was adversely affected much more so than me. Arriving back at the age of eleven, children in the two junior schools I attended in Hemsworth (St. Helen's) and then Brierley (St. Paul's), had been studying and revising for their eleven-plus exam, a test that would determine if they went to a grammar or secondary modern school. In Rhodesia, I had attended Nettleton junior, a prestigious school in Braeside, Salisbury (now Harare), that was founded on the legacy of Squadron Leader John Dering Nettleton of 44 (Southern Rhodesian) Squadron of the Royal Air Force in World War II. Nettleton was the only Rhodesian recipient of the Victoria Cross (the highest honour for bravery awarded by the British Government). Despite the significance of Nettleton's acknowledged bravery in defending democracy and fighting Fascism, the government of Zimbabwe changed the name of my former school, amongst many others, after Rhodesia became Zimbabwe. The school is now named after Tsitsi Munyati, a former Zimbabwean minister of education.

Like other white children in Rhodesia, if the colonial government of Rhodesia had continued I would have proceeded to a high school similar to the American system of education and remain there until I was eighteen or more with no 'division' into a two-tier system at the age of eleven, as was the case in England. Although I had always thought I was doing well at school in Rhodesia, and was in form 4A before I left, the reports my mother kept from that time indicated I was somewhat of a laggard as in the final report I came 19th out of 24 children in our class assessment. My form teacher had written that I would 'have to work hard to produce better results,' and that I was 'a quiet, polite and pleasant member of the class.' However, my headmaster, who didn't mince his words and had given me the corporal punishment of a beating on the backside with a leather belt, wrote (dated mid-year, 1963):

There is absolutely no excuse for such weakness. Wake up John and show us what you can do!

It would be some time before I did wake up, but, perhaps as a 'late developer' I would need a good reason to do so as my main focus was on sport and I had been picked to play football for Nettleton under my favourite teacher, a wily Scot named Mr MacKay, who taught us tactics as well as skills.

Because of being a 'foreigner' - the kid from Africa - in the eyes of some of the children in Hemsworth, I had several offers from boys to fight them and ended up with the odd bloody nose, even though I actually won the fights I was to take part in. I had done judo as a child in Africa, which helped me to defend myself in what, to me, were senseless 'tribal' rituals. However, once I had gone through this initiation process I won many good friends and some admirers due to my 'differences,' such as a Rhodesian accent and my sporting abilities. Rather unsurprisingly then, I failed my eleven-plus exam and ended up in one of the lowest streams of the first year at Willowgarth High School. However, I progressed up through the forms each year to reach '4:1' (fourth year, first grade) and made reasonable academic progress, albeit within a tier of schooling that was preparing its pupils for a career in industry and the service sector rather than the professions, as was the expectation in the grammar schools. To reflect this, the qualification I was studying for in various subjects was the Certificate of Secondary Education (C.S.E.), while pupils at the local grammar school in Hemsworth were studying for the General Certificate in Education (G.C.E.). Nowadays in England, of course, these qualifications have been combined into the General Certificate in Secondary Education (G.C.S.E.) and the term 'Secondary Modern' removed from the description of schools.

Whilst my academic achievements were terminated early through leaving school at the age of 15 before taking my C.S.E.s, I did fortunately excel at most sports and had represented my school or the district - comprising seven schools in the area - at football, rugby, athletics, and badminton, and was also the district cross-country champion and swimming champion. Indeed, through these sports and my life at school I had many very good friends and we actually achieved high standards in many aspects of our education. My closest friends were Leslie Foster, John North, Peter Waring, Steven Millthorpe and Paul Davison. John North, of a fairly quiet and modest disposition, was the captain of the football and rugby teams and an exceptionally skilful and intelligent player. Leslie Foster and I played alongside each other on the football and rugby fields – he played inside centre and I was outside centre in the rugby team and we were also badminton doubles partners. We therefore spent a lot of our time discussing tactics and making plans together. We were also fortunate to have an excellent P.E. and Science Teacher in Mr (Ron) Wilby, who really nurtured our talents and taught us how to play with style. Mr Wilby usually wrote good reports about me but this changed somewhat in my final year. This was because he had seemingly questioned my personal commitment by giving me a '2 minus' for games and writing (10th April, 1968):

Although he has outstanding ability, his attitude has not always been admirable this year

Photo 1 - Willowgarth High School Rugby Team, 1966

*Leslie Foster 4th, JN 5th, John North 6th, Steven Millthorpe 7th from left back row; Peter Waring 5th and Paul Davison 6th from left front row. **Source:** author*

[11]

When I read this I felt he had misunderstood my actions at times, which on my part were usually due to fatigue as I started my day doing a paper round in the village from 6.00-7.30 am, and represented the school in seven sports. My 'failings' were therefore not due to a lack of interest in the Saturday-morning rugby games, for example, I occasionally missed. However, I was aware of the fact that I did treat some situations with indifference for inexplicable reasons – a trait that would emerge more and receive some disapproval from those close to me as my life progressed. In that sense, Mr Wilby had been accurate in his appraisal of me.

Because of my sporting involvement with the school, the close group of friends I belonged to were very well known among the other children in the school. One of us was always being called onto the stage at morning assemblies to receive a prize or cup, or recognition for scoring a hatrick in a football match. I especially remember Leslie Foster was the first to get such an accolade, in the first year, which he claims today adversely affected his future playing career as he was so scared by the sudden 'exposure' and fame at assembly. We also had our names chanted regularly by other classmates and pupils when we were playing for the school. Consequently we spent a lot of time out of lessons and this meant my educational attainment wasn't as high as it might have been, although I did enjoy school very much and became a prefect/pupil councillor, and was made house captain for 'Ferrymoor.' I remain especially proud of the fact that many younger pupils in the school would often come to me and my close friends when they needed help when someone was bullying them, and fortunately we were strong enough to deal with the bullies and offer some protection to the younger children.

The girls in my class were also very important to me as friends and we had a close relationship within a mixed group. The netball team below shows many of them that I was closest too with one of our most popular teachers (for girls and boys).

Photo 2 - Willowgarth High School Netball Team, 1968

Back row left to right: Anne Clarkson, Annice Cooper, Mrs White, Barbara Bates, Carol Cummings.
Front row left to right: Christine Harper, Audrey Binney, Sylvia Kavanagh, Margaret Smith.
Source: *Annice Marshall (née Cooper)*

Presently, Uncle Bernard and I arrived in Barnsley, and the railway station, I could see, was just a few minutes away. After unloading my suitcase I said my good-byes to Uncle Bernard, who shook my hand, accompanied by that wide and encouraging smile he always wore, and wished me well. I showed the rail staff my Navy travel warrant for the journey from Barnsley to Ipswich, via Sheffield and London, and was issued with my ticket. After waiting for ten minutes on the platform my steam-driven train pulled in. As it was a fairly quiet period I boarded the train and managed to find a quiet compartment. Travel in those days was a much more luxurious and 'cultural' affair as the compartments had wide and comfortable seats, it was possible to open windows, which had curtains, and each passenger had a reading light above their seat. With only a couple of people in my compartment I settled down for the trip. At many towns around the country, hundreds of 15-year old boys like me were doing the same thing with the common destination of HMS *Ganges* in Shotley Gate, Ipswich.

I glanced at the travel warrant and noted it was signed by the regional recruiting officer I had seen in Barnsley. I reflected that the Navy had, in a sense, been my second choice similar to that of my father's, who was a member of the Royal Army Medical Corps (RAMC) during World War II (Nixon & Smith, 2006). Like him, my first choice had been the Royal Air Force (RAF) as I had been a member of the Air Training Corps (ATC), Barnsley 150 Squadron, since the age of 13 and had enjoyed it very much – attending weekly meetings at our own drill centre and visiting RAF flying establishments at Church Fenton and Finningley, where I had flown gliders and Chipmunk light aircraft.

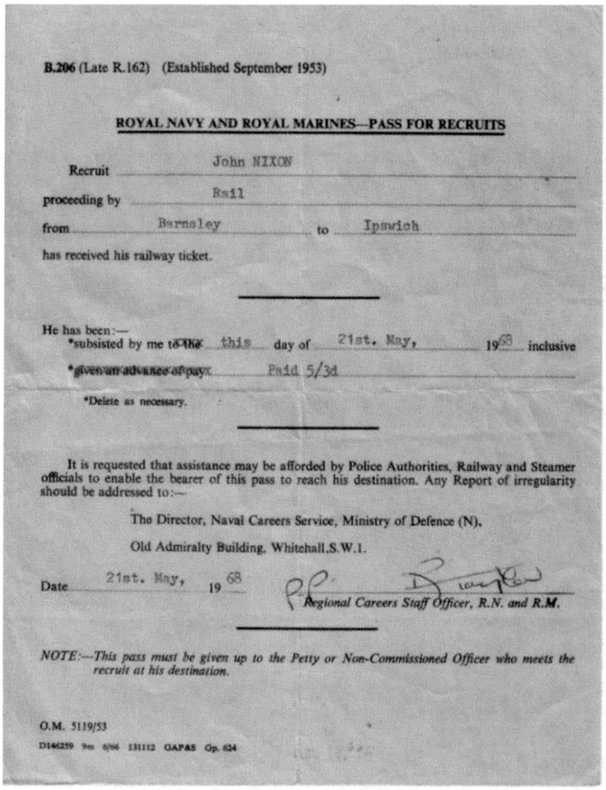
B.206 (Late R.162) (Established September 1953)

ROYAL NAVY AND ROYAL MARINES—PASS FOR RECRUITS

Recruit John NIXON

proceeding by Rail

from Barnsley to Ipswich

has received his railway ticket.

He has been:—

*subsisted by me to ~~the~~ this day of 21st. May, 1968 inclusive

*~~given an advance of pay~~ Paid 5/3d

*Delete as necessary.

It is requested that assistance may be afforded by Police Authorities, Railway and Steamer officials to enable the bearer of this pass to reach his destination. Any Report of irregularity should be addressed to:—

The Director, Naval Careers Service, Ministry of Defence (N),

Old Admiralty Building, Whitehall, S.W.1.

Date 21st. May, 1968

Regional Careers Staff Officer, R.N. and R.M.

NOTE:—This pass must be given up to the Petty or Non-Commissioned Officer who meets the recruit at his destination.

O.M. 5119/53

D146259 9m 6/66 131112 GAP&S Op. 624

Photo 3 - Travel Warrant from Barnsley to Ipswich

Source: *author*

I remembered that I had visited the RAF recruiting office in Sheffield when I was coming up to school-leaving age and had had an interview with the recruiters there. They were interested in me applying to join the RAF but indicated that I should complete my C.S.E.s and come back to see them later when I was 16 years old. This was a bit of a disappointment but I guess what they were telling me made perfect sense and it was not a rejection *per se*, as I may have interpreted it. Perhaps this was a significant event in my life, although I did not strongly interpret it as such at the time.

A few weeks later I had sent a newspaper application off for some Royal Navy recruiting pamphlets, from which I learned about the Boys' Service and in particular the famous training establishments of HMS *Ganges* and HMS *St. Vincent*. The pictures of young recruits drilling in their uniforms with gaiters and boots, the many sports they did, and Royal Navy warships exercising at sea, all stirred up my interest and I decided to apply to join. I sensed that life in the Navy would be tougher and more of a challenge than the RAF, but like many young boys I was tempted by the challenges of becoming a member of a famous institution like the Royal Navy with all its rich history. Sitting there pondering on these issues, I recalled the reaction of my instructor at the ATC in Barnsley, as he had been rather shocked about my decision to join the Navy and not wait for the RAF. I would later recall that he had given me a warning that life in the Royal Navy, especially at sea, could be extremely harsh, and that discipline was much more severe than in the RAF. In contrast, the RAF was the junior service and at that time had only been in existence for about 50 years. As such it had a much more contemporary approach to matters of discipline. Despite these warnings and the respect I had for my RAF instructor, I had ploughed forward with my application to join the Navy, which was a relatively smooth and uncomplicated experience, eventually resulting in me being selected by the Weapons Electrical Branch and for boys training at HMS *Ganges* where I would join as a Junior Electrical Mechanic second class (JEM2).

1968 was the time when the Beatles and Rolling Stones were at the peaks of their musical careers and most teenagers like me had a Beatles-style haircut. However, in the previous week I had been to the barber I always used in the village of Shafton. The barber himself, on hearing I was just about to join the Navy said, "Right then, it's a short back and sides for you, young man." Sitting now in the compartment with the other passengers I could almost sense that they knew I was off to join the Services due to my smart appearance for a teenager, short hair, and the suitcase plus other bags I had with me.

After about an hour, the train pulled into Sheffield station, my first change. My instructions were to report to the Royal Navy recruiting office in Castle Market at 9.00 am, where I would meet up with three other boys from South Yorkshire who were joining *Ganges* with me. When I arrived at the office I was greeted by the recruiting officer, and very quickly after this I met some of the other new recruits. They were all dressed in a similar manner to me, which probably helped ease the situation, and we quickly gained some comfort and support from each other as we clearly felt we were all in the same 'boat' together.

The first boy I spoke to was Kevin Calvert, who came from Doncaster. He was an immediately likeable person with a fairly quiet disposition and as I soon learned, had a good grasp of what lay ahead of us at *Ganges*. Kevin had clearly done his 'homework.' The second boy, Peter Kerley, from Wath-on-Derne, was much more outgoing and confident in nature and was already an established smoker, which made him appear more mature. His attitude seemed to be that "whatever they do to us we'll just have to get on with it and we can't be fairer than that, can we, lads?" Peter had the strongest Yorkshire accent among us and used a lot of 'thee' and 'thou' expressions, which was both amusing and homely to listen to. However, I suspected he also had some apprehension behind his confident exterior. As such 'Pete,' as we would call him in the future, seemed much more laid back about what we would experience in the Navy, whereas Kevin and I focussed on the details of our future life at *Ganges* and were trying to speculate about how best to cope. The third boy, called Bailey (I don't recall his first name), joined us and after a one-hour wait at the recruiting office we were escorted to the station and boarded the train for London Liverpool Street.

Finding our own compartment on the train, we chatted together and speculated about how we would settle into our new life. We already knew that some new recruits would not like Service life and everyone would have the option to leave after a few weeks, or at six months. Would we be in that group, we wondered, as we began expressing our hopes and determination to overcome the trials ahead of us. We were also aware of the fact that at *Ganges* our basic schooling would continue, which was important as we all recognised that we had left school at the earliest opportunity. However, integrated into subjects general subjects like Mathematics and English would be the other elements of our training such as naval history, parade ground drills, seamanship, sport, and our 'Part One' electrical training. If we passed all these hurdles successfully, we would proceed, after one year, to HMS *Collingwood*, which is the Royal Navy's Electrical Engineering School at Fareham in Hampshire. *Ganges*, we knew, would be more like 'boot camp' and *Collingwood* would be more 'cushy' and focus on our professional training. At this time, however, we did not consider what our lives would be like at *Collingwood* or at sea, only about surviving our first year at *Ganges*. The train journey to London took about four hours, during which time a sense of cohesion grew among us.

On our arrival in London we were met by another recruiting officer who had arranged transport across London to Liverpool Street station. When we arrived there, the number of boys that looked like us had grown to about one hundred. They had come from all over the country and the thing that struck me immediately was the number of different regional accents among us. Some came from the Midlands, others from the West Country towns of Plymouth and Bristol, and others from Scotland as well as several other areas of Britain. The train compartments were labelled alphabetically and a buzz of activity soon ensued as we all searched out our designated carriage and boarded the train with our luggage.

It seemed clear to me that there would be some sense of rivalry between our different sub-groups, and I considered, correctly as things later turned out, that this may continue through our training. 15 year-old boys, not unexpectedly, are competitive and partisan by nature. On the train to Ipswich the banter between groups became more noticeable, but I felt happy to be among those from Yorkshire as we had our own strong sense of identity and pride as young 'Yorkshire men.'

During the journey to Ipswich, the discussions among us became more focussed. We knew that the history of *Ganges* as a training establishment for boy sailors went back more than a century, and that training had originally started on de-commissioned sailing ships anchored along the river at Shotley-Gate; the setting for the present establishment. *Ganges* had, as its centre piece, a 143 foot mast which we would be required to climb as part of our training. After about a three-hour journey our train pulled into Ipswich station and we disembarked. At the end of the platform waiting for us were four Leading Regulators or Regulating Petty Officers (RPOs) who, we would soon find out, were the 'policemen,' for the want of a better description, of the Royal Navy and the principal enforcers of naval discipline.

We approached them in our groups with a good deal of apprehension, but I recall my spirits lifted as I fully realised that the long recruitment process of joining the Royal Navy and HMS *Ganges* was about to become reality. Although we had little idea of the particular demands, challenges and rewards that lay ahead, we had arrived.

II - HMS *Ganges* [1968-69]

The Regulators called out names, to which we were quickly told to respond, "Yes, Sir!" – we had perhaps thought that only commissioned officers were entitled to be called 'Sir' but at *Ganges*, as we were to find out, all instructors and Regulating staff were to be addressed in this manner. The first Royal Navy (white) logo I saw was on the side of the blue Bedford 'Pusser's' bus that was assigned to our group. Along with the other 'Yorkies' and additional new recruits we boarded this very functional machine and were soon on our way to the establishment, which was about ten miles out of Ipswich on the Shotley peninsula.

The first thing that struck me, once underway, was the deafening sound of the bus's engine, which was actually in the passenger area with us next to the driver, enclosed by a large leather casing. Having a conversation suddenly became a shouting match. I also noticed a strong smell of diesel fumes - combined with another quite unpleasant odour - that made me think of people suffering from travel sickness. We were also able to see how smartly dressed our Leading Regulator was, and I particularly noted his 'spit and polished' black shoes, the sharp vertical creases in his blue colour, and seven horizontal creases at the bottom of his trousers. We were later told that creases in trousers were ironed into naval ratings' uniforms as it had been tradition in Nelson's time for sailors to fold up their trousers neatly in order to scrub the decks, and seven was chosen because it represented the seven seas. As we exchanged chatter along these lines, we perhaps correctly anticipated that scrubbing and polishing decks was going to be a big part of our lives at *Ganges*.

At 4.30 pm we duly arrived at what we would come to know affectionately as 'Green Squadron,' which was officially known as the 'Annex' to the main establishment. As the bus entered the main gate, we noticed some young sailors in uniform who were controlling access. After mustering together in the small parade ground outside of each mess deck, we were assigned to our Chief Petty Officers (CPOs) and Junior Instructors (JIs). These were to be the people who would lead us through our first four weeks at *Ganges,* and teach us the basics of life in the camp and the Royal Navy. Although I sadly don't recall the name of my Chief, he was about 40 years old, rather portly in stature, with a patient and approachable demeanour about him. He wore a brown lab' coat with his peaked CPO's cap perched slightly to the right-side of his head. My JI, like all the other JIs, had completed his full year at *Ganges* and was therefore a year older than us, and his name was JI Patterson. He was slim, fairly tall and from his accent I could determine that he was from Scotland. Along with Kevin and Pete, I was assigned to *Tiger* Mess, and after some time we entered what was one of six corrugated-iron buildings, which comprised a large dormitory of about 30 beds in two neat, parallel rows. It had a large washroom, toilets, showers, drying/recreation rooms and a large cleaning-gear room. The Mess had a highly polished wooden-tiled floor, and the other rooms had polished floors and sparkling metal work - the smell of polish and 'cleanliness' was everywhere.

There was a lot of chatter among us as we weighed up our new surroundings when the Chief and JI allocated us to our beds and grey metal lockers, where we would keep all our belongings. We received our initial issue of kit as I explained in my first letter home the next day, which confirmed my approval of my new home and the new friendships I had started to strike up among my classmates.

The lads here are great. We don't quarrel at all and we are always joking. If it goes on like this I wouldn't come out if they paid me. We were issued with a lot of kit but get our main uniforms tomorrow ......we were given three pairs of dark blue working trousers, three light blue working shirts, three tee shirts with a square neck, three pairs of underpants and vests, two pairs of boots, two pairs of pumps and a pair of shoes, brushes, razors, a small attaché case, two caps and a load of other stuff.

As we soon discovered, our working clothes were called Number 8s and we also wore buff coloured gaiters above our boots. Having changed into our new kit we were given a brown paper parcel and told to put our civilian clothes (civvies) and other personal belongings into it for return to our homes the following day. I recall that my mother later said that she cried when they arrived back home, as she felt that she had lost her 'little lad.' This particular activity seemed to confirm my membership of the Royal Navy as the first and dominant master of my life from now on. This was affirmed more strongly when we all took part in a brief ceremony of swearing an oath to Queen and country. I recall an officer explaining this requirement and it seemed like the kind of thing we would be required to do, and all of us willingly complied.

The following morning we gathered outside our Mess in the quadrangle in our Number 8s and plimsolls for our initial drill sessions. JI Patterson, like all the JIs, was incredibly well turned out in terms of his uniform and general manner. I could not help but immediately admire him as the things he knew and could do at *Ganges* were those we would need to emulate. He had a very distinctive way of walking and marching - familiar to all former *Ganges* boys - that demonstrated and projected his confidence. There were also other small things that I noticed, such as the way he wore his cap lower on his forehead than the back of his head without it leaning to one side or the other, the neat bow tied on his black silk cap ribbon, the way his blue collar curled over his uniform and fluttered when in the breeze, the way he walked around with his hands clenched behind his back, and many other minor - but highly significant - details. The first order he taught us was how to come to attention, which took me a little by surprise as the command he used was, "Tiger Mess, *Ho!*" I was expecting him to use the command "Attention," which I was familiar with from my time in the Air Cadets, but as I was to discover there are many subtle differences in the way in which we drilled in the Royal Navy compared with either the RAF or the Army, and the use of the command "Ho!" was one of them. Other classes were being drilled around the quadrangle and we could hear the 'barking' sounds of the other JIs as they called out orders and explained and demonstrated all the drill moves in front of their classes. I also noticed very quickly that JI's did not accurately articulate the words 'left' and 'right' when calling out the step as their classes were marching around the quadrangle. Rather, they truncated these words to what became a familiar "aeft, aeft, aeft oit aeft!" pattern. We would practise several times each day from now on until we could perfect each drill procedure.

One of the most impressionable events on our first 'real day' in Green Squadron was the trip to the clothing store (or 'Slops' as it is known in the Navy) to receive our issue of kit. Under the instructions of our Chief, we formed an orderly queue in alphabetical order around the room, which had very wide serving surfaces so items of uniform could be laid out for inspection and sizing. I watched in some anticipation and impatience as my classmates ahead of me were shown a long list of items that were then brought out by the PO Stores Accountant (POSA) and his staff. We were measured for height, shoe size, waist measurement, neck size, inside leg length and head circumference. Some items were simply issued as they did not require any trying out but for our blue serge uniforms we were required to try them on to ensure they fit us properly. The SAs moved purposefully to and from huge racks and shelves piled up with uniforms and other items until the correct size was found. At this stage I recall I was size 9 in shoes/boots, five feet six inches tall, 32 inch waist, 28 inch inside leg and weighed in at just under ten stones – about average among the group.

As I waited for my turn, I got to know the person who would be my closest friend in Green Squadron - a tall, slim and friendly boy from Plymouth called Stuart (Ossie) Ostler. He had a warm and friendly sense of humour and getting to know him was reassuring for me as we would often walk to the dining room for meals together, take a pillow case of washing to the enormous self-manned laundry, and exchange ideas and thoughts on what we had to learn to do. As we moved slowly towards the front of the queue I registered the strong smell of moth balls (used to preserve serge uniforms), the highly-polished buff-coloured floor, and the smell of leather from mountains of boots and shoes on the racks. As I looked around the room I fixed my gaze on several black and white hanging pictures of destroyers ploughing through choppy seas, with their names inscribed on a brass plate below their frames. The combination of these sensory stimuli gave me the feeling that I was capturing some prominent elements of life in the Royal Navy. By the time I was attended to and issued with my uniform I was feeling a sense of commitment to my chosen cause. After trying on a few sizes, I walked off with my kit and 'Number Two' blue uniform, onto which we would sew our red badges (crossed lightning lines for the Electrical Branch). For our best uniform, 'Number Ones,' we sewed on gold badges and would only wear for ceremonial divisions or when out among the public. On other items we would sew blue and white badges.

Once back in the mess deck with all our issue placed on or around our beds, we very quickly began to be shown what would turn out to be pains-taking and highly detailed effort required to wear, care for, and present our kit. The phrase 'kit muster' would be something that we would hear regularly with some sense of dread in the coming months as it always involved judgement about how well we could formally present our kit and possibly involve punishment if we fell short of the expected high standards. We therefore spent many hours each day with our CPO and JI Patterson, gathered in the laundry or around an ironing board, learning how to press our uniform items to 'Ship's Book' size (a Blue Naval Rating's Manual that we all had a copy of), lay out our full kit on a blanket next to our beds, and make up our blankets and pillows in a neat pile each morning.

When the moment came to put on our Number One uniforms for the first time, we realised just how complicated it was to know what to do and get things right – our Chief and JI Patterson were constantly explaining, demonstrating and adjusting our uniforms to a level of precision that is difficult to fully describe here. However, this process was instrumental in forming friendships through comparisons and discussions about how to get it right. In the second letter I wrote home I described some aspects of our early life at *Ganges*:

Today for dinner we had cottage pie, mashed potatoes, carrots, peas and rhubarb pie and custard. On Wednesday all of us went to watch the European Cup final after an early supper. You go to bed here at 9.00 pm, lights out at 9.45 and you're up sharp at 6.10 am. We don't mind because we're all tired by 9.00. Anyway I'll sign off now as we've got to do our sewing.

Indeed, sewing and darning socks would become a major feature of our lives in looking after our kit. In the quadrangle each day we became more and more familiar with responding to commands such as: "At half-arm intervals, by the right dress," "Quick march," into line, right turn," "Mess halt - one still!" The 'one-still' indicated that we took one more step after the order before bringing the right heel into the heel of the left foot. We soon discovered, however, that everyone had a different aptitude for learning how to drill properly. In terms of marching, for example, we found that some boys had difficulty co-ordinating their arms and legs – marching is only 'smart walking' but some people simply tried too hard and their arms moved in the same direction as their legs, which we quickly learnt was known as 'tick-toking.' When JIs or our Senior Ratings (POs and CPOs) saw one of the trainees doing this it stimulated a barrage of loudly-shouted innuendos concerning the trainee's lack of co-ordination. What this taught me very quickly was that we were being intensely observed in every move we made and corrected or coached all the time. The contrast in styles of each 'leader' was also quite noticeable and was having a strong impression on me and others.

On the 1st June I wrote home explaining about the competitive aspect of life at *Ganges*. I recalled that we had drawn 4-4 with *Ashanti* Mess and that I had scored one goal and that 'we lost the cake by half a point.' The 'cake' was a weekly competition for best mess in Green Squadron. I also recorded that we were paid £3.30 per week but were advised to 'put something away in our credit book.' We were also told that when we went home on leave we would receive £17 plus an allowance for our keep, which I thought sounded very reasonable. In this letter I also related my first experience of leadership:

> *I was put in charge yesterday by the Chief P.O. because the J.I. wasn't here and I had to march them round to the lecture room. We are not allowed on shore leave until we have been here quite a while. We are off swimming tomorrow but we cannot go next week because we've got a whole lot of injections on Wednesday. We have a smart day tomorrow – we go to the cinema then have divisions with the Ganges Bugle Band, then sport all afternoon. I'm enjoying myself so you try (too).*

One of the most enjoyable recreational activities we did was to row on the river Stour – the correct naval term was 'pulling' rather than 'rowing' and we did this in a 'cutter' - not a 'rowing boat.' Learning the correct jargon, we quickly discovered, was important if we weren't to receive a dressing down from someone in authority. Learning to dress correctly in our main uniforms was indeed a lengthy and detailed task, which I outline in detail using the photo on page 27.

First of all, our trousers had to be pressed using a handkerchief to produce the seven razor-sharp horizontal lines and we wore a light blue canvas belt to support them. These also had a small money-pocket on the right-hand side of the buckle. Our socks were black - some others were also navy blue but these were not to be worn with Number Ones. Our shoes were spit-and-polished until the tips shone like glass, while the rest of the shoes were brushed using polish. Next we put on our 'white fronts,' which were white cotton Tee shirts with a square, blue-trimmed collar. The white front was pressed to have a vertical crease running exactly down the centre from the neck. The next step was to put on our blue collar, which had thin white lines at the edges. This was passed over our heads and secured around our white fronts by two white cloth ties that ran round our midriffs and tied in a bow at the front. We could now put on and zip up our uniform tunics but having done this we had to raise our blue and tunic collars to allow us to wrap our silks and lanyards around our necks. Silks were black and about one and a half inches across, and came to rest just below the level of the zips on our tunics. Just above this point were two black threads sewn into our tunics through which we passed a piece of black, tightly-knitted woollen tape about 12 inches in length and half an inch wide. At the ends of this tape we cut a neat 'V' shape, which had to be re-cut regularly as it tended to fray. To secure our silks to our tunics we had to tie a perfectly horizontal knot using the tape. This was quite a tricky manoeuvre as the knot had to follow a specific pattern in relation to the bow that was to follow. If we got this wrong the bow would be at an angle and be spotted by the Chief or an inspecting officer. Some boys took several weeks to learn how to tie a silk tape and we often struggled or had to ask someone else to do it before going on parade. Next came the lanyard, best be described as a thin white rope with a loop that went around the neck and a knot, which allowed only a single line of the lanyard to follow. The knot allowed the lanyard to be adjusted to exactly the right level – roughly half way between the top of the tunic's zip and the neck. Once the right level for the knot was achieved we then looped the single chord around the bottom section of the silk, formed it into a circle and then tucked it behind our silks and into our tunics. At the very end of the lanyard was a special knot to stop it from fraying or passing through the adjusting knot. We could now pull down both collars and adjust them to make sure everything was in its right place. Finally, our caps had a 'cap tally' with 'HMS Ganges' embossed on it in gold. The cap tally was black silk, which was pressed with an iron before tying it round the circumference of the cap using a neat bow, again horizontal and not at an angle. The bow for the cap tally was tied on the left-hand side of the cap when looking forward.

The photos of our classes in Number One uniforms that follow in this chapter show what the end result should look like. Today, various elements of traditional 'square rig' have been tailored into uniforms so the task of putting on uniforms is much simpler.

Photo 4 - The early days at *Ganges* rowing on the river

Tiger Mess, Green Squadron. JN front row (top photo with the watch on) **Source:** *author*

Days at *Ganges* were filled with activity. We were woken every morning at 06.10 by a bugle boy who sounded 'reveille' over the main broadcast - heard in every dormitory in the establishment. Within minutes the duty instructor arrived noisily in the Mess to hurry us out of bed in very sharp fashion - usually shouting and banging or shaking beds to ensure everyone was awake and on the move. There was usually a second visit to make sure people were up, or at the very least had one foot 'on the deck.' Having a 'lie in,' was to become a thing of the past for a very long time.

We started our days with early morning cleaning activities before breakfast – I remember polishing the cannons that were situated at the edge of the parade ground in the Annex with a messmate on many occasions. The daily rush to the bathroom for a wash and brush-up was always a hectic affair and meals were served in the Annex dining room. We always had a full English breakfast to enable us to get through all the marching, running and sporting exercise we participated in every day. The days ended at 9.00 pm with 'pipe down,' which was signalled by a ship's piper from the main gate. With 26 boys in each dormitory it could potentially be rowdy, so it was necessary for various duty people such as JIs, senior ratings and Regulators (affectionately known as 'bone heads') to walk through the mess decks with torches – often issuing threats of doubling (double marching) around the parade ground in pyjamas, oilskins and boots if people didn't keep silence or were running around and talking. On many occasions we did in fact experience this punishment to ensure we quietened down on our return. The mess decks had red lighting that came on at night time so people could move around safely and those in authority could observe if anything untoward was going on.

At this point I feel it would be beneficial to mention some issues concerning discipline and punishment in the Royal Navy, as one or two incidents remain quite prominent in my mind concerning this period of time. The first one occurred when we were on cleaning duties in our mess deck, which involved us getting into overalls and working in groups cleaning and polishing all areas of the Mess. The main activity involved polishing the wooden floors with wax polish using our boot brushes. It was normal for us to engage some banter or 'skylarking' - the Navy's commonly-used term for fooling around and not keeping to the task in hand. Whilst I don't recall the exact details of this incident, one boy was singled out for particular attention as he had given some back chat about being told not to smoke in a particular area that was off bounds to smoking. To cut a long story short he ended up being kicked in the groin in front of all of us by one of the JIs. The whole episode was rather distasteful and, in my opinion, a form of bullying and abuse of power.

The JI then pointed out that this was what would happen to anyone else among us who did not obey orders or argued with him, and he then invited any of us to come forward and take him on if we thought we were up to it. I have to say that I was sorely tempted to accept his challenge and I'm sure others among us felt exactly the same, but we quickly came to the view as we trudged back to our cleaning duties that we would have been defeated by the system one way or another. I probably assumed this kind of thing might go in to one degree or another and although I didn't agree with what I saw, it did have the desired effect of keeping large numbers of 15 year-olds under control, which could be difficult at times.

The second incident relates to the celebration of families' day, which occurred very early in my time at *Ganges*. My parents, two sisters and brother all came down to Shotley to give their support and see how I was getting on with my training. The Navy had set up tents in one of the fields due to the large number of people that would be attending and the lack of accommodation in nearby villages and Shotley. My parents were very impressed with the marching, sports and mast-manning displays that were put on over the week-end and I am sure they were proud to see that I was doing so well. However, they took me out for a few hours one day in the car and on the way back to Shotley my father accidently took a wrong turn in the road, which meant I would be arriving back at the establishment after my leave pass expired. There was some panic emerging in me as we tried to make up for lost time, but we did arrive late. When I reported to the main gate to collect my 'station card' (something we left at the main gate when we went on leave and collected on return) I was told that I was 'adrift' and would have to see the Officer of the Day.

I duly returned to the administration block as required and was greeted by the Master at Arms (MAA) and some other Regulators, marched into a room and given the order "off caps," which was followed by the reading out of a charge for being absent without leave – the precise words were, "JEM Nixon, Sir, is charged with being one hour absent without leave." The ordering of 'off caps' in this scenario always signified that the individual receiving the order was to be tried under the Naval Disciple Act (of 1957 at that time) and potentially receive some form of punishment. I have to confess that this was a scary incident for someone of my age and experience with the Navy, but smartly removed my cap and awaited the outcome of the procedure. The officer asked me why I had not arrived back on time and I explained, as best I could under the circumstances, that my father had taken a wrong turn and that was why I had been delayed. His response was immediate and clear in that it was 'my duty' to ensure I returned back to the establishment on time and that I could not attribute my 'guilt' to another person, even if it was my father and we were experiencing families' day. I had nothing more to add in terms of mitigation and was awarded one day's loss of leave and two hours extra work in the galley. The judgement was repeated by the MAA – "guilty of the charge of absent without leave; One day's number 14 punishment, on caps, right turn, quick march!"

These two incidents revealed to me that ratings in the Navy were open to abuse and punishment with sometimes little attention being given to mitigation, even though in theory one could appeal such punishments. In the case of *Ganges*, to expand on this issue a little more, the practice of punishing boys with 'cuts' had only been revoked by the Navy a few months before I arrived and the death penalty was permissible under the Naval Discipline Act. The regular administering of cuts had involved being beaten with a cane across the back such that the skin was broken and the trainee bled, something that went right back to Nelson's time when sailors could also be keel-hauled, given the 'cat' or hanged for fairly minor 'offences' (Howson & Nixon, 2006). It was clear that the things that my Air Training Corps instructor had discussed with me before I joined the Navy had some substance, although the initial punishment I received certainly succeeded in making me more responsible, which of course was a good thing in many ways and the underlying objective of naval discipline. In spite of these jolts to the system, my letters were overwhelmingly positive as exemplified in another one of my early letters home:

We all marched over to the main establishment last night to the cinema and on the way back our Junior Instructors were marching us with big lamps (to light up the street ahead) – we were marching down the road happily and I loved the experience. At the week-ends we all have a great time and play football, cricket, deck hockey or swimming the whole day long. On Sundays we have divisions and march over to the main establishment for church and then have sport or recreation all day.

For the purpose of writing home many of us used writing pads which were available in the N.A.A.F.I. that had the *Ganges* logo on top of each page, as shown below. This added to the sense of belonging to an establishment that was steeped in history.

HMS GANGES

SHOTLEY GATE   IPSWICH   SUFFOLK

Photo 5 - Letter heading on HMS *Ganges* writing paper

Source: author

After our initial six-week period of training we marched, accompanied by a Royal Marine band, from the Annex to the main establishment and joined our new mess decks according to our branch in the Royal Navy – I remember one of the tunes they played was 'Congratulations,' which the singer Cliff Richard recorded around that time and was the UK's entry in the Eurovision contest. As a JEM my new home, after a short stay in a transit mess, was to be 17 Mess of Drake Division, which was made up of most of the boys from *Tiger* Mess in the Annex plus some from other messes in the Annex I had not known so well. At this stage we were supervised by either Leading Juniors or PO Juniors, who were known collectively as 'badge boys.' They largely did the same jobs as JIs from the Annex and occupied the first two beds as one entered the mess deck and also had a specially embroidered 'counterpane' for their beds (which had a large blue anchor in the middle). We were eventually divided into Drake 320 and 321 classes, with my class being the latter. Our badge boys were Pete Ruddock and another boy from Wales, whose name I do not recall. They were both about nine months ahead of us in their training, which was the normal practice after being a badge boy for several months in mess decks accommodated by their own class mates.

My class instructor was CPO Gordon Jones, a Fleet Air Arm (FAA) Chief Electrical Mechanic. Chief Jones, with the 320 class instructor, PO Electrician Malcolm Allard, would be the ones to supervise all our mess activities, provide the pastoral care required to look after 30-40 15-year-olds, and instruct us in electrical theory throughout our 'Part One' training. Although there was a good deal of overlap in the duties of our instructors with regard to supervision of both classes, Chief Jones was naturally the instructor my class spent the majority of their time with. He was a person of immense integrity, strong personal religious conviction and kindness, and would oversee our development in the coming year.

The personal attributes of Chief Jones were arguably difficult to apply in such a disciplined environment but he would prove to be a person that knew when I, and my classmates, needed words of encouragement, or appreciation. In times of difficulty he was always there for us. The picture below reminds me of the values that were instilled in us at *Ganges*. "Young men," Chief Jones would often say, "if a job is worth doing it is worth doing well." PO Allard had a different approach and often barked out instructions in a forthright manner along the lines of, "right you shower, get this place looking ship shape or else!"

The values we learned from our instructors at *Ganges* have stuck with me and those classmates I remain in contact with. Paying attention to detail was the building block of our training and this applied to all aspects of our lives and the activities we undertook. There were many opportunities available to us that would help in attaining our true potential in life.

Photo 6 - 17 Mess after inspection with PO Allard and CPO Jones

Source: *author (Mr Fisk Photography)*

The routine at *Ganges* worked well in keeping us busy, and I particularly remember the rituals around preparing for, and taking part in, morning Divisions on the large parade ground we had. The Sunday morning routine was more elaborate as it involved getting into Number Ones after breakfast and mustering in our classes, initially on Drake Division's small parade ground. Having fallen in, our class instructors would inspect us and dust off every speck of fluff from our uniforms, trim tapes, make sure our caps were on straight and generally ensure we wouldn't be 'picked up' on divisions itself. Before we fell out our Divisional Officers, Lieutenant Commander (Lt Cdr) Kaminsky or Sub Lieutenant (S/Lt) Dodds, would also inspect us to make sure nothing had been missed – always giving a long hard and critical eye over each trainee and never slow to point out shortfalls in our appearance, or to give us praise when we merited it.

Once this procedure was over we gathered *en mass* at the edge of the main parade ground next to the mast and our 'markers' fell in, on command, just prior to divisions beginning. The markers were the tallest people in the classes – in our case these boys were Stuart Ostler and Vernon Beattie. Once divisions were ready to proceed, a POGI (Gunnery Instructor) would blow his whistle and everyone fell silent and came to attention. A few seconds later the GI would shout the command, "Parade, fall in!" This triggered a stampede as we all ran towards our markers and fell in smartly beside them in ranks of three. Some people used this as an opportunity to trip up their class mates or make some noise, in which case the GI blew his whistle again, which meant we came to a halt and stood to attention as quickly as possible. We were then given the customary warning, and sent back to the perimeter of the parade ground to start the whole process again. Once on parade, our instructor or badge boy gave the orders to bring us to attention, 'dress by the right' (to form straight lines), open order march, dress once more and then stand at ease.

As the band struck up, the more senior officers, who usually lined up either side of the Dias (some with accompanying wives or children), would march smartly over to their nominated classes in order to carry out a formal inspection. This prompted more drilling before we stood smartly at attention as the officer passed each trainee. They often made remarks to either encourage or criticise us, and many asked questions of a general nature, which were aimed at keeping up morale and showing an interest in the welfare of juniors.

Photo 7 - Captain Napper inspecting 320/321 classes on parade

Stuart Ostler (right), JN 5th from right. **Source:** *author (Mr Fisk Photography)*

After formal inspections classes were marched off by the GIs in such a way as to keep everyone marching in time as we manoeuvred our way around the parade ground and finally performed an 'eyes right' in salute of the senior officer on parade. Once divisions were over we attended church services according to our denominations and finally raced over to the Central Messing Galley (CMG) for our mid-day meal. This usually involved queuing up in a long line of boys and hoping that the chefs - who didn't appear to like us much - would serve up reasonable portions and not give us a hard time. Eventually though we were back in the mess deck planning what to do for the afternoon. Typically this might involve a trip to the bowling alley, dhobying (washing) and ironing our kit, spit and polishing our boots/shoes, getting into sports gear and climbing the mast, or something similar. The words of a famous Beatles (Lennon & MCartney, 1968) song were often heard when in the bowling alley.

Hey Jude, don't make it bad/ Take a sad song and make it better
Remember to let her into your heart/ Then you can start to make it better

During our time at *Ganges* we spent many hours playing sport and taking part in organised recreational activities. Our official 'sports rig' was something to behold as we wore a navy blue (or white) shirt with a white collar, white shorts that went down to our knees, our canvas blue belts and white plimsolls. The second photograph below of some of my classmates during a recreational afternoon, which must have been in winter as everyone is wearing winter 'rec' dress, is rather poignant to me as it shows just how young we were to be 'out in the big wide world.' Although life at *Ganges* was exciting and fulfilling in many ways, we quickly had to learn how to look after ourselves and those close to us as there was plenty of opportunity to be challenged one way or another. Indeed, we had many difficult situations to face with such little wisdom and experience, which is why our instructors, badge boys and divisional officers were so important in providing guidance.

After about eight weeks in the main establishment we knew that some of us would be selected to be badge boys and many of us aspired to this position as it came along with some extra privileges, the wearing of white gaiters and a stripe the left arm of all uniforms (hence the term 'badge boy').

Photo 8 - Stuart Ostler in our famous *Ganges* sports rig

Source: *author*

Photo 9 - A seven-legged race on one of our 'fun days'

Mick Ross, Colin Smith, Terry Rice, 'Tip' O'Keefe, Taffy Thomas, Dennis Barnard.
Source: *Michael Ross*

Understandably, at that age and in the regime that *Ganges* created, many of us were competitive by nature and our instructors instilled in us a desire to succeed and do well through a system of reward fully integrated with the potential for punishment. The two boys that were initially selected from 320 and 321 classes were Roy Brooks and me. Captain Napper, in a letter to my parents when I was promoted, wrote that 'badge boys were selected because of their leadership qualities, enthusiasm and example.' Having gone through an official procedure in the Divisional office that involved the issuing of our badges and some advice from our instructors, we were suddenly placed in a position that was associated with mixed blessings. We were given responsibility for drilling and marching our classes to instruction and on divisions. I was also selected to be guard commander when we performed that duty as joint classes. Like our role models such as JI Patterson, we learned to shout very loudly when giving orders on parade or marching our classes around the camp. We also took charge of cleaning routines, were allowed to go to the front of the queue in the CMG at meal times, did more 'cushy' jobs during work ship weeks, and got paid a little more than our class mates. Although I went on to have a long career in the Navy and was promoted several times to other rates/ranks, I don't think any of them made me as proud as the day I became a badge boy at *Ganges*. However, this new position brought with it some notable tribulations.

The first issue that affected me was the fact that some of my classmates who had been very close friends in the Annex and through nozzers' routine became somewhat distant. This is not surprising, however, given that one minute I was part of the group and 'enjoying' myself polishing brass cannons with a classmate at early morning cleaning stations, and the next I was giving out the orders. Also, it is not surprising that my colleagues became irritated at seeing their 'mate' with a pair of white gaiters on going straight to the front of the dining room queue. Dealing with this mixture of pride on the one hand and friction on the other gave me a few sleepless nights as I started to feel no longer part of my peers in some ways.

This affected me to the point that I applied to leave *Ganges* at our six-month option, and therefore the Navy. However, our instructors and other close friends like Roy Brooks, Pete Kerley, Stuart Ostler, Terry Rice, Mick Ross and many more, were clearly aware of these issues and gave me a considerable amount of backing and support. I recall it was quite a stressful experience to explain my reasons for wishing to leave in the formal setting of 'request men,' standing to attention with Chief Jones, PO Allard and my divisional officer watching on as I fought back my emotions in explaining that I 'missed my home.' They clearly thought I had a promising career in the Navy and didn't want to 'lose me,' which were difficult arguments for a 15 year-old to counter in such a formal scenario.

Photo 10 - Roy Brooks, JN & Pete Kerley (No.1 uniform explained)

Source: *author*

On hearing of this development, my parents became very concerned and urged me to leave the Navy if that is what I so wished. However, I withdrew my request once I had overcome this initial shock and settled into the role of badge boy. I always sought to do my best to undertake my duties with due concern for everyone in my class, although the system was designed to test people no matter which side of the fence you were on. After spending about three months in charge of my own classes in 17 Mess, I moved to 15 Mess in the 'Long Covered Way' to be the badge boy of some younger recruits with a colleague from 320 Class, Tony Evans, who had recently been promoted to Leading Junior. I think it is important to note, here, that once we had reached this six-month break point at *Ganges* we had committed to 12-years' service until the age of 27. This was a very long time to wait and I recall reading of two ratings who became distressed to the point of taking their own lives at some point after leaving initial training.

For this reason, the Navy later introduced the possibility of 'buying yourself out' and then the opportunity to leave after 18 months' notice. Indeed, we did lose many boys who requested to leave as our training went along. The first one I recall was in Green Squadron when a 'fashion-conscious' Scottish boy with long hair had decided he'd had enough after getting his first drastic hair cut in the Annex. It seemed like his pride had been badly damaged, but I did actually admire him for having his standards and sticking to them - only the ones who accepted rules and discipline, and could cope with high demands on their time and effort, remained with us.

Although I have recounted some challenging and 'disturbing' elements about life at *Ganges* there were many memorable, positive and humorous incidents. PO Allard, for example, was always on red alert looking out for the misdemeanours that our classmates were likely to engage themselves in, and the following provide examples of some of his successes as recounted to me during a re-union in 2004:

After Divisions on Sundays, juniors were required to fall in by Church parties. On one particular Sunday an un-named junior seemed to have gone missing and on enquiring of others, I was given a number of accounts as to where he had gone. Being somewhat unconvinced, another instructor and I decided to check the mess deck, when we observed a kitbag which seemed to be full and propped up in the shower room. This raised suspicions in me so with the aid of a broom handle we decided to operate the shower above the offending kitbag. As the kitbag got wet there was a sudden and frantic movement and out of the kitbag appeared the missing junior! Needless to say and irrespective of its originality, this trick was never used again!

On another occasion when entering 17 Mess I noted that there appeared to be a strong smell of toast, and not having a toaster in the mess I deduced that bread had been removed from the dining hall after a meal and the mess iron had been used as a 'toaster' as in the days when I was as a junior. On enquiring as to who was responsible, no-one came forward but a certain junior had a guilty look on his face. This seemed sufficient evidence and so as a punishment I ordered him to stand on a chair in the long covered way outside the mess and recite the words 'I will not use the iron again to make toast!' a number of times in a loud voice, which of course he did without question.

Daily activities at *Ganges* included classroom study, practical workshop training, marching and drill activities, exercises in the gym with the Physical Training Instructors (PTIs), lectures or films concentrating on aspects of life and training in the Royal Navy. During morning 'stand easy' we were treated to a large mug of kai (drinking chocolate) and what we referred to as 'sticky buns.'

The PTIs were extremely impressive individuals, both in the way they dressed and acted. They wore sleeveless white shirts with navy blue edgings and crossed blue clubs in the centre (which explained why they were affectionately referred to as 'Clubs' on board ships and other establishments), navy blue serge trousers with a smart crease down the centre, and immaculate white plimsolls. Their way of saluting officers always impressed me too as they brought both arms smartly and swiftly down to their sides and moved their heads to face the officer whilst momentarily pausing in their strides. They were also influential and important to me personally as I went on to represent *Ganges* at football, rugby and swimming, and PTIs were always the ones to spot those who had sporting abilities and bring them into the teams at *Ganges*. Several other boys in our classes represented the establishment at various sports, and the boy I spent most time with in this regard was Jim Mason from 320 class, who was goalkeeper for the football team and also swam (breast stroke) for the swimming team. I played in the position of striker for the football team, centre for the rugby team and swam freestyle in the 100 metres and relay for the swimming team. We led somewhat of a privileged life by representing the establishment as we were kept busy at week-ends travelling to various venues to play local boys' teams. Our record was very good and no matter which sport we played, we usually had high success levels. My day always started with Jim Mason as we went to the pool together to swim about 50 lengths before breakfast as part of our swimming training. Many of us were incredibly fit and lean because of the amount of sport and drilling we did. I was later selected to swim for the Royal Navy youth team but missed my opportunity as I contracted tonsillitis and spent a few days in the hospital ward.

The division I belonged to at HMS *Ganges*, Drake, excelled in many ways and was awarded the best division trophy by Captain Napper in our last term. As the head boy of Drake division I was given the honour of being presented with the cup at morning divisions. To win this trophy we certainly did a great deal of scrubbing and polishing, as well as performing highly in sporting competitions. Another highlight in the latter part of my year's training was being selected as joint guard commander for the *Ganges* ceremonial guard for a visiting admiral. The other guard commander was Leading Junior Wiltshire from Benbow division, and ratings from all divisions in *Ganges* were selected on merit to be part of this large 48-strong guard. Our march-past was recorded on Anglia television which my parents got a glimpse of at home and were very pleased to see. The photo below shows us giving an 'eyes right' salute as we marched past the Dias. We had spent many hours and weeks drilling for this event and everything had to done to perfection. For both Leading Junior Wiltshire and me, our responsibilities as guard commander contributed to our further advancement because soon after this responsibility we were promoted to the rate of PO Junior, which meant I now wore a stripe and crown on my left arm. This event was in my local press as only two or three boys at a time at *Ganges* reached this status, and Captain Napper's letter to my parents brought them a great deal of pride as it highlighted the qualities that were needed to become a PO Junior.

Our one year at HMS *Ganges* was fast coming to an end but in the spring of 1969 we were treated to a skiing trip to Scotland and also spent one week aboard HMS *Rapid* doing sea training. I recall the skiing trip to Glen Shee and the nightmarish trips in the back of a Navy lorry from base camp in HMS *Faslane* to the ski slopes each day. We collected our lunch packs and a large urn of soup, which we loaded into the back of the lorry, and then spent several hours en-route being rolled around in the back. The journey was not very comfortable to say the least as we sat along the sides of the lorry, under canvas, on hard wooden seats. I vividly remember a classmate, Colin Smith, waking up at the base on our return with a black face from the road spray after he had fallen asleep during the trip, much to the amusement of everyone else in the lorry.

Photo 11 - *Ganges* 48-strong ceremonial guard march past

JN front left guard commander. **Source:** *author (Mr Fisk Photography)*

Another 'unfortunate' incident happened to a classmate and close friend, who was pleased to be given a pair of skis that were just the right size for him at the beginning of the first day on the slopes. However, an accompanying officer, who hadn't been issued with skis for some reason, ordered my friend to hand over his pair. This meant that for the rest of the week he had to go tobogganing with some of the others who did not get a pair of skis either. This type of minor injustice was typical of what we all had to get used to as young trainees in the Royal Navy and was something that we referred to as 'pulling rank,' which none of us respected as a way of getting things done.

Our week aboard HMS *Rapid* during sea training was also a memorable experience. We were issued with hammocks - only used on older ships at that time - which we had to secure to the ceiling every evening and fold up and stow away the following morning. HMS *Rapid* (H32), a former R-class World War II destroyer that was later converted into a Type 15 anti-submarine frigate, was one of the fastest ships in the Navy and capable of a speed of 32 knots. I recall we had to do sea boat drills every day, which commenced with an announcement over the tannoy system of "man overboard, launch the sea boat." A buoy was thrown over the side of the ship, which then performed a 360 degree turn to return to the correct position. Those of us who were on duty that day had to rush to the upper deck and scramble into the sea boat, which was then lowered into the water after the ship had stopped. We then quickly rowed to the buoy, hoisted it into the boat, rowed back to the ship and, after coming alongside, were winched up to the upper deck once more. Coupled with all the other daily activities aboard *Rapid,* we were starting to get a feel for what our lives would be like in the future within the Royal Navy.

Unfortunately for me whilst on sea training I began to suffer from repeated nosebleeds for some unknown reason and spent much of my time in the Sick Bay. Although I was unhappy about this development, I did immediately find the atmosphere in the Sick Bay quiet and peaceful in contrast to the noise and cramped conditions in the rest of the ship. I also admired the work of the Medical Assistants (MAs) and on returning to HMS *Ganges* I seriously considered changing over to the Medical Branch of the Navy. However, for various reasons this did not proceed and I was eventually happy to remain in WE branch, which I had originally joined although like my father, who was a medic in the army during World War

II (Nixon & Smith, 2006), I retained a strong interest in medicine that I would take up formerly after leaving the Royal Navy.

In May 1969 I left the younger trainees that I supervised in 15 Mess and returned to my classmates in 17 Mess, where we all busied ourselves for several weeks preparing for our move to HMS *Collingwood*. At this point we were also categorised into Radio, Control or Ordinance Electrical Mechanics, abbreviated to REM, CEM or OEM. I was fortunate to have achieved good marks in my part one training so was able to select REM (the category requiring the highest marks) as my first choice, along with Roy Brooks, Pete Slynn and Mick Davis. At this point all the badge boys reverted to being ordinary JEMs like the rest of our classmates with the exception of Tony Evans, who chose to move to the Annex to become a JI for several months before joining *Collingwood*. This was an option I also considered applying for but declined as I didn't want to lose contact with all the close friends I had in both 320 and 321 classes, and then have to join *Collingwood* at a later date.

Photo 12 - Drake Guard performing the General Salute

Source: *author (Mr Fisk Photography)*

Photo 13 - HMS *Ganges* soccer colours with motto 'wisdom is strength'

Source: *author*

On the final day at *Ganges* we gathered up our kit bags, marched to the main gate and then boarded a bus for Ipswich railway station. Accompanying us on the journey all the way to Fareham in Hampshire was our instructor, CPO Jones. After five hours on a train and bus we eventually arrived at HMS *Collingwood* where we gathered in a room in one of our new multi-storey and modern accommodation blocks - in this case, Trafalgar block. As we moved through the building I immediately noticed the small 4-bed rooms that were in the mess decks, the comfortable chairs in the TV room and the relatively low-key atmosphere that permeated around the place. As we sat there chatting among ourselves in our best uniforms with kit bags and suitcases piled up behind us, I reflected on my year at *Ganges*. There had been many trials, triumphs and tribulations to experience, but Chief Jones and PO Allard had been ever-present to help us make the transition from school boys to young men who were ready to take up our place in the Royal Navy. The photo above of 320/321 Drake division guard performing the general salute – a sign of respect - depicts a memory of *Ganges* that captures something intangible about the place, and I think of it as a tribute to our two instructors. It was a demanding but significant time during which I learned an enormous amount about myself, other people and life in general. The motto of *Ganges* was 'Wisdom is strength' (photo above) and I had certainly gained in that respect over the one-year training period I had spent there.

After a short introductory talk and welcome by our new PO, Chief Jones stepped to the front to look all of us in the eye and say his last goodbyes in his own inimitable manner. He graciously wished us all well in our future careers, referring to us as "young men" as he had always done throughout our time at *Ganges*. I don't think everyone in the room realised just how much we had meant to Chief Jones, who I now know did not have a son of his own, and what he had meant to us during our time at *Ganges*, but one or two of us noticed him wiping a tear from his eye as he walked smartly and purposefully out of the door, alone. For me personally, nothing in the future would match up to our time at *Ganges* and the standards – both personal and those related to the Navy - set by Gordon Jones.

III - HMS *Collingwood* [1969-70]

At HMS *Collingwood* I was led to my bunk in 509D cabin on the ground floor of Trafalgar block, which formed *Temeraire* division. The first thing that struck me about *Collingwood* was that the regime, whilst still being highly disciplined, was much less demanding on our time and the need for excessive attention to detail in what we did – we rarely spent hours and hours, for example, spitting and polishing our shoes and boots as we had done previously. We also became part of divisions that were partly made up of older, and therefore more mature, ratings. Those of us who had entered the Navy as 15-year olds at *Ganges* or HMS *St. Vincent,* in Gosport, had to undergo one year of training and be subjected to a highly structured and busy training experience. In contrast, those who had joined the Navy over the age of 16 undertook only six weeks of training at HMS *Raleigh* in Plymouth – known by *Ganges* boys as 'six-week wonders,' before moving to *Collingwood* if they were part of the electrical branch. Approval of my new situation was reflected in a letter to my parents in early June, when I wrote:

> *I am in Temeraire division football team, volleyball team, athletics team, and cricket team. Temeraire division is definitely the best in Howe Section as we have not lost one game and we are in every final there is. We won the shooting, darts and football final 3-2 - so now we all get a medal and ten bob (ten shillings) which can't be bad at all.*

I also mentioned in this letter that I shared my cabin with a Jamaican trainee called Sam. He was quite a character who made the claim that he came from Brazil and was called 'Pele' during the football season, and from the West Indies and called 'Sobers' (after the famous cricketer, Garfield Sobers) when he was playing cricket. I also wrote about some regular but painful visits to the dentist, which were eased by the fact that the dentist's WREN assistant, whose name was Ann, always gave me a nice smile – she was by far the most attractive WREN in the establishment. I also mentioned in this letter that I had been to the *Collingwood* club for three dances and that 'Sam and I danced with every girl in the club.' I had been drinking quite heavily, including my father's favourite drink Drambuie, but that I 'knew my limitations and did not get drunk' like many others. I mentioned I would be home the following week-end and catch the long distance coach to Sheffield, which would arrive at 11.00 pm where my father always came to collect me from when I returned home if it wasn't Doncaster railway station.

Another aspect of mess deck life that changed the atmosphere was the fact that our divisions were under the control of a Leading (Radio, Ordinance or Control) Electrical Mechanic (LREM, LOEM or LCEM), who were equivalent to the rank of corporal in the Army. Known as 'Killicks,' they were accommodated in our mess decks and provided the necessary supervision of everyone in their divisions. They had served in the Royal Navy in one or two ships and were in their twenties or early thirties. This created a stronger hierarchy in terms of controlling ratings living in the mess decks in contrast to the peer-group supervision by badge boys that we had been used to at *Ganges*.

Our Killick was LREM Michael John Everett, otherwise known as 'Kenny' because of the radio and television celebrity of that time. He was also to become an influential person in my naval career and personal development as he would go on to serve with me aboard my first ship for two years after completing my training in HMS *Collingwood*. The first things that I noticed about LREM Everett were his intelligence, his well-spoken and refined manner, and his unbelievably sharp sense of humour. He immediately struck me as being of officer material, and I was unsure as to why he had entered the Navy as a rating, although he had clearly not had sufficient time to gain a degree and may or may not have been offered officer entry by what was known as the upper yardarm scheme, whereby ratings could be transferred to *Dartmouth* to undergo midshipman training. He helped us with our studies in radio electrical theory and often used the expression, "Oh come on, Johnny (or Ozzie etc. depending on who he was talking to), that's basic!" Whenever anyone at *Collingwood* used the term 'basic' it was a buzz word that implied if you didn't understand the principles that were being considered you were a half-wit or 'duffer,' to use the naval term. One example could be the application and manipulation of Ohms' law, which states that 'the current flowing through a conductor is proportional to the voltage applied and the resistance of the circuit,' in other words $V=IR$, therefore $I=V/R$ or $R=V/I$. Another formula we had to remember was that of the resonant frequency for circuits containing a capacitor (C) and an inductor (L), which we memorised with the mnemonic 'one over two pi root LC - that is the resonant frequency.' If anyone struggled with these concepts, or couldn't transpose simple formulae, someone was bound to utter those infamous words - "that's basic."

Kenny very quickly valued and acknowledged my leadership qualities, and soon after joining he selected me to be the 'Senior Hand' of our side of *Temeraire* division. This was a position that effectively meant I was his right-hand man in assisting him with the supervision and general management of *Temeraire* division. I felt this was an honour and of some credit to our time at *Ganges* as, although *Ganges* boys were among the youngest people in the division because we had joined the Navy at the age of 15, we had had the benefit of one year's general training before moving to *Collingwood*. My involvement in the sporting life of my division was also clearly taken into consideration. It was becoming clearer with every new month that I served in the Navy that sport was a key element of building up *esprit de corps* within Royal Navy establishments and ships. The main perk of being a senior hand, was that I was given a much sought-after 'blue card,' which meant I was excused the main-stream duties that were carried out on a 'one in four' basis. In contrast, blue card holders did duties only one in eight days and also had 'open gangway' until 11.30 pm.

Kenny and the other Killick in *Temeraire* division were extremely keen for our division to do well in sport, which is how I got to know and become friends with many of the other members of the division, especially those who were in the football team such as Brian Moverley, 'Bungy' Williams and Tommy Scott. Brian, who was a couple of years older than me, became a very close friend and taught me how to play the guitar, which is something I will always be grateful for as my guitar became a constant companion and source of comfort throughout my time in the Navy and the rest of my life. Because Simon and Garfunkel were very popular at that time, we often practised songs like 'the Boxer' and 'Sound of Silence.' Brian played in a finger-picking style and was certainly no ordinary 'strummer' - he always reminded me of the actor Steve McQueen, both in terms of his looks and his quiet but confident manner, and was someone I always looked up to and respected. Like me, he focussed on sport, music and his work as opposed to some of the other 'vices' life in the Navy would offer up to us. However, at this early stage of my life in the Navy, at least for a couple of years, I have to confess that I did make use of my free cigarette ration (issue cigarettes were affectionately known as 'blue liners' as they had a distinctive blue line running along the perimeter) and partook of modest levels of drinking at the *Collingwood* Club, where we attended dances and folk music evenings. Kenny, in particular, got me interested in attending folk evenings and learning songs that were popular such as 'Whisky in the Jar' and 'the Leaving of Liverpool,' which we used to sing along to with 'gusto.' He also used to sing, for light entertainment, several well-known songs where the original words were replaced by mini-stories about drunken sailors – the one that comes to mind is the Burt Bacharach and

Hal David song (1957) 'Magic Moments,' but in the interests of good taste I will refrain from repeating them here.

Whenever *Temeraire* division played football, Kenny - with fellow Killicks and other members of staff such as the block PO or our Divisional Officer in tow - was always there to give us his vocal support from the touch line. He would pace up and down with his blue uniform collar flapping in the wind, holding on to his cap and shouting encouragement in a very 'partisan' and loud (but refined) manner. He wasn't much of a sportsman himself – the correct term to describe his physique was probably 'lanky' or 'slim' - as he was more of a studious type and had a keen interest in politics and other cerebral subjects, but he certainly knew how to support his 'troops.' As mentioned above, we went on to win the Howe Section football tournament in some style, and also the 'Cock' trophy for best division, as shown in the photos below. Life in Trafalgar block had its own relaxed culture, which centred around the 'block office' on the ground floor - manned by our three-badge block PO ('three badges' indicates he had served for at least 12 years – see photo below). I remember him being quite a witty character who made many humorous 'pipes' over the tannoy system and had a very effective and charismatic way of managing people. At certain times of the day he also played music over the tannoy system so people on all four floors could hear it. We would therefore often return to the block at the end of instruction to hear songs in our cabins such as 'Good Morning Starshine' by Oliver (1969), or 'California dreaming' by the Mammas and Pappas (1965).

My very good cabin mate, Barry Pease, who's bed was next to mine, would often open his locker and unravel a packet of blue liners from its silver wrapping paper and offer me a cigarette. Over a cup of coffee we would often discuss what we had learnt that day from our courses and who had been up to what in our division. He was another mild but very intelligent and quick-witted person, who came from London. We spent many an afternoon or Saturday morning playing snooker and table tennis in the nearby N.A.A.F.I. club, where two friendly ladies sold us sandwiches, cakes, tea and all sorts of other goodies.

Photo 14 - *Temeraire* Division Cock Trophy winners, HMS *Collingwood*

Front row left (JN) then 'Bungy' Williams, Tommy Scott, Kenny Everett, Divisional Officer, Block PO
2nd row (left) Stuart Ostler, Barry Pease (5th from left),
Back row (right) Brian Moverley. **Source:** *author*

Photo 15 - Temeraire Division football team, HMS Collingwood

Winners of the Howe Division tournament – JN front centre. **Source:** *author*

As I was still a junior (under 17 and a half) I was also entitled to collect our 'nutty' rations (confectionary or fruit) twice a week from Howe Section divisional office with all the other juniors. These were therefore very enjoyable times for me, made even more special because of the friendships that I was lucky enough to have; prominent among these being my good friend and classmate from *Ganges*, Stuart Ostler, who was in the same cabin as me along with Barry and Sam. My studies at *Collingwood* were also very enjoyable and generally more relaxed than at *Ganges*. There were only four of us altogether on our REM's course, and our marching to lessons with our canvass study bags strapped over our left shoulders was easier to manage as class leader than thirty-plus at *Ganges*. After the lunch break back at the block we mustered on the main parade ground and were then marched off to instruction after giving an 'eyes right.' Although, as I have mentioned, life was more relaxed, the route from the parade ground to the instruction area was manned at regular intervals by Killicks or POs who wouldn't hesitate to order a class to halt, and then issue them with an infamous 'chit.' *Collingwood* was renowned for its 'chit' system, which referred to pieces of paper with instructions or information on them. In the case of a marching infringement, for example, the chit would instruct the class leader to report to Howe section office to be logged for a poor drill incident and be given a warning.

As well as being taught using conventional classroom arrangements for various radio and radar equipment we would maintain once we joined the fleet, we were taught basic radio theory through what we affectionately called 'teaching machines.' These were sited in cubicles and contained an instruction tape, which we worked through by reading material illuminated at the back of a viewer and pressing a selection of buttons. If we misunderstood anything we would press the wrong button and have to repeat that section. This went on until we had finished a unit, when we reported to our PO who issued us with a 'criterion test.' We had to pass each test before proceeding; the advantage being that we could work at our own pace. The system was well accepted by us and generated a certain degree of competition among the class members – the usual response by classmates to being slow in a particular unit was the familiar repost, "What's the problem, that one was basic!" I also mentioned to my parents in a letter that we had to be careful about the dangers of receiving electric shocks from the equipment we were training on, especially the 'JDA' radar display. We were required to focus the set by adjusting the cathode ray tube, which meant placing our hands close to an extra high tension (EHT) point of 14,000 volts. It seems that my classmate, Pete Slynn, received several 'belts' doing this and was becoming a 'nervous wreck,' as I put it in my letter. Fortunately these shocks were usually limited to a small area of the hand as we were required to stand on rubber mats and use insulated tools. However, they certainly made us jump and under certain circumstances they could be fatal, as I was to sadly find out in my future career.

Because of playing football for *Temeraire* division and scoring many goals in various games, I was spotted again by the PTIs and selected to play, with my friend Jim Mason from *Ganges*, for *Collingwood's* under-18's team. In a letter to my parents I mentioned that we played against *Ganges* in the first round of the Navy cup and only just sneaked a victory against them after extra time, 3-2. The cry from the touchline was to become familiar to me both then and in future years at *Collingwood* as the establishment was a regular winner of the Navy Cup – 'come on the Woods!' We went on to play in the semi-final against HMS *Heron*, from Scotland, but I am not sure if we went on to win the Navy Cup itself. This led to one of the highlights of my sporting career as I was then selected, after a period of trials with numerous other boys from all across the Navy, to play for the full Royal Navy Youth team. This was a genuine elevation as we went on to tour the Midlands and North of England, accompanied by our own Royal Marine band, which played before every game we took part in and therefore acted as a genuine crowd puller. I recall we played Derby County Boys at the Baseball ground where we were introduced to Myra Van Heck - Miss England of 1969 - before the match, Yorkshire Boys at Doncaster Rovers' ground close to my home, and Hull Boys as our final match. I believe we won at Derby, drew at Hull, and lost 6-0 to Yorkshire Boys. However, whilst I acknowledge Yorkshire Boys were a cut above us in terms of skill level, their team did contain players who were one or two years older than us and there is quite a difference between a sixteen-year-old and an 18-year-old in terms of physical development. Some entrepreneurial marine band members also set up a 'bacon sandwich and tea service' in our accommodation's kitchen. After a game of football or a hard training session, coming back to this kind of facility was really welcome. We were also invited to receptions after games, where lots of doting motherly types and their families entertained us – I remember one of them saying how much she 'liked the curl' I had in my fringe at that time. Life in the Navy was certainly looking like a wise move at this stage of my career.

Photo 16 - My family during a visit to *Collingwood* in 1969

Source: *author (photo by Michael Pointon)*

[37]

Whilst at *Collingwood* my family came down to visit me. Throughout my long career in the Royal Navy they provided constant support and encouragement, which I greatly appreciated as it helped me to make progress in my sporting and professional development. They seemed to enjoy their trips down from Yorkshire to the south coast and the warmer and sunnier climate there.

After 19 weeks of formal training we passed out as a Junior Radio Electrical Mechanics (JREMs) and waited with some anticipation for our first drafts to ships in the fleet. About this time we visited nearby HMS *Dolphin,* the Navy's submarine training establishment, to learn about life as a 'submariner.' We were shown films of how candidates were selected for submarines and how they had to go through very challenging escape chamber drills. This simulated an escape from a stricken submarine by going from the bottom to the top of a 30-metre tower filled with water while breathing out continuously and using the 'Davis' breathing apparatus. Breathing out avoided an embolism (a small bubble of air in the bloodstream) that could travel to the brain and cause death. If people were not breathing out sufficiently their instructors would swim out from strategic positions in the escape chamber and punch them in the stomach! We were also shown around a submarine that was tied up alongside at HMS *Dolphin.* Conditions aboard the 'boat' (the name for submarines) were extremely cramped and some members of the crew had to share their bunks with others (so called 'hot bunking'). There were also tiny toilets that looked more like cupboards, and some bunks were situated directly on top of very large, ominous-looking and brightly-painted torpedoes.

We had visited surface ships at HMS *Ganges* such as the Leander class frigate HMS *Sirius*, so we now had an opportunity to compare everyday life in both of our future sea-going possibilities. A certain percentage of trainees would be selected for submarine service, but after my trip to *Dolphin* I decided that the surface fleet would definitely be preferable, although I knew the choice would not be mine. The image that influenced my mind on this issue was that of the duty 'mess man' on the submarine, peeling a mountain of potatoes using a large bowl underneath the tiny amount of natural light that was coming down from the conning tower. Before joining the Navy, I had no real perception of just how claustrophobic life on board a warship could be, and in the coming years of my career I would have to learn to live and sleep in very cramped conditions, which would be a significant challenge bearing in mind my love of the outdoors and playing sport.

Back at *Collingwood* in November there was a chit waiting on my bed for me with instructions to report to the drafting section of the Administration Building. I knew by instinct this would mean me receiving orders to join my first ship, and headed off across the main parade ground with some sense of excitement and anticipation. When I arrived and handed over my chit to the drafting PO he rifled through a filing cabinet and pulled out some papers, reading out aloud, "JREM Nixon, D105750B, to join HMS *Bulwark* on 6th January 1970 at Plymouth." My heart skipped a beat as I knew *Bulwark* was one of the Navy's several aircraft carriers, converted by then into a Commando Carrier operating Wessex 5 helicopters, and listened with some intensity as the PO continued to fill in the details of my draft. I would leave *Collingwood* just before Christmas and join *Bulwark* on the 6th January, just before it departed home waters for an eight-month deployment to the Far East. I went back to my accommodation to tell my friends – Kenny Everett and several messmates or friends had either joined or were waiting to join *Bulwark,* which was good news. I would be joining with Roy Brooks and Mick Ross, my *Ganges* classmates. Pete Kerley and Stuart Ostler were both drafted to HMS *Ark Royal*, Pete Slynn to the Leander-class frigate HMS *Dido.* Other friends from *Ganges*, Gerry Taylor and Kevin Calvert, received drafts to the Ton-class minesweeper squadron of the Hong Kong Squadron, as had my good friend and cabin-mate Barry Pease.

[38]

It was therefore time to start thinking about my departure from *Collingwood* when somewhat of a sting appeared in the tail of my time there. The issue arose because it was necessary to move out of Trafalgar Block into *Lion* Section, which was made up of some older-style dormitory accommodation. The mess decks had 20 occupants, and were similar to what we had experienced at *Ganges*. Some former classmates from other accommodation blocks joined up together once more in this new arrangement. Among my former *Ganges* colleagues was someone who had vowed to 'take revenge' once we left *Ganges* as he had resented me giving him orders and for being a badge boy. He knew that I would lose my authority over him once we had left *Ganges*. I have to admit that he was a genuine 'hard lad' but as I was to find out much later in life, he had had a very tough upbringing and may have experienced bullying himself as he was growing up. Perhaps it was natural therefore for him to want to reciprocate against others, and he found it easy to come up with excuses to have grudges and threaten people. However, as I had discovered at school, bullies only ever tackle those who are significantly smaller and weaker than themselves, and usually meet their match one way or another. Although he was a bit bigger and possibly stronger than me, I knew he realised that the differences between us were too small for him to genuinely attempt to 'beat me up,' as he had done quite ruthlessly with other smaller boys at *Ganges*. As it turned out, and perhaps because we had all grown up since first arriving at *Ganges*, apart from some minor intimidation, his threats never materialised. In fact we enjoyed some pleasant times together playing the guitar and chatting with another close friend from *Ganges*, Terry Rice, who had also moved to this new accommodation. I knew that underneath his hard exterior there was a rather different person who would protect his friends as well as fight those outside his circle. I learned that it was necessary to get on with all types of people, even though they could literally make your life hell and you knew there was no freedom to escape because your life was in the hands of others. To exacerbate this, these types of challenges occurred within a large and often uncompromising organisation.

After spending many a day playing volleyball in a small recreational area outside the accommodation blocks, and doing communal work around the camp such as sweeping roads and washing up dishes in the galley, it was time to say goodbye to my classmate, Terry Rice, who was the last one to leave. Therefore, with my kit bag slung over my right shoulder and a green Navy suitcase in my left hand, I marched out of *Collingwood* and caught the train from Fareham to Yorkshire for Christmas leave. I felt fit, strong, well-prepared, and grateful for the comfortable time I had spent during my training. I had met numerous people I would describe as being 'out of the top drawer,' established myself as a Navy-level sportsman, and was tremendously excited about the future and the places I might visit at this early stage of my career.

****

As I arrived on the train at Doncaster station I climbed up the stairs there that led to the exit and saw my father coming into view, waiting for me, as he had done for all the times I had come home on leave since joining the Navy. At that time all servicemen and servicewomen wore their uniforms when travelling to and from home, and it was with pride in his eyes that my father greeted me with a hand shake and helped me back to the car with my luggage. On the way back in his Morris Mini we chatted and made plans for going to watch Rotherham United the following day. As usual, my mother and sisters gave me a warm welcome when we arrived back home in Brierley, commenting on how much I had grown since joining the Navy (from five feet six to five feet nine as it turned out) and we settled down with a cup of tea together. My younger brother, David, was now a toddler so was very much the centre of attention, especially for my sister Valerie who spent a lot of time looking after him - and doting over him like the second mother she had become for him.

After coming home from the football match with my father the next day, my mother mentioned that a Christmas gathering had been arranged by Uncle Bernard and that it would be nice if I could be accompanied by someone. Through various means, Carol Hardman, who worked in our local shop after leaving school and who I had known since my school days, was invited and I was pleasantly surprised that she accepted. Carol was an archetype of the 1960s and certainly turned the heads of several males in the neighbourhood, or those passing through, as she walked about the village. She had long blonde hair, blue eyes, always wore well-presented make-up and like most teenagers of that time, more often than not wore a short mini-skirt. After this 'date,' which did not go as smoothly as I might have hoped, Carol and I started seeing more of each other and I was introduced to her parents, Frederick (Fred) and Pauline (Peg), her sister, Maureen, and younger sister, Sandra, who knew me from school although I think I must have been in my final year when she arrived in the first year so I didn't know her very well. Fred quickly told me he had served in the Royal Navy during World War II and that he had also represented a team from the Royal Navy at football. On the sideboard in the home was a handsome portrait of Fred in his Navy uniform with a black war-time cap, so we clearly had a lot in common that we could discuss. He had previously been a miner after returning from the war, but had decided to leave the mines and work as a caretaker at the school I attended, and I recall he could remember me too.

My next date with Carol was a trip to the cinema at Barnsley, which we had agreed on after the party. Whilst I was pleased to know we would see each other again, on the night when I was getting ready to catch the bus, which Carol would get on a few stops along the route, I realised just how few clothes I had in my possession that would do for a date to the cinema. I remember my mother saying, "Try this jacket on," and "how about that nice jumper your grandmother bought you for Christmas last year" when I said the jacket wasn't 'cool' enough. I had my uniform, and considered wearing that, but thought it would make me stand out too much so eventually I wore something that just about passed my requirements. I caught the bus at the end of the road with some degree of trepidation. What I noticed about Carol as we rode on the bus together, and I'm sure I mentioned it to her, was how her bright blue eyes would dart around with some speed as she looked at, and talked to me. It was one of her mannerisms and told me she was not only intelligent but very fast when it came to assessing people's characters.

I guess our date to the cinema was when we started to become boyfriend and girlfriend rather than simply going out as an experiment or for company. I felt our relationship was developing but I could see that Carol was a very strong-willed person, something she almost certainly got from her father as he had been one for fist-fighting in local pubs and had a very 'short fuse.' Carol had been the only one in her family to pass the eleven-plus examination, attended the grammar school at Hemsworth and was very bright indeed – she was especially good at maths and working with figures as I had witnessed several times already in our local shop. Unfortunately, she had been hurried into leaving school at the age of 15 when she could clearly have expected to go on to do her O'levels, A'levels and then attend university if she had had the right backing. However, in those days girls were clearly disadvantaged, received lower wages than their male counterparts, and generally felt like second class citizens in many ways. As we chatted, these elements of Carol's thinking came out quite strongly and although I didn't register it at that time, it explained why Carol held the view that she would not, understandably, be type-casted into becoming an obedient and down-trodden wife, as perhaps many were in the mining area that we both were born into.

These thoughts were emphasised even more when we got to the end of the film as, in those days, every cinema played the national anthem ('God save the Queen') after the film ended and everyone was expected to stand up and wait politely until it had ended. Being a member of the armed services I was used to this and duly stood up when the national anthem started. However, Carol quickly voiced her disapproval, took me by the hand and we both walked straight out of the cinema together. When I asked her about this it became clear that she was not a Royalist as many people from South Yorkshire tended to have strong Socialist and working-class views regarding the Royal Family. By the end of my Christmas leave I had naturally spent quite a lot of time with Carol and probably my parents had registered this because I had less of my (limited) time to spend with them.

After joining *Bulwark* I would very soon, on the 23rd January, be setting sail and be away from home for eight months. I was unsure if my relationship with Carol would survive such a long period of separation and so I suspect we had tried to get to know one another well in the short period we could spend together, and there would only be one more week-end available before I departed.

IV - HMS *Bulwark* [1970-72]

The train journey from Sheffield to Plymouth was a very long one that lasted all through the night, and involved a change and a long wait at Bristol Temple Meads in the station café. As I would find out in the coming years, this was always a place where returning Navy and other Service personnel would congregate in the small hours of the morning as they took every opportunity to stay at home on leave with their families or girlfriends for as long as feasible. We were always warned that we should never leave our return journey to the 'last train' as we could end up being 'adrift' (late) in returning to our ships, and the excuse of 'the last train was delayed, Sir' was never accepted. However, most of us ignored those warnings and took the chance of being late and receiving various punishments. The ladies who served up tea in white cups and saucers, accompanied with sandwiches and pies, would be kept busy as trains came into the station from various destinations around the country all through the night.

At 7.00 am I finally arrived in Plymouth and caught a taxi to the dockyard, where I checked into the main gate and waited for Navy transport to take me to my ship. Although I was tired, I waited with great anticipation for the bus to arrive. I boarded the vehicle with some others who were joining various ships and we set off. As we drove through the dockyard I observed through the window that it was teaming with Navy personnel and dockyard workers in green overalls. There were also countless yellow cranes on railway tracks, and vast numbers of ships, barges and tugs of all sizes and shapes. The first carrier I saw was HMS *Centaur*, which was a sister ship of *Bulwark* so I thought we had arrived, but we continued further and finally stopped at the beginning of the largest jetty in the dockyard. I couldn't believe my eyes when I got out as there were three carriers all in a row and I became excited wondering which one was mine. As I walked along the jetty I looked up the large gangway and towering flight deck above the first ship and saw in large brass figures, 'HMS *Albion,*' another sister ship of *Bulwark,* so I continued to the second and saw it was quite a bit larger in size – it was HMS *Ark Royal*, so by a process of elimination I knew that the last one in the row had to be my ship, HMS *Bulwark*.

I walked to the edge of the gangway, which was a long wooden structure with ridged steps at an angle of about 10 degrees to the horizontal and tied to the ship. At the end of the ladder I saw the duty Officer and bosun's mate with several ratings walking along the decks and flight deck. Above them was the ship's name and emblem – I had arrived and was ready to climb the steps with my kit bag on my shoulder and green Navy suitcase in my left hand. I duly strode up the gangway and after placing my kit bag on the deck and saluting, was checked in by the bosun's mate and then told to report to the regulating office on four-deck.

This meant climbing down the steel ladders and walking through a number of passageways until I reached the correct compartment that served as the office of the MAA, RPO and other Regulating staff. After completing some next-of-kin forms I was issued with a joining routing pack, and told to report to the Killick of 5E2 mess, which was through the dining hall and then to the deck below (i.e. 5th deck, E compartment [5th from the front of the ship], and the 2 signified 'Port' [left] side). Once I arrived in the Pinkies' (the commonly-used name for members of the Radio Electrical department) mess deck I was pleased to be re-united with Roy Brooks and Kenny Everett, plus Jock Pettigrew who had been in *Temeraire* division at *Collingwood*. They had joined before Christmas and had already been involved in sea trials at Portland following the eighth commissioning ceremony in Plymouth on the 10th November. It was a warm welcome by everyone, with some of the 'old salts' making comments about 'another junior joining the REMs mess' (new juniors were referred to as 'skin' – meaning a young looking sailor who has not yet started shaving).

Photo 17 - HMS *Bulwark* (22,000 tonnes) in 1970

Source: author

The Killick of the Mess was 'Buck' Taylor, a very bright and well-organised person with black-rimmed glasses who came from Manchester. His first task was to allocate me a bunk and a locker, which I could immediately see were tightly packed into a fairly small area. In total there were 27 bunks within two areas containing 12 bunks each, and around a corner there were three bunks on their own. My bunk was the top one of the first sleeping space, which I quickly learned I had to haul myself up to by gripping two metal handles that were suspended from the deck head (ceiling). My modest-sized metal locker was right at the other end of the mess deck past the three separate bunks. The area we were accommodated in was about the size of two living rooms in an average sized home – which was shared by 27 people.

The space between one bunk and the one above it was about 2.5 feet and bunks were more or less placed end to end with very minimal gaps between them. The gap between one bunk and the one opposite was no more than three feet. This meant that a very strict routine of stowing away personal items of clothing in lockers had to be enforced. Seating in the Mess was achieved at specified times of the day by zipping up each mattress and bedding in our rexine (artificial leather) covers and then dropping the middle bunk so that it formed a backrest for the bottom bunk. The upper bunk was then raised upwards out of the way using the two straps that it was suspended from. This would be my 'home' for the next two years and it was clear that living in such a confined area with so many others would be a bit of a challenge at times. However, as I would soon discover, REMs were fortunate compared with some branches as we had access to many different compartments as part of our work, and these were always air conditioned and roomy even though they contained tightly packed radio and radar equipment – but we could write letters there or listen to music and so on.

We ate in two junior ratings' dining room areas directly above our Mess. Meals were obtained from serving areas attached to the galley and we ate from specialised metal trays that had several sections for each category of food (vegetables, main course, and dessert). Each of us had our own knife, fork, spoon, and plastic drinking cup. We used a designated shower room for 'Greenies' (the nickname for members of the Weapons Electrical Branch) one deck below the far end of the dining room which meant we took a fairly long walk in a towel and flip flops each morning and evening to get there. The toilets, known as 'heads' in the Navy due to the fact that in sailing ships they were at the head of the ship, were forward on four-deck. I quickly registered that they were very impersonal and arranged in long rows with only short metal doors and partitions, which meant that someone going into a toilet next to you could look down and see you, and often hold a short (unwanted) conversation with you. Because this did not suit my 'private' nature - to use an obvious pun – I soon learned to lock the toilet next to the end of a row and use the end toilet so no-one could disturb me. As I would find out in my sea-going career, finding privacy and peace and quiet would be a challenge for everyone.

On this my first day on board my new ship I was doubled up with Roy Brooks as duty REM as recorded in my first letter back to my parents that evening. I wrote:

> Roy and I were fire party today and we had an exercise. We had to rig a telephone from HQ1 to the scene of the fire. I will be working on the UHF section and went round and saw the equipment in the UHF office. It is all new stuff I haven't worked on but I'll pick it up as soon as I can. We are doing trials for 10 days then we call into Portsmouth so see you all on the 23rd.

After writing my letter I was required to pack up and carry my bedding in its cover to the duty fire Mess, and settled down for the night in a rather dowdy area of the ship with running machinery close by. As I was to discover, there was never a truly quiet area on the ship and we quickly had to learn to sleep or relax with all kinds of noise going on around us 24 hours a day.

The next day after a good breakfast with several friends I reported to the Electronic Maintenance Room (EMR) with all my fellow Pinkies. The EMR was the focal point for our branch where we mustered at the start of each day and for 'turn to' (start work) after the mid-day meal. I was required to discuss my work and general responsibilities with our Chief Tiffy (Artificer) 'Tug' Wilson, who was the person who allocated work to all junior and senior ratings in the Radio Electrical Branch. He was a short man in his thirties with dark hair and a beard. He immediately came across as an authoritative but approachable and likeable person, and was sitting on his stool at one end of the EMR next to the maintenance schedule board. I was then introduced to the PO in charge of the UHF Communications section, who would be my immediate boss. His name was POREL 'Bud' Abbot, and I was immediately sure that I would both enjoy working for, and learning from him. I was told to report to the UHF Office by Bud once I had been shown around the EMR and taken on a tour of the whole department by Roy Brooks. On the UHF section there was another more senior REM, who was a very quiet but friendly and helpful person affectionately known as 'Ginge' because of his red hair (a tag I was often given myself, especially by the PTIs). As the ship was in the dockyard there were literally hundreds of dockyard workers ('dockies') crawling all over the ship doing various repairs and maintenance work in preparation for the ship leaving port.

Once my tour of the ship was completed, Roy and I went to the Mess for stand easy. By this time the duty watch had scrubbed and cleaned the deck and folded down the bunks, which was something I would soon be doing myself. We could therefore all sit around with our tea and discuss work or anything else we wished to. I could immediately see that there were many strong and colourful characters among my messmates, many of whom I will describe in more detail as the book progresses as they would have a significant impact on my development, views on life and work. At this time the Royal Navy still issued rum, or the 'tot,' every day to those who were over 18 years old. I remember Buck Taylor saying to me that juniors could be invited by those entitled to the tot to have 'sippers' – which meant exactly that, a sip of rum, but if they were found to be drunk in the afternoon it would lead to serious consequences for both the junior and the rating sharing his rum. The tot was only to last another seven months before I reached 18, but I would be invited for sippers on one or

[44]

two occasions over the coming months – without getting drunk. After stand easy Ginge said, "Come on then, let's head off to the UHF Office," and we climbed up several ladders through the ship and up again into the ship's 'island.'

The island was the superstructure that rose up on the starboard side of the ship, and contained the bridge and several offices that controlled operations and flying in particular. One deck above the flight deck was the UHF Office, and we entered together. I had already signed for my new tool roll from Chief Wilson in the EMR – the two most important items in it, as I would soon find out, being the 'long red' screwdriver and a 'Pussers' torch, which had a green, corrugated metal case and a light at right angles to the main body. After having a quick chat, Bud started showing me round the equipment. There was also a small additional office at the end, which contained mainly smaller transmitters and receivers. The thing that struck me immediately was the regular whirling sound of the tuning motors in the larger transmitters (called 692 and 693) and receivers (CUH and CUJs). Bud explained that people on the Bridge, and in particular the Flying Control Officer (FLYCO), could change the channel (and therefore frequency) of any transmitter and receiver by simply moving a switch. This sent signals to the UHF Office, which triggered the motors to do the tuning. There were also several lights on the front of the sets, and when one was properly tuned the lights would be permanently on, and the tuning motors stopped. The warning sign that something was wrong would be when the motors did not stop and the lights continued flashing. Bud gave me some books of reference (BRs) to read on the sets and said I should work closely with him and Ginge until I learned how to help maintain the sets safely.

The environment was clean and air conditioned, and just outside the office was a porthole that would become a favourite spot for me to observe the helicopters taking off from and landing on the flight deck. In the coming weeks I continued my training on UHF and other equipment as outlined in a letter sent home on the 29th January:

I enjoy life on board a ship. It is a lot more exciting and relaxed than a shore establishment. I have got an exam on Tuesday on my section and also on other equipment on the radio and radar side of the ship. They teach you with a tape recorder and the PO in charge of you also gives help. I have already been given a few jobs to do by myself.

I quickly recognised that I was fortunate to be given such a good first job as an REM, although there would be one or two scary moments to deal with in the coming months. I also vividly recall the day I met Leading Radio Operator (LRO) Ken Quinnell, and his RO 'side-kick,' 'Big Al.'

Just before stand easy one morning LRO Quinell appeared in the UHF Office with a clipboard under his arm and commenced tuning the sets when I spotted him from our work bench. When we set eyes on each other there was some sense of, 'aye aye, who's this, then?' It was my first ship and I had never come across any other ROs before, and was therefore a bit unsure as to how the relationship between maintainers and operators worked in practice. He was of slim and not very athletic build with parted blonde hair and 'discerning' blue eyes, and had an assured and confident air about him. Perhaps without thinking of what I was saying but wishing to break the ice I said, "Morning, sparks." His reaction was muted with a slight smirk on his face as if to say, "Who is this cocky young Pinkie referring to me, *an LRO*, as *sparks?*" I wasn't even sure if that was the correct nickname for members of the Communications branch. After a few seconds, he turned to Bud and made some comment along the lines of, "Is this your new JREM, Bud?" I could immediately determine that he was very well spoken and professional in his work, but I also sensed he was likeable while being somewhat of a challenge, and I thought I might wish to reciprocate in some way. As our 'friendly' working relationship developed, when they came into the office the banter began immediately along the lines, "Excuse me Petty Officer Abbott, but are you sure you can trust JREM *One* – or is it *Two* - Nixon here with that screw driver? He might do some permanent damage to the gear. We don't mind if he gets a 'belt' – it might sharpen him up a bit - but FLYCO won't be too happy when he can't communicate with the *chopper* pilots." When I got the chance, while being aware of our difference in rank and me only being a 'sprog' (a favourite term Ken and others used to describe juniors), I usually responded by implying that he couldn't handle himself in a fight, and he only gave out these disparaging remarks because he had Big Al to back him up. They usually left the office, having tuned all the sets, implying they would "get me later" and clenching their fists in a mock threat (while laughing as they disappeared down the ladder to the Bridge Wireless office (BWO)). Bud thought this was amusing as in many ways it engendered a lively working relationship between us and the operators. As the months went by the exchanges between us became more and more 'imaginative,' focussing on accusations of incompetence, a lack of intelligence or judgement, coupled with idle threats while naturally remaining within the borders of naval discipline. This experience enriched my working life and I'm not sure I have ever worked in such a convivial arrangement since then – I suspect Ken knew it was a way of keeping up morale among the younger 'troops' and he also enjoyed a challenge himself.

In early January we set sail from Plymouth on a calm and sunny morning to head to Portland where we would continue with sea trials. I remember that as we sailed down the channel and out into the open sea I took the opportunity to look out of the porthole outside the UHF Office to get a feel for how the ship would handle herself and view other ships and the coastline. As I was doing this I spotted a line of helicopters flying towards the stern of the ship in its wake. Before long the Wessex Mark 5 helicopters of 848 Squadron were hovering impressively, one after the other, alongside the port side of the ship. One by one they manoeuvred above the flight deck where crew members of the Fleet Air Arm guided them onto one of the nine landing markings on the deck using a 'lollipop' that they waved about in the air. I could immediately see that the navy blue choppers had various identification markings – including their main alphabetic identifiers such as 'R' for Romeo and 'J' for Juliet, and 'Royal Navy' in larger white letters. I could smell the exhaust fumes that came out from a large and clearly visible exhaust system just below the pilot's position. I could also observe the pilots, in white helmets and flying suits with their gold-on black rank badges and squadron emblem badges. I quickly admired the skill and confidence they showed in bringing their aircraft safely down onto the flight deck whilst their air crew, in similar attire, stood or knelt next to the sliding door of the cabin looking out and below. They produced their own spray on the surface of the water, caused by the down draught of the rotor blades. Upon landing, the helicopters all waddled a little on the deck before reducing the velocity of their rotor blades and finally settling in a stable position. The flight deck parties then approached them with straps and secured them to the deck. Later, the aircraft handlers moved them to one of the two large flight deck lifts that took them down into the enormous hangar that housed them. For a 17-year old, this was all pretty exciting stuff, and soon I was back in the comfort of the UHF Office learning more about the equipment. Once in Portland the work we undertook was related in a letter home on the 18th January:

We were doing high speed trials on Thursday and the ship was doing 27 knots. We also did night flying trials and because the equipment I work on is used to communicate with the helicopters I had to stay up part of the night and make sure nothing went wrong. I must close now and get a shower. I will see you all on Friday.

I was therefore able to go home from Portsmouth for one last week-end before our deployment got under way. On Friday 24th I took the train back to Yorkshire to spend the small amount of time that was left for me to be with Carol and my immediate family members. It seems that my father in particular had felt the increased demand on my time because as Carol and I prepared to leave for the station together, and I said my goodbyes everyone, the atmosphere suddenly became emotional and upsetting. I was in uniform and carrying my case, and as I shook my father's hand and gave him a bear hug, as we always did, he broke down in tears and placed his head on the cupboard doors of the kitchen to cover his face. My mother also became upset and comforted him whilst also showing concern about me leaving. Although everyone was saddened by this as our previous goodbyes had been more 'matter of fact,' I don't think any of us knew the strength of the underlying reasons. First of all, as I have mentioned previously, my father and I were best friends and had done countless father and son-type things all through my life. He had also been similarly upset when saying goodbye to me when we left Salisbury to return to England in 1963. However, although my father never spoke about this at that time, he himself had left home in very similar circumstances during World War II and, as I would later discover and write about with my sister Barbara (Nixon & Smith, 2006), had ended up in Singapore, my main destination in the coming months, where he had been captured by the Japanese and spent three and a half years in captivity as a far east prisoner of war (FEPOW).

Thus, with this mixture of emotions I boarded the train at Doncaster station once more, waved to Carol and she waved back before heading for the exit. I sat down for the 10-hour journey ahead of me to Portsmouth, arriving at 7.00 am the following morning after changing trains in London. I wouldn't be back for the best part of a year and I was beginning to experience the mixed emotions that are associated with the loss of freedom encountered by someone who gives his or her life to the country's armed forces.

****

On Monday 26th January as I sat alone in the EMR late into the evening whilst on duty, I wrote letters to Carol and my parents under a green study lamp. In the letter to my parents I expressed concern for the fact that they had been so upset. There was nothing I could do about the effects of my departure and whatever the situation was it made me realise the strong bonds that existed between us. I mentioned that they had probably experienced similar issues with their parents when they were courting, and that it was natural for Carol and I to be spending my limited time together. The song many of us heard so often on the radio at this time was Peter Paul and Mary's 'Leaving on a Jet Plane' (Denver, 1966). For those who were married, in particular, or had close family ties or strong relationships with girlfriends as I now had, the words expressed something emotionally draining about the loss of control over where any of us wishes to be at a given time:

Oh my bags are packed, I'm ready to go/ I'm standing here outside your door
I hate to wake you up, to say goodbye/ but the dawn is breaking, it's early morn
The taxi's waiting, he's blowing his horn/ already I'm so lonesome I could cry
So kiss me, and smile for me/ tell me that you'll wait for me
Hold me like you'll never let me go/ 'cause I'm leaving on a jet plane
Don't know when I'll be back again…..

In the coming seven months the letters I would receive from Carol and my parents would be the 'umbilical cord' between my home on board *Bulwark*, the places I would visit, and my true home.

Amid a hive of activity on board the ship and flight deck the following morning, I watched out of my porthole near the UHF office as we slipped majestically out of Portsmouth harbour, observing some family members waving to their loved ones from the shore and various vantage points as people had done over the centuries for departing Royal Navy ships. Very soon afterwards we sailed through the Solent past the Isle of Wight and then into the open sea, heading in a westerly direction for Plymouth. There we would not come alongside but allow 848 squadron helicopters and personnel to embark and then commence our deployment for real as we headed south for our first port of call - the island of Gibraltar.

After experiencing a relatively smooth trip during the first day, the weather turned more inclement as we entered into the often turbulent area off the coast of Portugal as I recounted in a letter of the 29th January:

Well we are off the coast of Spain at the moment and due to arrive in Gibraltar tomorrow. We came through the Bay of Biscay yesterday and this time it was really rough. The waves were coming over the flight deck and the ship was rolling around quite a lot. Although I didn't feel sea sick it was awkward to walk around and it was hard to do a job without banging your head or something. I can tell we are off the coast of Spain because Roy and I have just been up and had a look at one of the radar displays and saw the coastline.

In this particular letter I also noted that Roy had been put on punishment that day for falling asleep on his bunk in the afternoon and therefore did not turn up for work on time. This letter reminds me of how lucky REMs were as we had access to all the operations rooms and radio and radar maintenance rooms, so we could often look at radar sets, in dimmed compartments, with their distinctive dark backgrounds and orange-coloured traces rotating around in time with the aerial outside in the upper superstructure; illuminating targets and areas of land as the trace rotated. It also reminds me of the fact that we were often tired from travelling through the night back to the ship and then having to work a full day, with the possibility of completing four hours as the duty watch late into the night or early hours of the next morning. However, it wasn't only their bunks that people overslept in, as had happened to Roy. I once saw another close friend fall asleep under some very loud running machinery in the UHF office annex, although I recall he had been suffering from a hangover as well as sleep deprivation, which had been Roy's only reason.

The following morning after breakfast when taking a stroll across the flight deck - the spacious area we were very lucky to have access to on board an aircraft carrier – the seas were blue and calm, dolphins could be seen swimming alongside us even though we were cruising at over 20 knots. The wake of the ship panned out to the side and stern with sea spray flying above the blue waves, and a fresh sea breeze refreshed my face as I gazed at the land to the port side ahead of the ship. We would soon be arriving in Gibraltar where, although I wouldn't have much time ashore as I was duty watch, I would have time to play my first game of football for *Bulwark* and rather gullibly buy my first 'rabbit' (present) - a fantastic-looking watch with a metal strap.

Soon after joining the ship I had made contact with the PTIs and the manager of the ship's football team, who was a wily member of the Fleet Air Arm (Wafoos, as we called them) with a typical sailor's beard and a keen interest in managing the team. I recall he came down to the Mess to talk to me about playing for the ship and knew that I had played for the Royal Navy youth team. I soon also got to know Able Seaman Mick O'Shea, the captain of the team and a budding PTI himself, who would become a good friend and someone I looked up to, both physically (he was about six feet two inches) and in terms of his character and footballing abilities. Although I don't recall playing any trial games during sea trials at Portland, I was lucky enough to be put straight into the first eleven as an attacking midfield player – my favourite position. Over the coming months and years, sport, along with playing the guitar, would be my saviour and a means of taking part in healthy activity in all the ports I would visit. I therefore looked forward to the few days ahead of us and went down to the EMR to muster with my colleagues for the day's work ahead. By now, like many of my younger colleagues, I had become adept at sliding down ladders' handrails whilst occasionally tapping my feet on the rungs. Later that afternoon the ship moored alongside in the harbour, and once cleared to do so some friends and I went on deck to take our first viewing of the spectacular 'Rock' of Gibraltar.

Photo 18 - *Bulwark* alongside in Gibraltar, 1970

Source: *author*

The next afternoon I gathered with the rest of the ship's football team on the jetty to catch a Navy bus for the match against our opponents that day - the Gibraltar Police force. The ship looked impressive against the background of white houses and apartments that made up the town, and the grey and green rock rising up into the blue sky. Once under way, we drove through the town and up to the stadium we would be playing on - with its sand (hard-surfaced) pitch. The match was a tough encounter – any game against a Police team usually was – and playing on a hard surface covered in sand put us at a disadvantage as they were accustomed to it.

I remember it rained half way through, but as it was warm rain it was more welcome than it would have been in the UK. The game was being watched by a good-sized crowd. I recall that our centre forward was 'taken out' by one 'clumsy' and heavy challenge. However, the game ended in a respectable 3-3 draw and I was pleased that my place in the team seemed to have been cemented. There were two other juniors who played for *Bulwark*; a Marine Engineering Mechanic (MEM) called 'Buck' Taylor and another 'Greenie' called JOEM Marsh, both of whom would go on to be my close friends.

I managed to spend some time exploring by walking some way up the rock and also through the very long tunnel that runs from the harbour-side of the island to Catalan Bay at the opposite side of the Rock. The scene there was idyllic with the blue Mediterranean Sea lapping onto a sandy beach and cafés with terraces, as well as the impressive Caleta Palace Hotel, overlooking the beach. I took a short swim in the water, which was warm and pleasant, but was slightly concerned about the risk of sharks being close by, but fortunately none appeared. The thing that also struck me about the island was the colonial feel it had. One could not avoid seeing the impressive governor's residence and guard room with its polished cannons and white exterior in the centre of the main town, and the Union Jack flag gently rocking in the warm breeze. I also walked past some nurses of the Queen Alexandra's Royal Navy Nursing Service (QARNNS) and doctors from the Royal Naval Hospital (RNH) and was struck by how smart they looked in their uniforms. It was also an impressive sight to stand high up on the side of the rock and gaze down at *Bulwark* looking so impressive in the harbour, surrounded by a blue ocean and other vessels. This would be a scene I would enjoy in the many ports we would visit over the coming two years. The final thing I did was to buy some presents for my family and Carol, and also bought my first 'deployment' watch with the aforementioned steel strap.

When I got back on board I proudly showed my new watch to several mess mates but didn't quite get the congratulatory response I had expected. I had bought it from one of the tourist shops in town and recall it impressed me as it had an unusual second hand movement – it may have been something like an arrow-headed arm, but I remember one of the Killicks, Dave Clegg, who had a wicked sense of humour and forthright manner, saying, "The cocky (cockroach) inside it that makes it work will die in a couple of days and you will have to bin it." The other more senior colleagues all agreed that I had bought a 'pup' and asked me how much I had paid for it – suggesting I had been 'robbed' when I told them - but as Kenny Everett reassuringly said, "Don't worry, Johnny, it happens to everyone on their first deployment." I have to confess that I have never been the most astute shopper to walk the shopping malls of the world, but I felt confident my new watch would survive longer than they all had predicted. Sadly, a few days after leaving Gibraltar when we were heading down the west coast of Africa, the watch duly died on me and there was no option left but to say goodbye to it. The advice I was given was to wait until we reached Singapore where I could buy a Seiko watch, which many people swore by in terms of reliability and had been wearing themselves for many years.

As we travelled south into warm and blue waters we changed into tropical working rig, which meant we wore dark blue shorts, lighter blue No. 8 shirts and a pair of leather sandals. Things were going well as I related in a letter to my parents on the 3rd February:

We are now only 2 days from the Equator. It is just like when we came back to England because we are on the same route as the Athlone Castle except going in the opposite direction. The weather is absolutely great, the sun is out and the sea is deep blue. We go on the flight deck every night and the sea air does you the world of good. Everyone's skin is slightly tanned. We have sport on the flight deck every week-end and have a really good time. We arrive in Cape Town on the 12th February and that is when this mail will go off and be sent home.

I also discussed a mission my parents had given to me in their letters, as I would attempt to locate some friends from Rhodesia, Helene and Peter, who had moved to South Africa about the time we left Rhodesia, as many white families had done at that time. The weather continued to improve and we were all given an extra two hours cleaning and painting of the ship after work in preparation for arriving in Cape Town. The First Lieutenant had produced a motto to help in this process, which was 'clean ship for fun in the sun.' Therefore, before supper each evening there were people being lowered over the side of the ship with paint brushes and grey paint, and my fellow UHF REM and I were given the task of painting outside our office. As a reward for all our hard work we were given a special but not particularly well thought-out reward.

Instead of continuing with our ship's painting work one evening the ship came to a halt near the equator and the decision was taken by the Commander to have 'hands to bathe' (free swim in the ocean). This seemed like a good idea as the sea was like a mill pond and looked blue and inviting. A frenzy of activity thus ensued as about 300 of us got into our swimming trunks and headed for the starboard boat bay, which was about 50 feet from the waterline and where rescue ropes plus the main ladder could be lowered from. This sounded like a unique opportunity so Roy and I, plus others from our Mess, shot off to join in the fun.

We were told that if sharks were spotted the ship's fog horn would be sounded and we should return to the ship as quickly as possible, and a cutter would be close by to assist any swimmers who got into difficulty. People were enthusiastically jumping into the sea and one or two dived in, which was my preferred method of getting into the water. The photo recording this adventure shows someone diving into the water from the position I had also selected. Some also jumped from the flight deck and thus made an enormous splash when entering the water. The sea was warm and I started swimming around like the others. I quickly noticed that it was actually rougher in the sea than it looked from above and I could see waves rolling along the side of the ship and exposing the black hull below the water line – the ship also looked enormous above us.

Then it happened. A loud noise boomed out from the ship's fog horns, which immediately instilled panic in the swimmers – we knew sharks were close by! The joke that this event generated was that 'Olympic records were broken' but it was actually a very scary experience as I explained in a letter to my parents on the 5th February:

We were swimming for about 10 minutes when two big sharks were sighted. The shark warning went and I have never seen so many sailors swim so fast in all my life. I don't think I will be going swimming in the middle of the ocean again!

When Roy and I eventually returned to the Mess muttering expletives about the 'good idea' it had been, I realised that all the Killicks and older REMs had declined the opportunity to swim in the shark-infested belt of the Atlantic Ocean – they clearly knew more than the best watches to buy. I remember complaining to Roy and a few others that I had started climbing up one of the ropes and could have managed to get to the top without any problem, but someone above me on the rope wasn't strong enough to go higher and had fallen on top of me and sent us both crashing back into the sea, which prompted me to swim at high speed to the ladder – ploughing over some people who were in my way. The people I admired most in this incident were those who actually swam 'away from the ship' and climbed aboard the cutter – that appeared to be madness at the time when I saw them heading off towards such a small sanctuary but in hindsight they could see it was sensible considering the chaos that was going on around the bottom of the main ladder.

As well as having a 'crossing the line' ceremony on the flight deck, which my letters indicate I missed due to falling asleep in the afternoon, I knew from my cruise on the *Athlone Castle* as a child that it involved Father Neptune coming aboard and administering various 'punishments,' usually involving copious amounts of water and mock surgery. In any event, there were numerous activities happening on the flight deck and also around the ship more generally due to the good weather and perfect sea conditions. I recall often sitting on the stern of the ship, watching the wake panning out behind us in the deep blue seas while knowing that below them lurked some significant dangers for would-be swimmers.

Photo 19 - Hands to bathe en route to Cape Town

Source: author

I continued to enjoy the voyage and life in general for this part of our deployment. We often played football on the flight deck but the balls that we made from masking tape and rags often got kicked over the side, and on one occasion we kept hitting 'Susie,' which was the small helicopter used for collecting and delivering mail to the ship. We were told to help move the helicopter before we could continue. Later, on a stroll over the flight deck in the early evening I watched some dolphins swimming with us and then spotted some strange creatures that looked like birds as several hundred of them were flying above the waves and then diving into the water. It turned out they were flying fish and I must say I was impressed by the agility of these little creatures. As the 12th February approached, however, we entered the famous 'Cape Rollers,' which were quite large rolling waves that were usually present around the Cape due to the meeting of the Atlantic and Indian Oceans. I remember coming up onto the starboard boat bay one morning and on seeing the new sea conditions, thinking how strong the contrast can be between various sea and weather conditions. As I would discover in the coming years, this variation could mean the difference between experiencing a sense of wellbeing in living aboard a warship, to that of being in hell – hence the commonly used expression 'you have to learn to take the rough with the smooth.'

On the morning of the 12th February the ship's company prepared for what was known as 'procedure alpha' in entering the port of Cape Town. Procedure alpha involved most of the ship's company of junior ratings, and nominated senior ratings, getting into their best uniforms – in this case tropical uniforms – and lining the outer edges of the flight deck and other decks. I had been allocated a perfect position next to the 'FU1' aerial - the distinguishing feature of *Bulwark* compared with her sister ships such as *Albion* and *Centaur*. It had a circular aerial at the end of its support and was on the starboard side forward of the island. As we mustered on the deck and started forming our straight lines we saw the magnificent view of Table Mountain with its flat top rising into the clouds above the city. Tied up alongside in the port were a number of cruise ships and other vessels. I described this event in detail in a letter dated 13th Feb:

We came in to a 21-gun salute to the Republic and another 21-gun salute to the Prime Minister. Our salute was replied to from a hill just to the right of Table Mountain. It felt really great as there were hundreds of us lining the deck in our whites and it looked a really impressive sight.

Photo 20 - Arrival in Cape Town

Source: *author*

Photo 21 - JN and Roy ashore

Source: *author*

A large picture of us appeared in the 'Cape Times,' which I told my parents I would try and get a copy of. The photo above records this along with a photo of Roy and I ashore the following day.

After being at sea for almost two weeks we were all anxiously looking forward to receiving mail on arrival. Everyone, in these circumstances, eagerly awaited the pipe over the ship's broadcast system that 'mail is now ready for collection.' This was the cue for someone from each Mess to charge down to the Mail Office and collect all the letters for their mess deck. If we were working in our sections at this point in time we had to wait until the morning stand easy break or dinner time. When I arrived in the mess deck I saw the columns of letters arranged according to our names across the top of a line of highly polished lockers. Luckily for me, Carol and my parents wrote letters very regularly and I was always pleased to see that my column of letters was among the longest of them all. The importance of our mail cannot be over-emphasised as many people were concerned about being away and missing their families, especially those with young children. I recall numerous occasions when I saw the looks of worry and longing on the faces of people around me, trying to make the most of their absence within often very cramped conditions. As providers and protectors of their families, wives or girlfriends, they felt vulnerable and naturally concerned about the risks of being away for so long. I recall an incident later in the deployment, when one of our mess mates with a baby daughter and wife, on hearing the pipe 'mail is now ready for collection,' ran straight up the ladder leading from our mess deck but didn't realise that the metal hatch had been closed, and smashed his head before returning to the Mess in some pain and embarrassment, rubbing his scalp. We all usually sought out a quiet place to open our letters and savoured the time spent reading them, often returning to read particular sentences or paragraphs repeatedly when something in them attracted our attention.

In Cape Town, we were visited by at least 250 guests and one particular couple, who were walking around the ship, invited Roy and I to their home the following day. With my South African past life in Rhodesia there were many opportunities for us to exchange views and stories about life in Africa. I also recall the football match that we played in Cape Town was against a Social Club, which we won comfortably 5-0 and in the evening we had a very enjoyable barbeque with our hosts.

One of the highlights of or brief stay occurred when I took part in an activity we always offered in visits of this nature - that of providing a party on board the ship for local children, many of whom came from challenging or disadvantaged backgrounds. In my letter of the 13ᵗʰ Feb I explained:

There were 220 children altogether. They really had a good time and we all dressed up as pirates for them. We set up all kinds of games and amusements and to tell you the truth I haven't enjoyed myself as much in a long time. After the games they had tea and then cartoons and they were very grateful. I am playing football for the ship on Sunday against the Technical College here so I am looking forward to that. I was presented with my Navy football Colours the other day so all I need now is a blazer to go with them.

****

On our departure from Cape Town we quickly encountered some very rough seas, which meant the Captain decided to change our original course. On the 23ʳᵈ February I was thinking of my childhood life in Africa as recounted in a letter home as our ship fought with the elements outside:

Well we are now between Madagascar and the main land in the Indian Ocean. I was just thinking if I look west and slightly north I will be looking at Beira where I used to swim when we lived in Rhodesia. Our original course would have taken us to Mauritius first and then on to Gan but we had to come up the West side of Madagascar because a typhoon was coming our way from Mauritius. The weather was rough before we changed course and we had really big waves coming over the flight deck. Some of the lads were sea sick, and I didn't feel so good myself but it was just a muzzy headache. I will write again before we reach Gan and I'm hoping to hear from you then.

As I went about the ship on rounds and observing the stormy seas of 'tropical storm Diane,' I recalled the long trip from Salisbury in Rhodesia to Cape Town by sleeper train, and joining the *Athlone Castle* in sunny Cape Town. I also remembered with affection the life and holidays we enjoyed in Beira, Portuguese East Africa, as it was then. It seemed strange to me that Rhodesia and Beira would not be suitable places for any of us to be in now, even though they had been home for many years. To get to Beira from Salisbury I recall the long trip by car when my sisters and I slept in the back of our black Morris Minor, which struggled to get up the very steep mountain road called Christmas Pass in the town of Umtali. We often stayed at a very comfortable hotel called the Mirima and enjoyed walks along the beach in the warm evening breezes from the Indian Ocean.

Leaving Rhodesia had been an enormous wrench for us and my parents had made a significant contribution in the good work they did in construction and at the main hospital. The nanny we had as children, Josephine, had wept in some distress at our departure as she had been like a second mother to me and my two sisters. The most devastating thing for me and my syisters was the fact that we had left our two dogs and cat to the care of I don't know who. However, I recall the steadfast manner in which my mother, in particular, had realised that it would be no place for a family like us to remain in, as many whites, including children, had been butchered in the 'Bush War.' In retrospect, the irony of post-colonial African countries such as Rhodesia/Zimbabwe, was that freedom, democracy and 'one man one vote' were the justification and means with which to usurp 'white' governments. But as time would tell, the principles of democracy and one man one vote would be trampled on by elected politicians with their own tribal instincts and desires, with often disasterous effects for ordinary Africans with other allegiances - effectively living in a one-party state for decades.

Photo 22 - Barbara, John, Valerie with dogs Trixie and Penny in Rhodesia

Source: author

Photo 23 - *Bulwark* in rough seas after Cape Town

Source: author

I brought myself back to the present as I returned below decks through the island's door hatch on the flight deck. In a letter I wrote on the 25th February, as we approached the island of Gan, I gave some details of my new pay rise to my parents and that I was now in a position to help them in their finances. At that time in working class families like mine it was accepted that children who were working helped their parents as my mother and father were certainly not wealthy. I also explained about my campaign to keep fit with one of my friends so that I could be fully prepared for my appearances in the ship's football team:

My mate and I are still keeping fit by running round the flight deck every morning and evening. It tired us out at first but it is getting better now as we get used to it. Well I suppose you have heard we are getting a pay rise pretty soon. I will soon be getting £20 a pay day (fortnightly) plus whatever we get from the pay rise. I am sending £3 per month to your Building Society account.

[55]

In the letter I wrote the following day I mentioned our brief encounter with the island of Gan. I described it to my father, making reference to his impressive knowledge of geography, as a 'dot in the Indian Ocean' and principally a US Navy base. Although it was very small it did look just like a paradise island as it was covered with palm trees and white sands that stretched out along abandoned beaches. We sailed around it for only two hours in blue and calm seas while our helicopters flew to and fro collecting mail and stores. I remarked that the Navy was clearly good at taking us to all these wonderful places around the world but not letting us ashore. However, we would soon be spending two weeks alongside in Singapore and that shortly afterwards we would be visiting Kobe in Japan for 'Expo 70.' The rest of the deployment would include visits to Hong Kong, Jakarta, Freemantle in Western Australia, Durban, Cape Town, Gibraltar and then Portsmouth on our return to the UK on the 20th August – still six months away at that time. At this point I gave details of the generous pay rise the Labour Government had awarded the armed services.

On pay days we all reported to the quarterdeck of the ship, which had scrubbed wooden decks and was astern of the ship well below the flight deck, and stood in lines that led to our pay officers. On stepping forward at the appropriate point we called out our ship's book number, rank and name, and were then presented our pay on top of our caps after the correct sum had been announced by one of the writers who scanned over enormous pay ledgers. I recall the pay rise day with some surprise and pleasure as I was impressed that our pay had almost doubled – I now received the princely sum of £17 per week (49 Shillings per day as I wrote in my letter). However, I noted that the tax man sadly took a greater share so I was beginning to appreciate the economic principle of diminishing rewards of increased pay although I was only interested in what appeared on the top of my cap like most 17 year-olds.

In this letter I noted my concerns about the way in which I would be dividing my time between my parents and Carol once I returned home. I explained that we had been discussing a possible holiday together with Carol's sister, Maureen, and her boyfriend. However, it is clear this raised some fears in my mind as I asked my mother not to 'go saying anything wrong to Carol' as my mother was possessive by nature, and could say things that were difficult for my fledgling relationship. It was quite a difficult situation for me personally because, as someone born under the sign of Libra, I generally sought balance in my relationships, but as I would discover in my Service life this would not be an easy thing to achieve in practice.

On the 1st March as we approached Singapore we rendezvoused with HMS *Fearless*, a former cruiser that had been converted into a helicopter assault ship. I watched her from the upper deck and my usual position outside the UHF Office as we ploughed through the warm, blue seas with a hive of noisy helicopter activity going on between the two ships. The reason for this was that, to coin a phrase appropriate for the permanent crew of *Bulwark*, the 'booties' were being transferred to us for an amphibious exercise called 'New Look.' The booties, of course, were the highly impressive Royal Marines of 42 Commando that joined us as all exercises approached, and there were a lot of them! – 900 to be precise. As the helicopters landed on the flight deck one after the other or several at a time, the marines jumped out with their extensive kit and made their way to their mess decks in an orderly fashion. I was aware that we had several very large mess decks that were empty, and now it became clear who usually occupied them. Queuing for meals, as we would find out, would become a longer process. Our mission was to undertake the planned five-day exercise at Wai Island before entering Singapore on the 9th March. As I explained in a letter home, dated 2nd March:

At midnight tonight we will be passing Singapore and that is when this letter will go off. We are taking mail on so I am looking forward to hearing from you again. We have had HMS Fearless

[56]

with us for two days and it makes things more interesting when you can look at another ship. We also saw a very large Japanese oil tanker the other day. I was listening to the football results yesterday and heard Rotherham lost 3-2 but still, all good teams lose now and then. I will be playing out here in Singapore but I don't suppose it will be the same as playing on an English pitch.

In a letter dated the 8th March I explained that the exercise we took part in was just off Brunei in Borneo, and outlined some of the details:

All the booties were flown ashore in the helicopters with their equipment and the ship just remained off the shore while the helicopters flew back and forth taking stores and supplies to them. The idea was to try and capture a terrorist company of marines. The 'terrorists' were Malayan and on the ship for a little while as well. According to the Commander it was a success so everyone was happy. Bud and my colleagues on the UHF section kept the equipment going during the exercise.

As the Commissioning book for our deployment (HMS Bulwark, 1971) indicates, the Sultan of Brunei paid us a courtesy visit around this time, arriving by fast patrol boat and leaving by helicopter. Although known widely as the 'Rusty B,' it was a happy ship and I was fortunate to have many good friends and colleagues with little reason to complain, except for being separated from my family and Carol.

With exercise New Look over, we entered Singapore on the 9th March for a one-month maintenance period. As we moved up the channel towards our destination, the first thing I registered was the odour that engulfed us on the flight deck. Singapore would prove to be a marvellous place, but it definitely did not have a pleasant aroma when approached from a seaward direction.

In the early morning of the 9th March I walked down the gangway of the ship, which was berthed alongside the dockyard, with a towel and shaving gear as the toilets and shower rooms on board had had their water supply removed. This was the first time I had stepped onto dry land for three weeks and the warm and sunny day made me feel encouraged despite the 'inconvenience' of our temporary arrangements. We would be in dry dock for a small maintenance period (SMP) for one month. The thing that was mostly on my mind was that I would be playing football for *Bulwark* this coming Thursday under floodlights at HMS *Terror* on number one pitch. I had been told about this by older members of the team and that we could expect large crowds to watch the games. I was hoping my keep fit regime of running every morning and evening around the flight deck would have kept me in good shape.

The following evening I went on a trip around Sembawang village, which would be a regular staging post for shopping and buying 'egg banjos' (a large egg sandwich cooked out in the open by the locals) after a game of football or 'run ashore.' The first thing I noticed is that all the local shopkeepers had clearly been expecting me as everywhere we went among the air-conditioned shops with shiny bright electrical goods and watches, including the famous Seikos, they called out, "Do you want to buy a watch, John?" or, "Do you want to buy a camera, John?" I was amazed but quickly realised that 'John' was the common name used by the locals to address us. Clearly a lot of Johns from the Royal Navy had visited Singapore over the years so it seemed logical that the locals would use that name to gain our attention and entice us into buying their goods. I also spent time, when not on duty, at the well-known club for Naval personnel called the 'Sailors' Rest,' which had its own swimming pools and was an ideal place to relax with a cool beer in the warm and pleasant evenings. Thursday night duly came along and the night of my first match, as recounted in a letter of the 12th March:

I played football for the ship last night. We were playing under floodlights and even though it was evening the heat was still very bad. It is the thin air that makes you feel the worst. We were doing well at first and at half time we were winning 2-0, but we weren't used to that type of weather and the other team knew how to play. We lost 4-3 but after a couple of more games we should be used to it.

The photo below shows our team just before the start of a game, which brings back fond memories as football had been the love of my life and would continue to be the thing I looked forward to as we continued our visits abroad and back at home. In the same letter home I noted some difficulties that one of my close friends had been experiencing, perhaps because of the long period we had spent at sea before arriving. It seems that he had been put on punishment and had had his leave stopped for two days as he had returned to the ship an hour late one evening and a little under the influence of alcohol. However, as I wrote, 'he wasn't satisfied with that because he tried to get off the ship in just a pair of shorts and when the officer of the watch told him to get a shirt on he started arguing back. So he has been given some more punishment and had his leave stopped. I don't know what that lad is playing at.' This was to be a regular feature of life in the Navy as many people naturally felt a need to 'let their hair down' after being at sea without the freedom to act as they pleased.

Photo 24 - *Bulwark's* 1st XI football team at HMS *Terror*, Singapore

JN back row 3rd from right. Our captain, Mick O'Shea, is front row centre. **Source:** *author*

Over the coming months the football team established its own routine in preparation for the matches, often arriving early and having a haircut or cold drink in the bar. We certainly enjoyed a tremendous following from the ship's company and went on to become one of the stronger teams that competed with HMS *Triumph*, the maintenance ship HMS *Forth*, HMS *Terror* and other visiting ships. After the matches in Singapore, the team always gathered in *Terror* bar to either celebrate with several pints of Tiger tops (Tiger beer with a shot of lemonade) and sing along with our supporters, or drown our sorrows and look forward to the next game.

I recall we lost a great deal of body weight during those games, and needed to drink several pints of iced water even before we got to the bar, although I mostly opted for an 'early night.' We were certainly all lean and fit because of the regular games we played. From my commissioning book I note that in Singapore, *Bulwark* played 13 matches altogether of which 6 were wins (including 5-1 against *Fearless* and 4-1 against *Forth*), 1 draw and 6 were losses.

By this time I was establishing friendships with many people and also learning from them and their mannerisms and characters. I would like to mention, as this chapter progresses, some of those that particularly impressed me in addition to my good friendships with Roy Brooks and Kenny Everett. The first one I recall is LREM Dick Wolsey. Dick was about 25 and a married man with young children. He was quietly spoken and immensely polite and thoughtful by nature. Whenever I took a problem to him he always listened very carefully and gave his full attention, and then offered intelligent and thoughtful answers. He was also technically astute and readily willing to teach the younger ones interesting and useful things about the radio and radar equipment we worked on. However, because Dick was such a strong family man and of a quiet, even gentle disposition, he genuinely suffered because of being away from home. The main thing he had to 'bear' because of his nature was a great deal of ribbing from his mess mates over some of his mannerisms. For example, he wore his Navy-issue pyjamas every night, unlike the rest of us who took to our bunks in colourful boxer shorts made by the Chinese tailors we had on board. He preferred non-alcoholic drinks and was basically teetotal. However, Dick always stood his ground and never once did I see him crumble and 'go along with the crowd' – I admired his position in that he knew what was appropriate for 'him' and no amount of peer-group pressure was going to have an impact on him. Some of the attention he received must have adversely affected him, but at the same time he was genuinely respected by everyone. Over the commission I became attached to him and he returned my respect and support by inviting me for meals at his home where I met his lovely wife and children. He was very much in the 'Chief Jones of *Ganges*' mould, which meant that life could be problematic for him at times. As someone who focussed on sport, there would be many times when I also had to stand my ground, like Dick Wolsey, in the face of peer-group disapproval because of my own conservative preferences.

****

One of the attractions of this period is that the ship's company were accommodated at HMS *Terror* and that we worked what was known as 'tropical routine.' On the 18th March my letter home, in which I describe our mess on board as a very happy Mess with everyone getting on well together, I describe this new arrangement in further detail.

We are on tropical routine, which means we work from 7.00 am to 12.30 pm. We get up in time to catch the busses from Terror to the ship, and at 1.00 pm we go back and have the afternoon to ourselves. Terror is more like Butlins than a Naval base as we have our own swimming pool (just like Cranborne in Rhodesia), our own club overlooking the football pitch and the thing we all like most – a good comfortable bed and a nice cool mess. The accommodation blocks have verandas to stop water getting in. I'm very much enjoying life at the moment. We played HMS Whitby on Sunday and won 6-0 – I scored a goal. We are gradually adjusting to the weather.

On that particular evening, as I explained, I was on board the ship as duty personnel remained there. That night we had a film to watch after supper - films were shown in the large dining room using a Bell and Howell 16mm cinema projector. We also watched films in our own mess deck when at sea – various members of the Mess were qualified to operate the famous if noisy reel-to-reel projectors, which were connected to their own loud speakers and created a genuine small-scale cinema atmosphere (it wasn't like watching a modern DVD, for example). For a screen, one of us donated a sheet from our clean laundry and we sat on the bunk beds in their non-sleeping positions. These were always pleasant occasions with either a can of cold beer or an ice cream 'goffa' (soft drink with ice cream similar to a milk shake) from the N.A.A.F.I. During most films there were one or two breakdowns as the film had a habit of slipping or breaking, which meant a short interlude with time to collect another goffa or relieve oneself. The two films I recall watching in HMS *Terror* cinema at this time are the James Bond classic. 'You Only Live Twice', and 'Mackenna's Gold' with soundtrack 'Old Turkey Buzzard,' performed by one of my favourite guitarists/singers, José Feliciano. The cinema itself was cool and comfortable with its own air conditioning – there was absolutely no better place than to watch a good film than the cinema at HMS *Terror*.

Around this time I received my favourite photo of Carol. She had arranged for it to be taken especially for me in a local photographic studio in Selby where she and her family had moved to due to her father's work. In *Terror* it was possible to put personal photographs on the tops of our large wooden lockers – on board ship we only usually took our family and personal photos out when writing letters, and kept them in our writing material cases at other times. In my opinion Carol outshone every other girlfriend's photo (although others naturally felt the same about their girlfriends of wives) and many friends voiced the common opinion that she looked very much like Judith Durham, who was the lead singer of the Australian group 'the Seekers.' Many had bought expensive stereo systems from the shops in Sembawang and as I sat down on a bamboo chair at a desk in our accommodation to write letters I often heard the words and music of Simon and Garfunkel, or indeed Judith Durham singing the song her own biography in the distant future would be named after - 'Colours of my life.' (Durham & Reilly, 1967):

Colours blend with love to show I'm happy with you/ I can never be the same again;
Now my eyes are looking past the life that I knew/ I'll be shedding black and grey;
To take on red and blue/ Colours I can feel by touching you.......

Photo 25 - Photograph of Carol I received in Singapore

Source: *author*

[60]

The combination of music and the environment created a relaxing atmosphere but also tugged at our emotions and made us think of home. The magic of life in HMS *Terror* was enhanced by the fact we could clearly hear the music in good quality hi-fi sound, unlike on board when loud speakers had to compete against fans and other equipment that were constantly running near to where we were in 5E2 mess. By this time I had also bought my first guitar and a genuine silver-strapped Seiko watch in the magical shops in the village.

As our dockyard maintenance period progressed we saw and heard the ship being repaired, painted and cleaned every day. I say 'heard' as we quickly became accustomed to hearing the famous 'windy hammers' used by the dockyard workers. These were pneumatic hammers that were used to remove paint and made unbelievably loud noises that reverberated around and above us wherever we were. On the UHF section we also carried out our planned maintenance, which led me to experience one of the scariest times of my career as an REM2 (having reached seventeen and a half the 'J' for junior was now removed).

The incident came about as Bud Abbott gathered us at the side of the ship, which was now in dry dock so there was a very large drop that went right under the keel of *Bulwark*, so the height from the bottom to the top of the ship was about 200 feet or more. Bud, in his calm but assertive manner, said, "Okay, our task today is to do maintenance on the UHF aerials up there attached to the mast, and we need a volunteer to go up there with some tools and a bucket of water to clean them and check the connections." At this point I asked how we were going to get up there to do it. "Easy," said Bud, "that enormous crane above us has a bucket attached to a steel line and one of us gets hoisted up there while giving instructions to the crane driver with hand signals. This sounded like fun, if a little dangerous, and it seemed that the long tradition in these situations was for the youngest member of the section to have the 'honour.' Reluctantly but 'bravely' I accepted the challenge and after a few minutes a rusty yellow bucket appeared next to us with a long line attached to the top of the 'bucket.' It didn't look that safe and I wondered how skilful the crane driver was – perhaps 'he' was the youngest crane driver on duty that day and also his first time for performing this particular job! With Bud and my REM1 colleague, Ginge, smiling and saying, "It'll be a piece of cake, John, don't worry about it," the bucket was hoisted slowly upwards with the flight deck and dry dock becoming smaller and more distant below me. As I approached the aerials using hand signals I realised that as I leaned out to perform the required maintenance the bucket swayed back and forth so I had to grip the aerial supports to steady myself. It was made more precarious as the aerials were on the Port and Starboard sides of the main mast so there was quite a lot of manoeuvring for the crane driver to do. However, I managed everything okay and returned to the jetty to smiles and claps from Bud and Ginge. I took an extra-long coffee break but at the same time felt a sense of achievement in the knowledge that someone else would do that job when it came around again.

Being a 'Pinkie' was something me and my colleagues were proud of as to become an REM meant achieving good marks in our basic training at *Ganges*. Indeed, I was keen to get hold of a blazer badge of our branch as part of the 'Far East Fleet.' At this stage in my life I never actually wore a blazer but the badge impressed me a lot. Therefore I took a visit to our Chinese tailors on board, who could make absolutely anything one needed in the way of clothes, and purchased one. It would remain with me until the time of writing this book.

Having received Carol's photo I arranged to visit a photographic studio myself to have my photo taken to send back to her. I duly booked an appointment at Lee's photo studio in *Terror* and went along for the shoot. I posed as best I could and waited a few days to have it developed, but didn't realise that the studio would be using enhancement techniques on the final version to make it look more like a painted portrait.

Photo 26 - Royal Navy Far East Radio Electrical Branch badge

Source: author

Photo 27 - My 'enhanced' portrait taken in Singapore for Carol

Source: author

Therefore when I collected it I was fairly amazed to see I had been given a more 'angelic' look than the average photograph. I have to confess that I had mixed feelings about the enhancements, but at the age of 17 I was naturally young looking and most probably at my best in many ways - it showed off my wavy chestnut locks if nothing else.

To mention another mess mate now I recount a fellow REM who was also quite a character and someone I worked with a lot. His name was David Catton. Dave was my age and had been a few months ahead of me in basic training. He was an interesting person as he always asked very demanding questions of the senior ratings who supervised him or the Killicks in our Mess. He never accepted at face value anything he was told about, for example, radio electrical theory or the equipment we maintained, and always wanted to know 'why' something worked or didn't work. This tended to irritate those who had to deal with his questions, but I absolutely admired his tenacity as it often induced some fairly abrupt responses from his superiors.

However, unlike some people who would accept anything and everything they were told, Dave, also perhaps like Roy, really did understand what he was doing. Some people possibly regarded him as arrogant and rightly noted that he did not exhibit the same amount of attention when it came to the more menial tasks we had to perform, such as scrubbing the EMR floor when doing the morning watch (4.00 am – 8.00 am), but in a similar way to Dick Wolsey, he stood his ground and did not bow to peer group pressure.

The other person in our Mess who was very much like Dave, was 'Wiggy' Bennett as he was very sharp in terms of his knowledge and sense of humour, and didn't bow to discipline or the views of others without good reason. I also remember Wiggy loved to arm wrestle with me but got extremely irritated when I almost always won - he was a few years older and didn't always appreciate 'vitriolic' celebrations from me. However, nothing I recall in 5E2 mess was done with bad intent and I would say we were a pretty talented and decent collection of people.

As our maintenance period progressed I continued to enjoy playing sport although I did acquire a large blister that turned septic and led me to attend the Sick Bay to have it lanced and dressed, as I noted in a letter home dated the 25th March. In this letter some expressions of being home sick were also present:

We are leaving Singapore on the 4th April and sailing for Hong Kong. We have an exercise called 'flying fish' first and we are in Hong Kong for 12 days. Anyway, August is getting nearer all the time, and although I enjoy myself a lot out here I will be glad to get home again. Anyway when I get home I can say I have been half way round the world, and at 17 it's not bad is it? I will close now and get a shower and try to get to bed early. I hope to hear from you soon.

It was about this time in our deployment that a devastating event happened to one of my closest friends, who I won't mention by name as it is a matter of privacy and my intention here is only to illustrate the strains and potential 'losses' associated with long periods of absence from home. One morning during our 'stand easy' break at 10.30 am I descended the ladder to our Mess with my long red screw driver in my pocket along with my colleagues, and looked with anticipation over the locker tops for mail from Carol and my parents. However, although I was pleased to see my two letters in their blue air mail envelopes ready to be opened, one of my close friends was holding his mail but rather than showing pleasure, he was clearly distraught and in tears. Some of our friends in the Mess were standing next to him showing concern and offering comforting remarks such as, "Don't worry, it happens to all of us at some point in our careers." It turned out that my friend had received a dreaded 'Dear John' letter from his girlfriend back in the UK, saying she had decided to end their relationship because of their long separation. We all moved to the bunk spaces where we could have our coffee and try to talk over the matter. Some of the Killicks made remarks to the effect that it usually is the best thing as strong relationships survive long periods but those that are meant to fail will ultimately fail. However, as I have mentioned previously, letters from home were the things that kept our spirits up and knowing someone was waiting for us was so important to our morale. I naturally felt sorry for my friend and did what I could to encourage him, but without wishing to feel confident about my own position I looked at my letter from Carol, with its faint fragrance of perfume and the codes (such as H.O.L.L.A.N.D. – which I will leave to the reader to interpret) and crosses we used on the back of our envelopes, and was grateful that I seemed to be surviving the trial of separation thus far. We all returned to our sections around the ship to continue working, but this brought a cloud down upon many of us for a time as we knew – even those with wives and children – that this was always a possibility for any of us.

****

On the 28th March we all moved back to the ship from *Terror*, which I noted in a letter dated 30th March as it was a drastic change compared with what we had become accustomed to. To compensate, along with several of my close friends, I had spent a lot of time at the Sailors' Rest because of its pool and relaxing environment. The thing I loved most about HMS *Terror* was the excellent food – at lunch time we had omelette counters, salad counters, fish counters, steak counters, dessert counters and many more enticing options to choose from. The Chinese chefs were certainly difficult to beat and we were, undoubtedly, spoilt for choice. However, there were the less savoury elements of life in Singapore and other places like Hong Kong that were encountered on a regular basis.

Like all British and other national servicemen who visited Singapore, we were constantly being invited to do some typical 'sailor' things when we were out in the evenings walking around the place. While none of us could claim to be saints, I was probably fortunate to be among the ship's sports teams and was usually with the football team training or playing, and preferred the Sailors' Rest to other places. I also had some excellent mentors and role models, such as Mick O'Shea in the football team, and Dick Wolsey and Kenny Everett. Although no-one should claim saintliness as a virtue, I must have been one of a very small band of people who never once visited the infamous 'Bugis (Boogie) Street' in Singapore, known for its various 'attractions.' To a lesser degree, these were also in evidence in Sembawang village but my attention was usually on food such as egg banjos and buying a guitar, a new watch or presents for Carol and my family at home. In this setting, however, we often discussed issues such as separation is good because 'absence makes the heart grow fonder,' which was contrasted by one of my friends with the expression 'what the eyes don't see the heart won't grieve about.' For a 17 year-old, these were highly philosophical and moral issues to grapple with. It is worth noting, however, that people in our situation were deprived of any physical contact or comfort from anyone, least of all from those they loved, and it cannot be ignored that people regularly faced the issue of being 'between the devil and the deep blue sea' with regard to their physical, emotional and psychological needs as human beings.

On the 3rd April, the day before we left Singapore, I wrote that:

I was playing for the ship against HMS Fearless. We won 5-0 and everyone was happy. The supporters said they had never seen a team play so well out here before so we were satisfied. We are putting to sea tomorrow to do an exercise with 50 other ships. Well April is with us now, time does seem to be going fast and I hope it keeps up like this until August when I can once more be at home. I look forward to hearing from you soon.

At sea the following day our usual routine resumed. I recall relaxing in my bunk after the daily shower and 'dhobying' we usually did before taking a shower – washing our underwear and socks and then hanging them up next to our air vents in the Mess. The Ship's Radio Equipment (SRE) loudspeaker was close to my bunk and I heard the familiar words of Norman Greenbaum's famous and enduring song, 'Spirit in the Sky' (Greenbaum, 1969) coming from it:

[64]

Never been a sinner, I've never sinned/ I've got a friend in Jesus
So you know that when I die/ He's gonna set me up with the Spirit in the sky
Oh set me up with the Spirit in the sky/ That's where I'm gonna go when I die
When I die and they lay me to rest/ I'm gonna go to the place that's the best
Go to the place that's the best

Roy Brooks and Kenny Everett were two of the resident disk jockeys for 'Radio Bulwark,' and we heard their programmes every week. I also regularly recorded the ship's quiz in the Wardroom for later airing over the SRE. The SRE, which provided the necessary technology for Radio Bulwark, was connected to every mess deck throughout the ship and was a great source of entertainment for the ship's company. Overhead and in the calm waters of the South China Sea, our helicopters busied themselves with night flying missions to land marines ashore as we sailed in convoy with the other nations' navies, including ANZAC (Australia and New Zealand) vessels. One sunny morning around this time departmental photographs were taken in the lift well of the flight deck and although I do not appear in the photo below, presumably because I was duty or possibly playing football for the ship. However, it shows the Weapons Electrical Branch with many of my colleagues and friends included in it. PO Bud Abbot is 2nd row fifth from the right, Chief Wilson is front row third from the right, Toby Tyler (yet to be mentioned) is third row far left, and our section officer, Lt Tull, is front row eighth from the left.

Very shortly after exercise 'flying fish' we entered the impressive and exciting port of Hong Kong shortly after the 10th April. The first thing I remember is coming up on deck on the sunny morning of our first day anchored in the harbour to see a group of Hong Kong ladies with hats on and an enormous amount of painting materials. I soon learned that they were the famous 'Jenny's side party' who took on the task of painting Royal Navy ships that visited Hong Kong. Her team of about 36 ladies also served ice cold soft drinks, on the quarterdeck and other parts of the ship, from large wooden barrels with water and ice in them. Their efficiency and dedication to their tasks was absolutely admirable and the results they produced over the time of our stay were better than what the ship's crew could manage. Over the years they would paint an enormous number of visiting ships and could be seen in their Chinese hats sitting on planks of wood suspended on ropes working away in the beautiful backdrop of Hong Kong harbour. Jenny herself would eventually be awarded the British Empire Medal in 1980 by the Governor of Hong Kong, Sir Murray MacLehose (Daily Telegraph, 2012).

At the first available opportunity some of my friends and I went ashore and took the famous 'Peak Tram' to the top of Hong Kong to witness a breath-taking view of the harbour and *Bulwark* lying gracefully in the middle. In our white tropical uniforms, it felt truly magical to be part of the Royal Navy and to be able to visit, as it was then, an important part of the British Empire, which acted as a free trade area at the edge of Communist China.

Because of its geographical location and links to Britain there would always be some friction over the governance of Hong Kong. However, there was in fact no real evidence of hostility towards us. While looking over the harbour I noticed the flotilla of Royal Navy minesweepers that were based in Hong Kong and realised that my good friend from *Collingwood*, Barry Pease, had been drafted to HMS *Bossington*. I spoke to Kenny Everett about the plan I then had to go and find him to see how he was getting on, and he gave me some advice about how to do this. The next day after work I set off on my own to the part of the harbour where all the minesweepers were tied up, and eventually located Barry's ship.

Photo 28 - *Bulwark's* Weapons Electrical branch in tropical uniform

Source: *author*

Photo 29 - Post card of Hong Kong Harbour, 1970

Source: *author*

Feeling rather pleased with my success I went up the gangway, saluted, and showed my identity card to the bosun's mate. A pipe was made and eventually Barry appeared and we shook hands. He showed me round the ship, which was tiny compared with *Bulwark* and he explained how much these small ships were thrown around in rough weather at sea. Because we were only visiting for a few days and Barry was duty we didn't have the chance to socialise, but spent a pleasant few hours chatting over a cup of coffee in his mess deck.

Bulwark played against a Royal Navy team on a very hard pitch, which I remember caused us some problems as the ball bounced much more than on a grass pitch. I recall we scored an own goal and lost the game 2-3. The main events in Hong Kong were recorded in a letter of the 12th April:

I went into the city with a couple of friends and we went to the Hong Kong Hilton. It's the best hotel here and was really a great place. We drove there in a big red taxi and an Indian in a turban and purple suit opened the door for us. We went into the lounge and the service was excellent. We had a vodka and lime each and it cost 19 dollars (about 28 shillings) but it was worth it. We didn't stay long otherwise it would have cost too much.

I remember this particular evening very well as a Spanish group of musicians came into the lounge and played 'Guantanamera,' which really impressed me and gave me more encouragement to continue learning to play the guitar. However, learning to play was a bit tricky on board as everyone else could usually hear the 'struggles' that are necessary in learning to master any instrument and I was often asked if I could play 'over the hills and far away.' A good friend and I often practised together in the starboard boat bay or in the EMR and gradually both of us became reasonably competent and I remember we learned to play the tune 'Born Free,' (John Barry, 1966) which may have reflected the confinement and lack of liberty that we felt from time to time.

We duly sailed from Hong Kong and made a grand entrance into Kobe, Japan, on the 23rd April in full procedure alpha with a small armada of ships escorting us and water jets being projected into the sky. In a letter home on the 24th April I mentioned that the weather in Japan was similar to that of England as the two countries ranged over similar latitudes, and therefore we had transferred from tropical to our regular blue uniforms. In this letter I gave my first impression of the Japanese people, which have remained constant throughout my life:

Well I can truthfully say that I like Japan, and the Japanese people. They are very friendly and always have smiles for us. I went on a tour today with my mate, Jim (Turner) to Kyoto. There were some really interesting places to see there. Apart from us there were bus-loads of school girls aged about 11 or 12 and as soon as they saw us they were crowding round us and asking for our autographs, address of the ship and a lot were taking photos of us. We visited a few more places but the one I liked most was a Buddhist temple up in the trees on a hill, leading up to it was a road full of shops like those we used to visit in Beira.

Photo 30 - HMS *Bulwark's* grand arrival in Kobe, Japan

Source: *author*

In this letter I also explained about the problem of storing the large number of presents I had been accumulating on our deployment as we had very little spare room and I started using extra suitcases I had bought along the way. Unfortunately, this lack of space led to one of the most impressive Japanese drinking vessel sets, bought on this day in Kyoto, being stolen before I arrived back home. In fact it was quite common for items of clothing, and especially shoe laces, to 'go missing' due to petty theft. However, on this particular day, Jim - a tall, quiet and thoughtful close friend - and I enjoyed a sophisticated day as tourists together among people who treated us in quite a different manner compared with those in Singapore and Hong Kong.

This contrast was possibly because of the lack of a colonial link even though, as my father had experienced, they had been our enemies in World War II. No-one said, "Do you want to buy a watch, John," but simply bowed and smiled politely as we looked around the shops. The main reason for us visiting Japan, of course, was the attraction of Expo '70 in Osaka. After representing the ship at football in the four matches we played and won - in a refreshing and much-appreciated spirit of friendship and respect - several of my friends joined me on a train ride to the incredibly impressive Expo site.

I recall noting how clean and efficient the trains were, and how the Japanese passengers smiled again at us as we sat there in our uniforms directly across from them in long seats next to the window. Little did I know at that time that the Sailor's uniforms, which we observed were worn by so many Japanese school children, were introduced because of the link between the British and the Japanese Navies. In the early 20th Century the British had trained Japanese officers and built their first major warships. After arriving at our destination we joined the enormous international crowds strolling around the impressive exhibitions that made up Expo '70 and finished the evening sitting around on some steps next to the Canadian exhibition, chatting among ourselves and with other visitors over a drink and sampling some of the excellent food that was available from various national stands.

Photo 31 - Tower at Expo 70

Source: author

Photo 32 - Japanese visitors, Kobe

Source: author

As with all courtesy visits to foreign ports we held a party for local children and the ship was open to visitors from the public. The number of people that visited the ship was almost overwhelming – we seemed to be able to compete with Expo '70 itself, as shown in the photo. Next to it is one of the Japanese artist Taro Okamoto's most famous works, 'Tower of the Sun,' which became the symbol of Expo '70. It represents the past in its lower part, the present in the middle section, and the future (face) of the human race at the top.

On the 28th April we left Japan and returned to Hong Kong for a maintenance period between the 1st and 14th May. The deployment continued in much the same vein as I have described, but perhaps one of several life-changing events that occurred in my career emerged at this point in time. Chief Wilson asked me to stay behind after one stand easy break and then explained that I would be moving to 'communal' duties for the next three months, which meant I would leave the UHF section and work in the kitchens and dining rooms of the POs and CPOs. In a letter to my parents, I explained that although this was a wrench in some ways as I would be away from the day-to-day life of the Radio Electrical department, I did get quite a lot of spare time between my daily chores. I had been studying towards my next promotion to REM first class (REM1) which would mean I would get a star above my branch badge and extra pay, so perhaps I had more time to dedicate to this too.

Every morning for three months I would get up at 5.30 am and go to the galley to start my day, which consisted of operating very large dish washers for the plates and cutlery used in serving the hundreds of meals that were produced three times a day. We also had to scrub floors in the galleys, lay tables before meals, and do a task that would lead to be being Christened 'Smelly in the Mess.' This is because I had to carry large sacks of potatoes from a storage locker, high up in the ship, down ladders to the galley every morning. This could be a potentially hazardous task as it wasn't possible to look down and have a clear view of the steps of ladders and it wasn't unusual to slip. I also no longer wore my usual working uniform of Number 8s but a white tee shirt and working trousers – in contrast to the smart appearance of the other REMs who worked on the Radio and Radar sections.

The main problem was that some of the potatoes had gone rotten in their hessian sacks and as I carried them on my shoulder they squashed into my tee shirt and made a mess. Despite showering twice a day as we all did, the aroma of rotten potatoes went with me into my mess deck at stand easy and other times and this was registered by my colleagues. One day I was therefore given the tag of 'Smelly,' which was all in good fun as all the younger REMs had to do their time on communal duties, but it focussed my mind somewhat. For example, I used to feel slightly embarrassed when the senior ratings I had worked with until then came in for meals and saw me behind the counter washing pots and pans. They did say encouraging words along the lines of, "Don't worry, everyone has to do it sometime," but occasionally they would ask me for something such as a clean spoon, which was in contrast to the fault finding I had done with Bud especially on the UHF equipment when he might ask for an oscilloscope or a signal generator from me. Clearly I wasn't doing the job the Navy had trained me for but there were many common tasks, such as storing ship, that meant we all had to abandon our normal duties and do these things that often lasted the whole day; passing stores and equipment down a long line that went from the jetty to the required compartment on the ship.

What communal work induced in me more than ever, was a sense of ambition, despite it being wholesome and necessary work. I knew that anyone above the rate of Killick did not do communal work so I set my sights on studying and gaining promotion as fast as the Navy would allow me. This meant studying in the evenings, learning from others such as Kenny Everett and Dick Wolsey, and taking a much greater interest in the technical aspects of my career. Other friends of my age were of the same opinion, particularly Dave Catton and Roy Brooks, so we were able to encourage each other to get on, share notes and ideas, and do our best to succeed.

One interesting thing that happened in our second visit to Hong Kong was that members of the football team took a trip into Red China to watch a game in a very large stadium between a Chinese team and a combined armed services team for those stationed in the region. The stadium was filled to its capacity of about 30,000. The main thing that struck me, however, was the clear antagonism between the teams and the partisan attitude of the Chinese supporters. The British element was clearly in a small minority and there were some hysterical responses when a Chinese player was tackled heavily, in contrast to the cheers when the opposition were tackled in a similar manner. It looked a little like a bear pit and perhaps revealed something of the underlying 'true' feelings of the Chinese people to British rule in Hong Kong. I don't remember the score but on the bus trip back we discussed such things among us. Indeed, in a letter home I had expressed the opinion that although we usually beat Chinese teams when I was playing for *Bulwark*, I didn't generally enjoy the games.

This episode also reminds me of one event during inter-departmental flight deck sports competitions. The Chinese contingent on board was fairly substantial as the they provided all laundry, cobbler and tailor services and lived in their own mess deck just below the N.A.A.F.I. On one sunny afternoon the flight deck was a hive of activity as teams from different departments competed at volleyball, deck hockey and football. The football semi-final was between the Chinese local employees and the marines. Rather like the game I had watched in Red China, there was a good deal of fouling and squaring up going on and things started to get rather fraught between them. After one particularly bad foul by a Marine, there kicked off a mass brawl between every team member on both sides that looked like something from a Kung Fu film. Karate kicks and chops were flying around at a frantic rate for about a minute when the referee plus a few helpers managed to split up the fighting. Although it was quite amusing to watch, again it did uncover an undercurrent of resentment and conflict of cultures and customs.

Below is one of my favourite photos of *Bulwark*. It reminds me of those occasions when, after supper in the evenings, I would jog or stroll around the flight deck under a setting sun with calm blue waters beneath us and a tropical background on the horizon. Life in the Navy was often frantic, but I found that it was within my character to enjoy 'ordinary' and routine days the most.

Photo 33 - *Bulwark* in the setting sun of the South China Sea

Source: *author*

On the 7th June I noted some aspects of our plans and concerns for my sister, Valerie, who was expecting her first child:

We are leaving Singapore on the 12 June to do an exercise with Australian, New-Zealand and Malayan ships called 'Beatu Padu' and it will last until the 1st July. We then come back to Singapore for six days. The name means 'complete unity.' I hope Val's high blood pressure won't create any complications. I hope she will be alright – I received a letter yesterday and it's nice to hear from her, and I enjoy reading her letters very much. I hope I am home in time for her going into hospital in August.

What I wrote in the above letter reminds me that 'complete unity' among the Australian and British services was not always in evidence, especially when it came to sport and recreation when there was a lot of rivalry – not all of it pleasant. Although our football team could beat any Australian ship's team, the rugby games were very fierce encounters. In fact they often reminded me of the game I had seen in Red China or between the Royal Marines and Chinese local employees on board *Bulwark*, but the difference was that the two teams more often than not made up for it over a Tiger beer afterwards.

I do recall, however, one very unsavoury event that made me lose my respect for some of the Australians who were there at that time. The event became known by most of the ship's company. What happened was that one of our crew members was walking back to the ship on his own through Sembawang village, when an Australian sailor came up to him and said, "Excuse me, mate, can you come over and help one of my shipmates as he has been attacked by some of the locals." Wishing to help, our colleague followed the Australian over to his friend, who was lying on the floor and holding his face. The sailor from *Bulwark* bent over him to ask how he could help when the one on the floor, who had absolutely nothing wrong with him, laughed and punched his helper in the face. The two Australians and others then attacked our shipmate so badly that he was taken to hospital. It was difficult for us to comprehend such an underhand trick on an innocent person who was only wishing to be a 'good Samaritan' to someone in need of help. Although I would go on to have some very good Australian friends, this event certainly left a lasting impression on me and perhaps, again, revealed the adverse effects of our colonial links with other countries. On the 7th June, however, I reported some welcome news about my move back to my department:

I will be coming off night work on the 18th and returning to the Radio section again. I will be working in the EMR – this is where all the work is done (outside of section offices) and the maintenance is controlled from so it should be okay. It's not long now before August will be here, and I can tell you I'll be glad to get home and have a good rest. So until I write again, I'll look forward to hearing from you again.

A new adventure was planned to compensate for our long stretch at sea of three weeks - it was what we called a 'banyan.' This meant a day in recreational clothes on an island we were passing during exercises to relax, spend time on a beach together, and take along with us some cans of cold beer and food. Practically all our Mess members took part as life was busy on board with 1,000 marines embarked. However, we had one or two precautionary words from the Commander to consider. In a letter home of the 17th June I explained that were told to be careful of sharks or stone fish if we swam in the sea and to watch out for sea eggs when walking on the beach (which had large spikes jutting out of them). We all had to take an anti-malaria tablet before setting off on the ship's cutter – on this occasion to the island of Pulau Tioman. During the day itself we all had a good time, as I related in a letter of the 25th June:

> *We got ashore at about 7 o'clock as it was just getting dark so we lit a big fire on the beach. It gave off a lot of light so we had a game of beach football. Every time the ball went into the water we all piled in after it so we got soaked in the first ten minutes, but the nights are very warm so it didn't bother us at all. Some of the natives sold us coconuts and bananas which were good to eat and didn't cost much at all.*

After this it was back to the ship and ever-more crowded conditions; before arriving in Singapore for the last time before our long trip home we would have 2,300 men on board and hoards of equipment, associated with the marines, secured to the flight deck. Many people chose to sleep on the upper deck at night due to the warm, fresh air up there, which was in contrast to the cramped accommodation below decks. The conditions on board ship indeed were a shock to some people and the marines in particular as their accommodation was extremely cramped, and they had fewer 'home comforts.'

Through the three months on communal work I had moved eventually to night cleaning duties which involved mass cleaning operations in passageways and mess decks throughout the ship. The standard term for this was 'glifting and gleaming' whereby we first cleaned the floors with 'glift' and then polished them with 'gleam' – both being high-powered chemicals that were slightly intoxicating to work with.

On the 18th June, I reported to Chief Wilson and was pleased to be back in my REM's uniform again and quickly ramped up my studies towards REM. I enjoyed working for him as he was very relaxed in the way he dealt with any number of technical difficulties, or welfare issues being experienced by the staff. My main task was to manage and maintain the large stock of electronic maintenance equipment we kept in the EMR, order and collect stores and spare parts for all our equipment, and keep books of reference (BRs) for equipment up to date. I had a small enclosed compartment at the end of the EMR that I worked from with all the BRs above my desk in large book racks.

By now the separation from my family and Carol was beginning to tell as I wrote that 'there were only 9 weeks and one day' before we got home' in a letter of the 17th June. For those with young children, it was becoming more worrisome the longer they were away. One of the Radio Mechanicians on the High Frequency (HF) section, Wilf Manion, often chatted to me about these pressures as he had a wife and at least one young child back home in Plymouth. In fact Wilf had what one might term a general malaise about life in the Navy and being away from home as he used to 'swear blind' that wherever *Bulwark* went a black cloud always followed the ship. Clearly this was not the case, but in later years I would certainly appreciate the perspective he held. He was another Killick but a 'mechanician' rather than a 'mechanic.' These distinctions were important to know about for anyone interested in advancement through the ranks and would increasingly attract my attention in due course.

On the 5th July we departed from Singapore under procedure alpha to commence our long journey home. In one of my letters home I mention that the sea conditions had become rough, perhaps an omen of future experiences in the more hostile and unfriendly northern waters that I would encounter in the future. I explained that I had bought a final batch of presents for everyone in the family, including a racing car with two-buttoned control for my brother, David. I had placed them all in a new, large suit case. Our destination after Djakarta would be Freemantle in Western Australia, where we would stay for only five days before re-tracing our route home via Durban, Cape Town and Gibraltar – due to arrive in Plymouth at 12.00 on the 20th August. Unfortunately, we lost our last two games of football at *Terror*, but as I explained, we had been at sea for three weeks prior to those games and this affected our levels of fitness. However, football had been, in many ways, the major motivator of my life and the thought of a game always made other things related to work pale into insignificance. I signed off the letter 'keep smiling and God bless' – the latter part being the phrase my mother always used to sign off with – and headed back down to my bunk with the ship pitching and rolling more than we had been used to whilst in the Far East.

Our stay in Djakarta was very brief and I recall the city had much contrast in terms of wealth and poverty. As we drove towards the town I noted a rather unsanitary river with people washing clothes in and living next to, while the main city itself was very modern and clean in appearance. The ship's football team played at a very large stadium against the Indonesian Navy. I recall it was a close game and eventually ended in a 2-2 draw. The Indonesian players were typically smaller in build and height than us, but they were quite skilful and played together well as a team. Again, we left under procedure alpha with me being one of the chosen to line the flight deck in whites. I realised our next stop in Freemantle would be more like a home-coming as the Australian culture there was basically that which we shared. Once we were out into the open sea we were dismissed and I returned to the EMR.

The cruise down to the West coast of Australia was uneventful and life in the Radio Electrical section went on in the usual manner. Chief Wilson and our resident Chief Radio Electrician (CREL) gave regular instruction to me on the technical aspects of the test equipment I looked after. CREL Quentin was rather an eccentric person to say the least as he was extremely bright and knowledgeable, but had the habit of 'flying off the handle' if he thought people were mis-informed or didn't know what they were doing when he clearly thought it was all too obvious himself. I remember he used to stalk around the EMR coming out with witty and philosophical comments but was always at the ready to give someone a ticking off whilst glaring at them intensely. His main interest was in looking after all the SRE equipment and I recall he had his own bunk bed in the control room, which was right next to the EMR. As duty REMs we often had to wake up POs or CPOs in the small hours of the morning if there was a technical problem on their section that we, or the duty senior Radio rating, could not fix ourselves.

I recall that one night when I was duty I decided, rather foolishly, that Chief Quentin was the correct person to wake up to deal with a particular fault – perhaps to do with the correct piece of test equipment to use for a task I had to perform. I therefore pressed the intercom that went to the control room and called out his name. After a few seconds the intercom clicked into life and I clearly got the indignation he felt at being woken up, interspersed with a large volume of expletives, and was ordered in no uncertain terms to wake up Chief Wilson. In his calm manner, Chief Wilson got out of his bunk (Chief's shared cabins with three colleagues) and dealt with the issue I had reported. Needless to say, I didn't attempt to disturb Chief Quentin again! All staff members, no matter what their rank was, were very cautious in the way they dealt with 'Sam.'

Early on the 14th July after only four days at sea we entered the port of Freemantle under procedure alpha, with our helicopters flying overhead, to be greeted by quite a sizeable crowd of people on the jetty – some of whom, I would find out, had relatives on board. At this time the British and Australian populations were much more homogenous than would be the case in future years and for this reason it felt like we were arriving in a familiar place. The next day, when we were entertaining hundreds of visitors, I had many conversations with people who had settled in Australia from various parts of the UK, including Yorkshire. On the 19th July I summed up our stay as follows:

Well, I must admit that Australia would be the place I would choose to live in other than home. Everyone is so helpful and friendly and they all seem very happy out here. They seem so free and easy and know how to enjoy themselves. Unfortunately for me I have been duty for three days out of six because a friend of mine has relatives here, and I did his duty so he could be with them for the weekend. Although Roy and I had a good time on Wednesday when we went out together, I'm afraid we had one or two too many and came back to the ship the worse for wear. But it's not very often we do get drunk and with us being on our way home it seemed all right to celebrate. We beat an Australian Air Force team 6-2, and after being 4-0 down to HMAS Luelin at half time, we made a come-back and won 7-4 in the end. We are sailing on Monday morning for Durban. We had a party for all the kids around here yesterday – they were everywhere and all seemed to enjoy themselves very much indeed. Well it is only 4 weeks now before I'll be home again. I'm looking forward very much to seeing you all again and I look forward to your next letter. Write soon.

Photo 34 - *Bulwark* arriving in Freemantle, Australia

Source: *author*

At the dance that Roy and I had been to, we were entertained by our own ship's rock group, who were very good and the bass player was one of the REMs. I remember the quaint and sociable way in which Australians served beer as it was placed on tables in large glass jugs. We were then given our own glasses to fill up at the tables we were seated at. We both made good friends with the locals there and entertained them the next day when the ship was open to visitors. The warmth and friendliness of the Western Australians really touched many of us – I think we must have been a link to the roots they had in the UK and so they clearly treasured our visit. They certainly made up for the unsavoury incident I related in Singapore when one of our ship mates was attacked by some Australians. I had especially enjoyed looking after the children who came to our parties as we always dressed up as pirates, put out all kinds of games such as rings that had to be moved carefully along a metal curvy wire – a buzzer was sounded if the ring touched the wire and they had to start again. We also showed them cartoons in our enormous dining rooms while they had tea and jelly, and we finished by chasing them around the flight deck - armed with wooden swords.

When we finally left Freemantle on Monday, many people had a tear in their eyes as we saw the crowds on the jetty waving goodbye to us. Standing on the flight deck in my best uniform, I recall looking down and seeing people I recognised running along the jetty to get a last wave and to throw a kiss in our direction, but the sad thing was that we could not move to reciprocate as we were standing to attention. It must have been especially painful for those who had relatives there as the prospect of seeing one another again soon would have been remote. This experience reminded me of our departure from Rhodesia, when friends, Valerie's boyfriend, 'Kookie,' and my father had run along the station platform at Salisbury waving to us in exactly the same way. Saying too many goodbyes in one's life does not come without a cost.

Photo 35 - *Bulwark's* procedure alpha and sad departure from Freemantle

Source: *author*

Our journey across the South Pacific Ocean straight to Durban was slowed down a little as we were low on fuel due to our supply ship being kept in harbour to undertake repairs. My letters now were mostly about counting down the days to when we arrived back in the UK. Apart from a game of football in Durban against a team from Natal there was not much new material to write home about, although for the Royal Navy itself a landmark decision was taken at this time to end the long tradition of the 'tot.' The MoD had signalled its intention to end the daily rum ration on the grounds that it was not sensible to allow its sailors to drink rum every lunch time in view of the increasingly complex and hazardous equipment we all had to operate and maintain. Gone were the days, for example in Nelson's time, when sailors could drink themselves into a stupor and crash out on the deck to sleep it off. Incredibly, until 1740 the daily ration was half a pint of 'neat rum,' rather than the mixture of two parts of rum to one part of water that was issued to people in 1970. Therefore, on the 31st July 1970, which was to become known in the Navy as 'Black Tot Day, the sun passed over the yardarm for the final time and free rum was retired from navy life.

As I had not reached the required age to receive my rum ration I did not miss it like the older members of the department and there definitely were some grumblings of discontent going on among people. However, I generally agreed with the position of the Navy as drunkenness on board ships was an issue that caused a good deal of grief as well as 'merriment.' Alcoholism was always in evidence throughout my career and probably one reason for my eventual teetotal preference in the future. I can recall several times throughout my career when I would be woken up by drunks returning to the ship, although on some occasions I was undeniably among them myself. My relative prudence was often regarded by some in a negative light but like my colleagues Dick Wolsey and Dave Catton, I would learn to stand my ground and not be easily persuaded by peer-group pressure.

During our stay in Durban one of our crew members was sadly attacked and killed in the dockyard by some locals on his way back to the ship late one evening. Although these incidents were rare, we always had to be careful and ideally move around in groups. It was never wise to return to the ship alone as we were sometimes seen as easy targets in unfamiliar and far-away places. I felt some relief, therefore, when we set sail, navigated around the Cape of Good Hope, and headed north towards Gibraltar and then Plymouth. I recount my thoughts as we made this final leg of our journey on the 15th August, five days from home:

Well I hope you haven't been worrying about me. We have been at sea for 11 days and arriving in Gibraltar tomorrow. The next stop for me will be Brierley! I am really looking forward to getting home again because it has been such a long time since I saw you last. I am not sure of exactly when I will be home but if I catch the right trains I will arrive at Doncaster at 9.00 pm on the 20th. Carol is going to go to the station from her house and wait until about 9.00 and if I don't arrive on that train she will go through to our house. I have been anxious to hear how our Val is getting on. It is murder for me not knowing how she is. This will be the last letter I can write before I get home and in a way it sounds nice to be able to say that. I'll see you all on Thursday night everything permitting. So goodbye for now, and God bless you all. Love, John.

After our passage through the Bay of Biscay, which was thankfully calm, we finally sailed majestically into Plymouth Sound on a warm English summer's day under procedure alpha and were tied up alongside at about 12.00 noon. Like many colleagues and friends, I returned to 5E2 mess and frantically busied myself packing my clothes and my very large suitcase full of presents as souvenirs of my long and eventful trip of more than 30,000 miles across the major oceans of the world.

I collected my travel warrant for the long train journey up to Bristol, Sheffield and then finally Doncaster. The excitement and anticipation on the 20th August was palpable as everyone contemplated being home again with their families and girlfriends. The 'umbilical cord' of letters from Carol and my family had followed me to the other side of the world and back. I had learned a great deal about my work and had some wonderful memories of all the places we had visited, the games of football I had played in for *Bulwark*, and the people I had met. But now I would soon be back with the people that really mattered in my life, who are all captured in the photo below - taken a few months after arriving back in England.

I duly arrived home at about 10.00 pm with my large suitcase of presents and banged on the front door of our modest but cosy and comfortable home in Brierley.

****

Everyone was naturally pleased to see and greet me, and very soon I was doing the things I had been deprived of for eight months – drinking tea and chatting while sitting on my parents' comfortable rocking chair, holding hands with Carol on the sofa, watching some television, having a long bath, wrestling with my father, checking out my sisters' and brother's progress with their lives, and acting like father Christmas as I opened up my large case and gradually allocated all the presents I had bought for them.

However, I'm not sure if I got all allocations of presents correctly balanced among various family members and Carol due to fact that some of them had gone missing on board ship during the long voyage home. But for now I could finally sit back and relax for the one week's leave I had been granted and enjoy all the comforts of home.

Photo 36 - Family photo with Carol after returning from the Far East

Mother, Grandmother (Rose), John, Father
Valerie, Valerie's new baby (Joanne), David, Barbara, Carol. **Source:** *author*

During this period of time my father and I managed to get to watch 'The Millers' at Rotherham, my mother and I caught up on several things and Carol and I spent time with her parents over in Selby and with her wonderful grandparents. Carol's mother knew I had a soft spot for custard slices and would often bring me one back from her shopping trips to Selby, which I really appreciated and enjoyed. Carol's grandparents, Louis and Edith (Fletcher) I have to say, always offered a nice welcome and prepared wonderful afternoon teas for us. They were gentle folk who took an interest in what we were doing, and Louis in particular was always keen to discuss anything and offer advice. He introduced me to 'Bic' razors for shaving, and I have used them ever since. Valerie's baby, Joanne, was born on the 31st August. I was touched that my sister wanted to name her child after me as far as possible, so Joanne received her name as it was the closest girl's name to John.

Once I returned to *Bulwark*, we went into a long refit phase in Plymouth and moved to live in Drake Barracks. The accommodation was better than we had on board but rather basic. We walked to the ship each day to do our jobs amid the hustle and bustle of activities carried by the dockyard workers. The refit would last for about six months so it was possible to establish a routine for getting home at week-ends and a social life within the city – we had our own local pub where my Radio Electrical section friends and I often gathered to play darts and pass our time. During this period I also took driving lessons with my friend Dave Catton, who sat in the back of the car while I had my lesson and vice versa. Because of this we effectively had a double lesson with our excellent Scottish instructor in his green Vauxhall, and both duly passed our tests first time on or around our eighteenth birthdays.

When home at week-ends, Carol's father took us to the local pub in Thorpe Willoughby on Friday evening and eventually, once I passed my driving test, I used to drive his much cared-for Ford Anglia with Carol and her parents on trips around Yorkshire. This was very good practise for me as I was a new driver. Fred always spoke to me about his time in the Royal Navy during the World War II, and had any number of interesting and harrowing stories about being sunk four times while serving in destroyers. He had also been part of various enterprises he and his colleagues had set up to make extra money. The routine we developed was that Carol always met me on Friday evenings on Doncaster station, we caught a taxi to her home in Selby where I stayed for the night, and the next day I went to

Brierley to stay with my parents. Carol came over in the evening, after finishing work, to stay with us for the night and I caught a train back to Plymouth on Sunday afternoon.

My letters home during this six-month phase were less frequent as I was there at every opportunity, and much of the subject matter concerned catching trains, making arrangements to be collected from various stations and life in the barracks of HMS *Drake*. I was fortunate enough during this time to be selected to play for the Plymouth Command football team, which was quite an achievement at my age as players could be selected from any ship stationed in Plymouth or any shore base, which probably amounted to about 20,000 or more Royal Navy personnel.

I recall that another episode of naval injustice happened to me whilst in Drake barracks. Whenever going 'ashore' from a ship or shore establishment it was necessary for us to hand in our 'station cards' to the gate staff. When returning from shore leave we collected them again, which signified that we were on board the ship (or shore establishment). I returned from week-end leave one evening at some point after midnight and said to the gate staff on duty at Drake main gate, "REM Nixon." One of the duty personnel then looked through the pigeon hole under 'N' in the usual manner but couldn't find mine. He returned to the window and said, "Sorry, I can't find it so you'll have to report back here in the morning to check again." I duly returned to the ship and went to bed. After breakfast I walked from the ship to the gate and arrived at about 8.30 am. I explained to the day staff what had happened and that I was returning to collect my station card. The RPO duly found it in the wrong pigeon hole and returned it to me, but then promptly said that I would be charged with being 'absent without leave.' Looking at him in my working clothes, and clearly knowing that he had seen me approaching from the ship and not the streets outside, I was flabbergasted and asked him why. He replied, "Ship's regulations state that all personnel returning from shore leave and not being issued with their station cards are to report to the main gate before the expiry of their leave." My leave had expired at 8.00 am. Despite my obvious innocence in that I had clearly returned several hours before my leave expired, and that the fault lay with the duty staff who had placed my station card in the wrong pigeon hole, I had to face the Commander later that day, remove my cap, and explain my case. Despite the obvious logic surrounding this event for everyone concerned, I had, unknowingly, broken the rules and was given one day 'Number 14s' punishment. This meant me doing extra work in *Drake* barracks and losing shore leave. However, when I reported for my extra work the CPO who listened to my story was equally astounded by what had happened (could such as case be so clearly a miscarriage of justice by anyone with an ounce of common sense?) and he gave me a very small task, and then let me play snooker for the rest of the afternoon.

****

Early in the New Year, Carol and I made the decision to get married and she made arrangements for us to visit the vicar at the Church we would be married in, which was at Brayton in Selby. Although our decision came as a bit of a surprise to our parents, we both had the intention of making a new life outside of Yorkshire and I now had the opportunity of acquiring a married quarter for us to live in. Also, our relationship had survived long periods of separation and seeing each other only at week-ends was not ideal. Our decision also focussed my mind on gaining promotion so that by the time I finished my time on *Bulwark* we could live together close to HMS *Collingwood* and then hope for a shore-based draft for two years, which was a reasonable expectation after service at sea for two and a half years.

Carol worked as a chief cashier in Selby so between us we were able to save a reasonable amount of money. In my periods of absence in Plymouth and at sea, she competently took on the tasks of designing the bride's maids' outfits and other aspects of the wedding such as the reception and photographer. The ship had come out of refit by now to undertake two periods of sea trials before sailing for courtesy visits to Stockholm and Helsinki. On this trip we were accompanied by the frigate HMS *Andromeda*. As we were sailing into the Baltic area ships of the Soviet Bloc began to shadow us as they usually did whenever possible. I recorded the details of this encounter in a letter home as I vividly remember standing on the flight deck on a crisp and sunny morning watching this event unfold.

> *On Wednesday we had an East German patrol boat following us all day, and since Thursday we have had a Russian Frigate on our tail. Today we put on a bit of speed, and left the Russian ship back on the horizon but now we have slowed down it is back with us.*

As we increased speed to about 30 knots the Russian ship did try to respond but seemed to produce an enormous amount of black smoke out of its funnel with no significant increase in speed, so it fell behind us. I think a few of us cheered and waved it goodbye. This was the time of the Cold War and Western and Soviet forces were constantly monitoring each other and probing here and there on various fronts.

The approach to Stockholm was particularly impressive as we passed numerous small and picturesque islands with summer houses nestled neatly among the trees. They seemed almost within touching distance of the flight deck as we stood in line for procedure alpha and moving only at about five knots. I could immediately see that the Swedes clearly had a good standard of living if so many of them could afford one of these summer homes. The next day after our arrival we received an amazingly lavish reception from the city as a banquet was arranged for most of the ship's company – several hundred of us were waited on for lunch in the magnificent Civic Hall, complete with speeches from the mayor of Stockholm.

In terms of football matches, we played a Swedish Naval team and drew 2-2 – I remember scoring the equaliser from an acute angle in what was a tight game against a well organised team. In Helsinki we went down 1-4 to a combined armed services team – perhaps not a surprise to lose to a team that was selected from such a large pool of players.

Photo 37 - The civic hall in Stockholm

Source: *author*

Once these two trips were over it was time to prepare for the big day back home in Yorkshire. Our wedding was arranged for when *Bulwark* was in Plymouth between visits – the next one being planned for Istanbul and Gibraltar again. I recall being in a slight panic because as we approached Plymouth there was a great deal of fog and our entrance was delayed for a few hours. However, we finally tied up alongside and my bags were already packed and I was ready to go. Two friends accompanied me to Yorkshire from *Bulwark*, Roy and my good friend – also from Yorkshire - Tony Linstead, who was my best man. My long-standing friend from *Ganges*, Pete Kerley, and another colleague from HMS *Ark Royal*, joined me in what was a traditional Royal Naval wedding in uniform. At weddings we used white tapes to secure the silks on our uniforms, as shown in the photos. Carol and I later took a honeymoon in North Wales.

Our principal concern now was how to grapple with the needs the Navy had for me and setting up a home together once the time was right. If I could go back to this event in my life and change anything it would definitely be the speech I made at the reception. I was clearly relatively young when I got married (just under 19 years old, which was not unusual for that era) and the demands of getting home on trains and organising my own family's needs meant I didn't really dedicate any time to what I would say once everyone was gathered at the reception. In subsequent years I would be much more adept at writing things down beforehand and practising them, but I realise that the words I used were inappropriate – the main issue, I suspect, was that I made some comments that only my comrades from the Navy were privy to so it came across as a private joke in parts. However, looking at the group photo at the time of writing this book I can see how young and attractive everyone was, and how happy they looked.

Photo 38 - Carol and John at their wedding

Source: author

Photo 39 - The family photo at the wedding of John and Carol

Left to right: Auntie Olive (Benson, née Nixon), Valerie with Joanne, my father with David, my grandmother, Rose, my mother, Tony Linstead, Maureen, John, Carol, Sandra, Barbara, Pauline, Fred, Edith and Louis (Carol's grandparents). Photo: Michael Pointon. **Source:** *author*

Carol's father was tall and good looking, and clearly enjoyed talking to the rest of my friends from the Navy. Peg and her parents look like the gentle people they were, and my family to the left of the photo are generating the warmth that existed among us. The bride's maids, Sandra and my younger sister, Barbara, also look very attractive as does the chief bride's maid, Maureen. Naturally I was pleased and proud of the way Carol looked – In my opinion she most definitely was the 'epitome of young Anglo-Saxon womanhood.' The best man, I recall, was rather too zealous in his congratulatory kisses for Carol and I remember I asked him to 'behave himself' with my bride.

These photos, in fact, were not part of the official collection we had taken by the photographer we employed, but taken by my brother-in-law, Michael (Mick) Pointon, who was and remains an excellent photographer. Once I returned to *Bulwark* I joined the Royal Naval Dependence Fund (RNDF), which all married people joined to ensure we had life cover for our wives in case of our death in service. In due course I set up an 'allotment' (monthly allowance) to Carol. I also seriously set my mind to the task of planning my career in such a way as to have Carol, and any future children, with me as soon as possible. I knew that I would have to map out what was possible for me and when, all being well, I might achieve each stage of promotion.

In Figure 1 I have produced a schematic diagram of what I knew so well at that time. It represents the 'other letters' of my career in the Navy as, without a doubt, we were all driven by the use of letters to denote our rating or rank, and letters after names are related to educational qualifications or professional associations. The first thing to establish was where I could go from now – I had successfully taken the local examination in November, 1970, to become an REM1 – denoted by one star above my branch badge as shown on the first wedding photograph. This exam was carried out by our section officer, Lt Tull, who was a very mild and polite person by nature but certainly did not let anything 'pass him by' and had a steely side to his character. He often called in to see his staff as they went about their daily activities and had discussions with them concerning equipment, personnel and welfare issues.

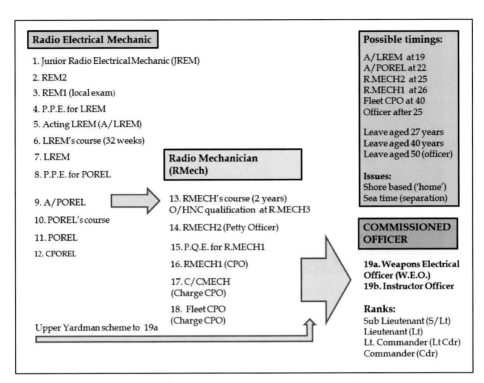

Figure 1 - Career path possibilities and issues/timings

As I was in the 'mechanic' category I could expect to progress down the left-hand side of Figure 1 to possibly reach POREL by the age of 27, and then leave the Navy at that point if I wished to having completed 12 years' service. This would mean passing PPEs for LREM and POREL and then completing relatively short training courses at *Collingwood* before being confirmed in those rates. I could sign on to complete 22 years at some stage in this line, in which case I could expect to reach the rate of CPOREL. This line would not, however, lead to any formal qualifications of its own accord and these would have to be gained by another means, such as following a City and Guilds correspondence course which was run by an educational department in *Collingwood*. If I stayed on the mechanic's line, there could be a possibility of being selected for commissioned officer through what was known as the 'Upper Yardman's' channel. People selected for this would proceed to Dartmouth to train as Weapons Electrical Officers. This was a route that my friend, Roy Brooks, had been offered at *Ganges* but had turned down to remain with our classes and friends there.

For those mechanics doing well on their qualifying courses at *Collingwood* and obtaining suitable recommendations from their section officers, it was possible and common for mechanics to transfer to the Radio Mechanician (RMECH) line at the level of POREL. This would mean two years' formal education at *Collingwood* that lead to formal qualifications at Ordinary or Higher National Certificate (ONC or HNC) level. Following this there would usually be rapid advancement to RMECH1 (CPO) by about the age of 26. About 50% of WEOs came from the RMECH or Artificer pool - a similar line in terms of advancement prospects but artificers joined as apprentices from the beginning and were trained at HMS *Fisgard* in Plymouth. There was another, less commonly-used route to officer, whereby CPOs who were either artificers or mechanicians could apply to attend teacher-training college for one year and then return as an instructor officer (IO) - otherwise known as 'schoolies.' The main concern in thinking about my promotion prospects was to acquire more income and therefore a better quality of life for my future family, and to test myself in seeing how far I could climb up these ladders.

With this diagram set out before me one evening in the EMR, I clearly knew that my first objective would be to study for, and pass, my P.P.E. for LREM. If successful, this would guarantee me being drafted to *Collingwood* for a year once I left *Bulwark*, where Carol could join me in a married quarter. I had many willing tutors to help me, with Kenny Everett especially being my principal advisor and advocate, so I took down the advancement BR from the shelves above me and started to work out a plan of action. I realised that I would have to study hard around my normal responsibilities and duties to achieve my aims, so one of the first things I did was put together a study journal that I could fill with notes and diagrams based on the guidance I had before me.

At the same time, my thoughts remained focussed on my work on board, my parents and other members of my family. After studying my diagram and the advancement BR whilst still on duty in the EMR, I wrote:

> *One day last week it was very rough indeed. Quite a few people were sea sick and things were flying around all over the place. It was the first time at sea for some of them so it is understandable really. I didn't feel too good for a while, but I wasn't sick and felt alright after a couple of hours.*

This excerpt is rather interesting to me as the issue of sea-sickness is one that dramatically affected some people such that they became almost incapable of performing their duties. Again, the Navy had its solution as anyone being found to be incapable of performing their duties due to sea sickness may be placed on a charge if they had not taken anti sea-sickness tablets (Stugeron) before leaving harbour. Luckily for me, I wasn't too badly affected in a ship the size of *Bulwark*, but I knew that many people on small ships such as minesweepers and frigates faced a much greater challenge in living with the consequences of sea-sickness. This facet of naval life was something that could greatly affect anyone's career prospects.

In terms of my plans for my next promotion I knew that I would have to wait one year after being rated REM1 before I could take my P.P.E. However, I quickly acquired the sample theory questions we had to study and to some extent, learn by rote in discussions with others. This included circuit diagrams of amplifier and radio circuits, block diagrams of transmitters and receivers, radar principles and various other things such as memorising the colour code for electronic resistors. The second element of the P.P.E. would be an oral exam conducted by the Radio Section Officer and others. What I needed now was a job change to extend my knowledge of radar in particular. Luckily that would come in due course but for now I concentrated on studying theory and memorising the example material in the P.P.E. book.

****

On the 20th July I wrote home to highlight an issue that would develop into something more serious for the remaining time I would serve on *Bulwark* concerning the island of Malta. I explained:

> *I suppose you will have heard our ship being mentioned on the wireless concerning us going to Malta to take a Commando unit there. Originally we should have gone but Malta has a new Prime Minister and he has demanded £13 million from our government to have British service personnel stationed there. We have offered £10 million and they have been arguing about it. We were put on 48-hours standby but it was lifted today so we definitely won't go there for at least 7 weeks.*

The new Prime Minister of Malta was Dom Mintoff and he would subsequently go on to seek the removal of British forces from Malta and this was something we were aware of as we would clearly be in the front line of any evacuation of British personnel and resources. In the coming six months we took part in several exercises in the Mediterranean with Commandos embarked, with visits first to Liverpool and then Istanbul, Cyprus, Malta, Venice and Trieste. For Carol and I, our first child was now on the way and would be born just before we returned to the UK in December, so I was very much in the category of 'married man' that I had described during our deployment to the Far East. I still enjoyed my work and being with my good friends, but nagging away at the back of my mind always was the thought of when I would get home again. I was also aware that I would not be home for the birth of our baby, so Carol would have to manage everything with the support of her sisters, parents and my family in Yorkshire. However, Carol was a strong person and I knew I could rely on her even though my absence filled me with a sense of guilt and, to some extent, resentment about my lack of freedom to be where I needed to be.

In between periods at sea doing exercises we visited Gibraltar once more, and I returned to Catalan Bay as I had done before to relax and contemplate the new challenges ahead of me, both in the Navy and with regard to my new and increasing family commitments. About this time I had somewhat of a shock as I was assigned to another three months of communal work in the kitchens, which I wasn't pleased to find out about as it would delay my progression and I felt I had already done my fair share of this type of work.

Photo 40 - Catalan Bay, Gibraltar in July, 1971

Source: author

One evening after washing the hundreds of dishes I had to do in the senior rates' galleys I returned to 5E2 mess and took up a typical after-work conversation with Kenny Everett over a can of beer. I wasn't happy about doing what appeared to be an extra session in the galleys and said to him that "I felt I should have been treated with more respect and consideration as I was now a married man with a child on the way." Kenny replied by going straight to the point and explaining, "Listen, Johnny, you are still an O.D. and you can't expect any favours from the system just because you happen to be married – I can appreciate how you feel but you just have to accept it, mate." 'O.D.' was the general term used to describe people at the bottom of their rank structure, and literally meant 'ordinary.' Although

I didn't welcome this point of view, I accepted that he was right - and I acknowledged that to him. However, it made me even more determined to take my P.P.E. for LREM because my qualification period to do so was fast approaching. Starting the following day, I went about increasing my efforts in studying and preparing myself for this objective.

On the 9th October I wrote a letter to my father to wish him happy birthday and also mentioned some aspects of our exercise in the Med' and about Carol's progress:

> *We are off Crete now and anchored in a bay with five American ships. Tomorrow we are off to sea to do a big N.A.T.O. exercise called 'Deep Farrow.' There will be 31 ships involved from Britain, America, Turkey and Greece. USS America is the biggest of them all – she is anchored on our starboard side and I should say she is about 40,000 tonnes, and nuclear powered. The exercise will last until the 21st of this month when we arrive in Malta to spend three weeks doing a self-maintenance period. Carol seems to be doing well and if she's had any trouble she hasn't told me.*

When we finally anchored in Malta I was getting rather concerned about our 'new arrival' back home. I knew that I would be informed by telegram to the ship from Carol's parents once the baby was born, and everyone kept saying to me, "Not long now, Johnny." As usual I played football for the ship and went ashore from time to time in the famous gondolas that transported us to and from the ship in Valetta harbour. I was always fond of Malta as a place to visit as it was clean and had a certain ambience that reflected its colonial links with Britain. I even mentioned in a letter home that I would be asking to be drafted to the island once I finished my time on *Bulwark*. On the 7th November I wrote that:

> *I am sorry about not writing sooner, but I can't seem to concentrate on anything else but when this baby is going to be born. I still miss you all though, and I think about everyone very much, but I can't seem to put my mind to anything else.*

In this letter I go on to expand in some detail about the fact that although I was now married I still cared for parents and brother and sisters as much as ever. I think that because of our 'isolated' life without our extended family in Africa we became a very close nit unit. In Rhodesia there was only a minimal welfare state so in times of financial difficulty because of intermittent employment for my father, everyone had had to pull together to get by. Probably for those who married into our family, our closeness to each other was a barrier in some ways.

Each day I listened intently to every pipe that was made over the main tannoy system and felt a sense of disappointment when my name was not mentioned. Then, one morning at stand easy while sitting in the Mess, with many of my friends and colleagues sitting around having coffee, the main tannoy clicked and the announcement came: "REM Nixon, report to the Bridge Wireless Office." Rather like my mess-mate who had run up the ladder to bang his head on the closed hatch on our Far East deployment, I set off up the ladder with a chorus of cheers and encouragement from my friends and colleagues. To get to the correct office I had to run up several ladders as the Bridge Wireless Office, was up in the island of the ship. When I made it I was handed a telegram that said:

> *Baby girl arrived safely, 7lb 4oz. Mother and baby doing well.*

It is difficult to describe the sense of relief I felt as I descended back down the ladders to my mess-mates and to pass on the news, which resulted in a flurry of back slapping and hand-shakes. I was a father now at the age of 19 as well as a husband, son and brother. I waited with anticipation and impatience now for my next batch of letters from home to hear all the details of how Carol had been during the birth. After about a week I finally received details of our daughter, who would be called Lisa Jayne, and the first photograph that had been taken of her. I would, however, have to wait until the 14th December to see her.

In the Navy there was a term that was used to describe how ratings normally celebrated the birth of a child – known as 'wetting the baby's head.' Although I would have much preferred to do this over a beer with my family in the Three Horse Shoes pub back home in Brierley, or even having a cup of tea or coffee at home, there was an expectation of all new fathers to do this by over-indulging in alcohol consumption. Whilst ashore with a group of my closest friends the following day, therefore, I did go through an evening that was perhaps out of character for me and one that would put me in degree of danger.

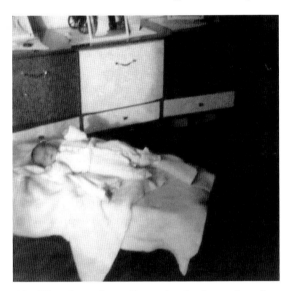

Photo 41 - The first photo I received of my daughter, Lisa

Source: *author*

This is because, in a large social club in view of Valetta harbour, I was offered an enormous number of vodka and cokes – my preferred drink at that time – by people from my department, the ROs and many others who knew me because of being in the ship's football team. They all had good intentions of course and I really appreciated their gestures, but I was left staring at about 20 glasses of vodka and coke on a round table. I knew it wouldn't be sensible to drink all of them but to show my appreciation I did my best to raise a glass with many friends and receive their congratulations. However, although I thought I had managed the situation well, on walking outside a couple of hours later I suddenly became very intoxicated indeed and, according to Kenny Everett and Roy Brooks, extremely belligerent and insulting towards some of the locals who worked in the watering houses we subsequently visited. In the end, and I don't know how, I returned to the ship on my own without any recollection of how I achieved it. Although this was an amusing occurrence for me and my friends, it really wasn't my idea of how to celebrate the birth of my child. I also had great concern for Carol's ordeal during her labour. Luckily, however, I survived this event but over time I would learn how to protect myself more in similar circumstances. I was therefore pleased to get back to normal with my work and sport as quickly as possible and my forthcoming Christmas leave on the 14th December.

The other good news for me at this time was that I had a job change to the 'Tactical Section,' which meant working on the main navigational radar system, called '978,' and other operations rooms' radar displays under the leadership of LREM 'Toby' Tyler. My fellow-REM on this section was 'Tex' Peach. Toby can only be described as a 'one off' as his personality was at the extreme in many ways. His main characteristic was that he 'didn't suffer fools gladly' and had any number of 'bespoke' expressions to describe people who did or said silly things. Over the months ahead I would often see him returning from the operations room after checking a radar display that had been reported defective by an operator or one of the officers. If the problem had been, for example, the 'gain control' turned down or if a switch had been placed in the wrong position (the general term we used for these 'faults' was 'finger trubs' – i.e. finger trouble), Toby would come into our maintenance room and let off, in his West Bromwich accent, a torrent of expletives that left us all in fits of laughter. I soon learned that if I fed him a little more information about the particular operator or officer with the 'finger trubs' he could be kept going for an age, and usually ended his outbursts with a well-known expression among us: "He's a total duffer!" One of the PO Artificers I worked with also had one of these all-encompassing expressions to sum up a difficult situation – he simply smiled slightly and said, "Gloom."

Tex Peach, who was from Southampton and had a strong south-coast accent, was also a one-off in his own way and wound Toby Tyler up no end with his 'daft questions,' which I think were deliberate in many ways. But the interaction between Toby and Tex was a sight and sound to behold and kept me amused practically all day long. The reason I was pleased to be on this section was that I could finalise my revision and studies for my P.P.E. for LREM, which I was scheduled to take in early December. Toby was a great help as he did his best to encourage and prepare me for this important exam that would determine what would happen to me, and Carol, after leaving *Bulwark*.

After visiting the beautiful city of Venice, a major problem in the ship occurred as we approached the Italian port of Trieste. We were due to enter the bay on the 25th November but were prevented from doing so by very bad weather, so we remained at sea close to shore waiting for conditions to improve. At 6.15 am whilst lying in our bunks asleep, the loud and piercing call for "hands to emergency stations" came over the main broadcast system. In these situations we usually heard the prefix 'for exercise,' meaning it was a drill, but this time there was no such prefix. Quickly our Killicks were up and telling everyone to get out of bed and rush off to emergency stations, which were on the flight deck. Once we got up onto the deck we could see vast amounts of smoke coming out of the funnel and realised something serious was happening. I recorded the incident in my letter home later that day:

At 6.15 a fire started in one of our boilers and we had to go to emergency stations, which is one below abandon ship. It took about an hour to put the fire out and really it was a lucky thing we didn't blow up. If the boiler had gone we would have been in trouble as it is next to a magazine full of live ammunition, and if the fire had spread into that we'd probably be at the bottom of the ocean now. Anyway it didn't get far due to the way everyone worked to put it out. The engineers who were down there were trapped for a while but a rescue team was sent down to fish them out. Some of them were burned a bit and will be in sick bay for a week.

I remember this incident very well as several hundred of us were standing in lines with the land to our right as we rolled around in rough seas trying to speculate about what was happening. In fact we had been saved by the heroic actions of two engineers who were subsequently awarded the B.E.M. for Gallantry. They were POMEM Joseph Thompson and MEM1 Peter Simcock. The citation *(Burns, 1986)* for the latter read:

[87]

Simcock, only 19 years old, spent 20 minutes almost alone in a compartment filled with heat, flames and smoke (in his fire suit) of a major fire and carried out the task he had been given.........the trapped men were recovered unharmed and it became possible to close down the compartment and fight the fire in time to stop it getting out of hand. MEM Simcock's courage, devotion to duty and coolness in the face of considerable danger were in the highest traditions of the Service.

The boiler fire had eventually been extinguished by a process called 'steam drenching.' This entails closing down the boiler or engine room and evacuating everyone. The compartment is then flooded with steam, which starves the fire of oxygen and therefore puts it out. If anyone remained in the compartment when this happened they would have died almost immediately – which is what PO Thompson and MEM Simcock were honoured for doing in getting the young engineers who were trapped out to safety. Unfortunately, steam drenching does enormous amounts of damage to the equipment itself, which is why we had to limp back to Plymouth on one boiler and be limited to a maximum speed of 13 knots. However, we would make it for Christmas and I would be able to see Carol and Lisa, and the rest of my family fairly soon, but before then I had the not insignificant task of taking my P.P.E. for LREM, which was scheduled for the 8th December if I passed the written part first.

Because I had spent so much time studying whilst on duty and receiving so much support, I passed the written exam without any difficulty. Now my task was to finalise my preparation for the oral exam, which would be with Lt Peckham plus one or two others in the department. These oral exams would always be a nerve-racking experience for most people and I was no exception. The format was that any weaknesses in the written paper, covering theory, would be brought up first and the candidate would have an opportunity to clarify. Following this there would be fairly in-depth questions on the equipment worked on to date, and then more general questions on other sections of the Radio Electrical department – in our case there were six. I recall making sure I was smartly dressed for the exam and when the time came, reported to one of our quieter offices in the island of the ship for my exam, along with two other friends who were taking it at the same time. Although I felt rather anxious I managed to answer most of the questions well enough and was called in to see Lt Peckham a little later. He congratulated me with the good news that I had been given a 'very good' pass.

This was naturally welcome as I could start climbing my career ladder but, more importantly, it would initiate a series of drafts that would mean Carol, Lisa and I could start living together as a family whilst I was ashore for, hopefully, several years. Kenny Everett, my main supporter along with Toby Tyler as my section boss, were especially pleased as I had accomplished this milestone at the earliest time possible at 19 years of age. I owed a lot to their help, along with our senior ratings and my friends and colleagues in 5E2 mess. I probably partook of the odd beer with one or two of them in celebration.

Once we returned to our base port of Plymouth we were soon on Christmas leave and I returned, after six weeks of not seeing my first child, to see her myself for the first time. She had blue eyes like her mother, and golden locks like her father. Lisa was a very healthy and robust baby who needed feeding well and regularly from the very start and I soon began to do my share of looking after her to give Carol some respite and hopefully became a 'modern Dad' from the start of being a parent. It was also at this point that I decided to stop smoking cigarettes – something I had been doing for about three years as was common for people in those days and especially with my free allocations in the Navy. Not only did I not want to smoke around Lisa, I had also noticed being a little more out of breath than usual when playing football for the ship.

Photo 42 - With daughter, Lisa, Christmas 1971

Source: author

I therefore made it my New Year's resolution for 1972 and luckily or otherwise, I would encounter and manufacture some of my own luck in this intention. It was wonderful to be home again in a comfortable and peaceful environment. However, Mr Mintoff's actions in Malta would trigger *Bulwark's* new mission to the island and a long family separation period early in the New Year.

****

On the 13th January, 1972, *Bulwark* left Plymouth for the Mediterranean on what would be my last deployment. Over the Christmas leave period there had been various items in the Media concerning the likely withdrawal of British forces from Malta. In essence, Mr Mintoff wanted the British out of his island and a great deal of diplomatic negotiation was going on between the British and Maltese governments. For our part, *Bulwark*, being a commando carrier with a large number of helicopters and marines, was the ideal ship to undertake operations on and around the island in order to protect British interests and personnel. Several thousand people connected with the military and their families were stationed on Malta, and our task would be to protect them and oversee their exit. Indeed, the mission we were now to take part in was given the title of 'Operation Exit.'

We were held back from sailing for 24 hours due to bad weather, and immediately after departure hit rather inclement conditions which were forecast for most of the passage to Malta. I recall talking to Toby Tyler and Tex Peach in our maintenance office, which had its own porthole so we could observe the sea conditions outside, and saying that although I felt a bit unwell it did stop me from wanting to smoke cigarettes, so I was helped in some ways by the sea conditions. To increase my likelihood of success I put a £5 bet (quite a lot of money in those days) on with Kenny Everett that I would be able to stop. As usual, he was always keen to help me improve myself and, to his credit, did all he could to help me as a young father with family responsibilities. I felt sure he would stand the loss of his £5 for the greater good of my endeavour to stop smoking.

The voyage was rather gloomy all the way, and what we mostly saw out of our porthole were grey seas, white-capped waves, and rain drizzling down from dark and heavy clouds. There was also some uncertainty about how long we would be away for. Our initial estimate from the Captain was that we may have to face the prospect of being at sea continuously for 82 days and remain in the area to land marines or evacuate British citizens when and if required. I did not relish this prospect and I was aware that I would be missing Carol, Lisa and other members of my family. Lisa would have changed considerably before I would see her again, another thought that wasn't welcome but one that I was familiar with having observed and listened to my married colleagues.

When we arrived off Malta, where the sea was now thankfully calm and blue, our first task was to circle the island to establish contact with those ashore and send out our helicopters on various sorties. Due to negotiations, our task was uncertain but very soon our initial plan would change and we would be anchored in Grand Harbour. We would soon become involved in a full-scale evacuation amid unrest and antagonism towards British forces' personnel in general. These aspects were fully explained in a letter to my parents of the 4th February, a few weeks after our arrival:

We are helping with all the stores that have to be moved out by sending working parties ashore every day. We are more than a month ahead of schedule in the withdrawal and since being here I have only been ashore twice to work. I think you must have heard about the occasional demonstration here. I haven't seen any myself but when I do go ashore I make sure everything is quiet although I don't feel at ease as you get stared at wherever you go. Actually, one marine has been killed and one is in hospital after they were attacked by a mob of Maltese people but there isn't anything to worry about as it has all calmed down. I always go to Sliema, which is away from the trouble spots, and no trouble ever happens out there. We are scheduled to arrive back in the UK on the 11th April but some people say it could be earlier. I told you I had a draft to Gibraltar after Bulwark, but I have requested to go to Collingwood for LREM's course and see what I get after that. It will be much better if I want to get on in the Navy if I can go straight to Collingwood.

Reading this letter again I recall very clearly the two occasions I was ashore clearing out the homes of British families who had returned to the UK. I remember being in the lounge of one such home, which had quite an eerie atmosphere due to there being so many personal items of furniture and equipment in it but no family members. We put on the radio to listen to music as we carried out sofas and cupboards to a removal van outside. Playing on the radio was the song 'Mother of mine' by Neil Reid (Parkinson, 1971), the words of which filled me with some sadness and sentimentality:

Mother of mine, you gave to me/ All of my life, to do as I please
I owe everything I have to you/ Mother, sweet mother of mine

Although I felt only slightly vulnerable in this potentially hostile environment, I was aware that life in the Navy could be risky having in mind the killed marine from our ship and the general hostility of locals. At times like these it was easy to get sentimental about those I cared for and missed at home.

Another task we undertook was to load the cars of evacuated people onto a merchant ship for transportation back to the UK. I remember going off in the ship's transport with Kenny Everett and Dave Catton as there had been a call for qualified drivers to volunteer for this work. We were driven to an enormous parking area near the ship which was filled with just about every kind of vehicle one could imagine. I remember also bartering with Kenny and Dave over who would drive the next sports car or classic car. For the whole day we therefore jumped into cars, which had their ignition keys already in place, and drove them up a ramp into the cargo ship where we parked them. We then returned for our next choice and so on for the whole day.

[90]

Photo 43 - *Bulwark* in Grand Harbour, Malta during Operation Exit

Source: *author*

Although our days were filled with activity and our helicopters carried out 1,000 landings and more, life was getting to be rather tetchy as we sat in the harbour for two and a half months while further negotiations went ahead. During this time, Kenny Everett and I hired a car on one or two occasions and went on tours of the north of the island to get away from the focal point of the mission we were on. Kenny also taught me something about social etiquette as we often used to call into high quality restaurants for a meal. Although I had had a reasonable grounding in how to behave when dining in more formal places and during our cruise from Africa to the UK, we were on what was affectionately termed a 'smoothy's run ashore,' in contrast to what most people would associate with a sailor's normal mode of recreation. Having a four-course meal with a good bottle of wine – I remember Kenny's most highly recommended wine was a good bottle of *Châteauneuf-du-Pape*, and a cigar and cognac at the end was, without wishing to appear aloof, more agreeable to me. My phase of being a heavy drinker was rather short for more than one reason, and my natural preference has always been that of moderation or even abstinence when it comes to alcohol. As a reminder of the perils of family life in the Navy, however, I was called to the bunk of one of my closest friends one evening back on board ship.

He had returned from shore after having some drinks that didn't make him drunk, but did release his normal inhibitions to reveal something that was deeply troubling him. I put my hand on his shoulder as he lay there sobbing uncontrollably and said, "What's wrong, mate, - what's happened to you?" At first he just continued sobbing but after a while he said, "Johnny, I've never told anyone else but I was married for a short period of time but it ended. I've got a son and I haven't seen him now for years." This had clearly been wearing him down through worry in not knowing how his son was doing. I had no inclination that he had been married as he never mentioned anything about his family life other than his siblings and parents. I did my best to listen to him and offer empathy, but again this was a recurring theme for many people for any number of reasons. The Navy's divorce rate was certainly among the highest of any social group in the UK and here again I was witness to its consequences in a very close and much-valued friend. I think he felt better after getting his grief off his chest and I was gratified to know he had felt he could do this with me as his friend.

Throughout this long period the ship's company took part in a mass of games and sports, both on the flight deck and in one of our naval bases on the island. The pitches were rock hard with a sandy surface that was problematic for footballers like me. I was regularly playing once or twice a week for the ship or my department. After so much stress from the pitch I developed a serious injury that could easily have ended my playing career. I explained the details in a letter of the 4th March:

Every time I play football I get severe pains in my knee (after a couple of hours). The doctor said it was caused by rough edges of bone in my knee cap that are rubbing on the joint and causing the knee to swell up. He said the only cure was to have the knee cap removed so he advised me not to play for six weeks and then only every two months.

This was a worrying development but as usual my colleagues in 5E2 mess took my mind off the situation with their witty comments as I climbed down from my top bunk and then screamed out in agony before limping off. Getting up ladders was especially difficult as I had to jump up with my good leg and keep my affected leg perfectly straight. People standing at the top of ladders got impatient watching me hobble upwards in slow time – going down was okay, however, as I could slide down holding on to the hand rails and stick my leg straight out. I was relieved that after the six weeks of rest I could resume playing even though it continued to swell up after games for quite a while.

In this particular letter I also mentioned that my draft to Gibraltar had now been cancelled and I was now programmed to join *Collingwood* for LREM's course on the 5th May, and that we would be arriving back in the UK on the 6th April. Very shortly after that I would leave *Bulwark* for the final time on three weeks' leave during which, as I mentioned to my father, I wanted to buy a car for when Carol, Lisa and I moved down south to our married quarter near *Collingwood*. I asked my father, who had mentioned in his letters that he had been without his own car for some time and was cycling to watch football matches at Rotherham, to look out for a 1966 or 67 Morris/Austin 1100. This popular British car of that era had been recommended to me by Kenny Everett and as usual I respected his advice – although on this occasion he may have been somewhat mis-informed as they had a number of troublesome design features that often caused their owners problems, including rusty sills, failing hydraulic suspension and clutches that developed a judder. However, it is true that cars of that era often had similar issues - especially British-built models.

My life ahead was now mapped out and we would soon depart from Malta; the crisis now having died down and an agreement reached between the two governments. After what was a long ordeal, we finally set sail in procedure alpha to majestically move out of Grand Harbour with our helicopters flying overhead. Malta had been my first brush with danger in the Royal Navy but as usual we just tried to go about our business in the normal way. As we sailed into the open ocean my mind was firmly fixed on getting back to see my family. On the voyage home I could reflect on my time aboard what was a very happy ship for me. She was large and powerful but her power had been put to good use in the many exercises, courtesy visits and operations we had taken part in. She was like a surrogate mother in many ways; providing us with shelter, food, and all the facilities to sustain life no matter where we were across the globe. She was the ultimate 'mobile home.' There were many literal 'calm waters' to enjoy in the Mediterranean, Indian and Atlantic Oceans, and the South China Seas. There had also been many occasions, however, when we found ourselves in stormy waters in the Bay of Biscay and off South Africa in particular.

There had also been many sporting occasions that I had been lucky enough to take part in all across the globe – Singapore under flood lights in such a warm climate was the pinnacle for me. I had also served with many good friends from *Collingwood* and *Ganges*, I had got to know and work with some excellent people – many of whom had been supportive and good role models. I particularly learned important principles for my own life from them, and always to 'be true to myself' and not cave in to peer-group pressure – even if it attracted an unpleasant or even hostile reaction from others. I didn't realise it at the time, but it is true that certain professions, academic areas or specialisations attract like-minded people, and within the Radio Electrical branch I felt I had found many such colleagues who thought and behaved like me. Indeed, I was proud to be a 'Pinkie' and hoped that my friendships from *Bulwark* would continue into the future one way or another. I had also visited an enormous number of interesting places around the world and met some unforgettable people.

Photo 44 - *Bulwark* departing Malta for our final voyage back to the UK

Source: *author*

At the same time, some psychological and social 'troubled waters' had raised their problematic heads. The Navy, as I had experienced before, often punished the innocent at times by its rigid application of discipline without due consideration of the evidence or the application of common sense. It was also clear to me, as a young married man now with a wife and child to provide for, that long periods of separation often had adverse effects and risked the very survival of Service marriages. As I reflect now I believe that a transition occurs in such situations – a transition that makes people *stop living in the present and start living in the future* when separation from their families or loved-ones would end. I had begun to appreciate my colleague Wilf Mannion's perception that a black cloud can follow one's life, no matter how sunny the weather is outside.

At least for the foreseeable future, however, I would return home to re-commence living much more in the present. My destiny from that point had been manufactured through much hard work and effort to gain promotion as early as was feasible, and now I could think about the next step on the ladder to, hopefully, a better life for me and my young family. In my final letter from *Bulwark* to my parents on the 29th March, sitting in the EMR whilst on duty as I had done on many occasions for two years, I heard the familiar words and music of one of my favourite songs, 'The Sound of Silence' by Simon and Garfunkel (Paul Simon, 1964) on a cassette player next to me. It was past midnight as I wrote.

I'm sorry for such a short letter but I'm very tired now as we've been putting in quite a lot of overtime getting all the equipment ready for sea. It's all working well now but we've lost a few hours' sleep in getting it that way. Anyway, I'm hoping to see you all on the 11th in thirteen days' time, so until then God bless you all and I send you lots of love and kisses. John

Once back in Plymouth I was fortunate to have Carol journey down to meet me immediately after we had docked. We had arranged to do this as I would have to wait for three days before being relieved, so we found a suitable place to stay in town, while Lisa was being looked after by Carol's mother. There was a square in town full of good restaurants that we went to in the evenings and enjoyed this rare opportunity of being together without family around us. Carol had previously travelled by train to meet me when she was about seven months pregnant, and unfortunately she had had to stand nearly all the way from Doncaster to Plymouth because no seats were available. Therefore, I was pleased to know this, and similar experiences when travelling, had not diminished her wish to come down to collect me before returning home together.

On my final day I said my farewells to the many and never-forgotten close friends and colleagues I had; sad to be leaving them for the final time. I walked down the gangway with my kitbag over my shoulders and a suitcase in my hand, to a taxi with Carol patiently waiting for me in the back seat. I looked back once more to the ship, towering above me with a hive of activity going on as usual, and knew that the memories I had of *Bulwark* would stay with me and grow in importance as the years went by. *Bulwark's* motto was: 'Under Thy Wings I Will Trust' – I had done that and she never let me down, but for now I was pleased to be moving to new pastures. I said to the taxi driver, "Railway station please," and watched out of the back window as HMS *Bulwark* gradually slipped from view.

V - HMS *Collingwood* & HMS *Mauritius* [1972-75]

When the train finally arrived in Selby, Carol and I caught a taxi and after 45 minutes we were greeted warmly by Fred at the front door. I was very keen to see Lisa after three months away as I knew she would have changed quite a lot. Carol led me into the lounge where Lisa was sitting quietly on the sofa in a small dress with her grandmother smiling and making sure she was safe. Lisa was propped up with some pillows and I could immediately see she was much more alert and quickly spotted that a 'strange person' had suddenly come into the room. Carol said, "Lisa, your Daddy is back," as I knelt down to look at her and hold her tiny hand. As one might expect, her bottom lip started to protrude and shake, and she immediately burst into tears and looked longingly up at her mother. Carol took over the situation and after a day or two of similar incidents I was finally accepted, but in fact my absence during Lisa's early days had understandably strengthened the bond between her and her mother, and it would take many months before Lisa would regard us as equals in terms of who she was happy to be with.

Over my leave period before joining *Collingwood* Carol and I visited my parents several times – my family naturally doted on Lisa as she had clearly inherited many characteristics of the Nixons, and I was pleased to be able to sleep in a proper bed again and walk through woods, visit the seaside and generally relax. After a few days, Carol and I decided to buy our first car. Carol's father helped us to scan the papers and we came across an advertisement for an Alaskan blue 1967 Morris 1100, which was being sold privately in Selby. We duly called in to see it and after a test drive, bought the car. It felt good to be able to drive around as a family and have our independence – I was also in regular contact with the married quarters' people in Hampshire, who fairly quickly allocated us to a new flat in the Navy's 'Rowner' estate in the town of Gosport. We finally got our address as '54 North Path.' This meant that all the jigsaw pieces were now in place for when I joined *Collingwood*.

On the evening of the 4th May as my leave was due to expire, I loaded up the car with as much luggage as I could manage and set off for the long journey to Fareham on the south coast. I would return after two weeks to collect Carol and Lisa once all the arrangements had been finalised at *Collingwood*. The journey south would prove to be somewhat of an ordeal as I had never driven on a motorway before. I recall having to learn very quickly how to dodge traffic that was speeding along in three lanes, and how to overtake other cars while looking in the mirror to make sure it was safe to do so. The journey took about 8 hours in total and I recall feeling very stiff and uncomfortable when I finally stopped at the main gate to report my arrival. The duty PO informed me that I was to proceed to Trafalgar block, where I had been accommodated on REM's course, and that I could park my car immediately outside the block. These two pieces of information were very welcome and I duly drove up the main road of *Collingwood*, and passed the parade ground on my right to park my Morris 1100 next to another Morris 1100 and check in with the block PO. I was allocated a cabin on the second floor with three other people who had joined *Collingwood* for Leading Rate's courses. I quickly made friends with a Scottish colleague who, as it turned out, owned the other Morris 1100, so I certainly felt in good company. The surroundings of Trafalgar block felt very familiar and comfortable as I unpacked my bag and settled down for the evening. One of my close friends from *Bulwark*, Stuart Mowbray, was also in the same accommodation so we would be able to keep each other company over the coming weeks.

Early in the following morning I reported to the main administration block and was allocated my course number and start date. As there would be some delay before I actually started my course, I was given a job working in the Pay Office for the Chief Writer. This turned out to be a rather pleasant and relaxed period of time and after the first week I saw the Captain to be promoted to acting LREM, which meant I was required to sew the badge of a Killick – which was an anchor – onto the left sleeves of my uniforms. I remember the Chief Writer ribbing me somewhat about this as he had noticed that I suddenly started walking with my left arm inclined to the front so that everyone could see my new badge. It seemed that this was a natural response for newly-promoted personnel like me. Back in Trafalgar block, as we both awaited the start of our courses, my new friends and I exchanged stories about our cars and information regarding our forthcoming courses.

After three weeks at *Collingwood* the day arrived to start my new course and my new colleagues and I assembled one Monday morning in one of our teaching rooms to give our introductions and learn more about our course. It was at this first meeting that my relative inexperience and shyness revealed itself. This was because, without any warning, our class instructor stated that we would all be required to come to the front of the class and give a short introductory talk on our backgrounds. Although I had been given lots of responsibility as a PO Junior at HMS *Ganges* and had worked for two and a half years on board a ship, I suddenly found this task to be extremely daunting. I suspect this was because it was the first time I had been required to talk about 'me' personally, and for some complex and unknown reasons at that time, it made me feel extremely nervous. This might have been expected as I was the youngest person in the class and had only served in one ship whereas many others had had two or more drafts outside of training. However, I did overcome my nerves to one degree or another and said what I thought was relevant but was happy once I had returned to my seat. It was reassuring for me, therefore, to find out the other members of my new class had also felt the same but it was probably an indicator that being under 'public' scrutiny could be problematic for someone with my personality.

I quickly became friends with one of my new classmates, whose name was Steve Marsh. We were of a similar age and had so much in common as he also had a young wife and daughter, and like me, was a keen guitarist. We would also go on to be those who were first in the queue for the 'goodies' that were served up by the N.A.A.F.I. at stand easy each morning in the main instruction area, called 'White City,' following our first lesson. The things we usually focussed on were ham and salad crusty baguettes in large wooden trays, steak and kidney pies, and tea with a jam doughnut for 'desert' (this was well before lunch!). He also lived on the Rowner estate with his family and I knew that I would be living near to him very soon. Another classmate who would become close friends was another Steve – Steve Champion – who would become a neighbour and the three of us would travel to *Collingwood* each day in my car and share exam tips as we progressed through our course. My priority now was to finalise everything for Carol and Lisa to join me and the following week-end I returned to Yorkshire to collect them.

I imagine Carol's parents were sorry to see their new granddaughter and daughter leaving home but at the same time I am sure they were happy to know that we had our own place to live in now. After a long journey on the Sunday that we left Selby we finally pulled up outside our flat, which was on the top floor of a brand new three-storey block of impressive-looking apartments. At the bottom of the stairs we had our own storage room for Lisa's pushchair and when we opened up the front door the fresh smell of new furniture and wood greeted us. The flat had two bedrooms and a separate lounge and kitchen/dining room. Although we didn't strongly register the point at the time, it was true that Carol, like many Service wives, was taken away from her extended family hundreds of miles away from 'home' and we would have to learn to be an independent unit as quickly as possible. In a letter home in early June I mentioned some aspects of life on the south coast:

Carol, Lisa and I are keeping well, but since we came down here Lisa has really cried a lot. I think it must be because everything is so strange to her. Carol is pleased with the flat and seems to like it down here although we would both probably prefer to live in Yorkshire, but it is a good substitute down here and we have got all we need now.

In fact the impact on Lisa at the age of six months was quite dramatic to begin with. This is because, for many weeks, Carol could not lose sight of her without her screaming, and she even had to take Lisa to the bathroom with her. As well as her new surroundings, this was almost certainly because Lisa was used to a house full of people and the constant attention she received in an extended family arrangement. The sudden change to only having Carol with her during the day, and the two of us at home in the evenings and week-ends, took some careful parenting skills to address. However, we all started to explore new areas near to where we lived, which was only about two miles from the sea. One place we became fond of, and where Carol walked to with Lisa when I was at *Collingwood*, was 'Stokes Bay.' It had a large beach area, vast open spaces of grass and a wooded park nearby. We would spend many a Sunday morning there with Lisa and later had her Christened in the local church in Rowner. Once we were all settled in our new home I could concentrate on doing well on my course and Carol also regularly listened to my struggles regarding the theory I was now studying.

Photo 45 - Carol and Lisa at Stokes Bay after moving south

Source: *author*

In this regard, I recall coming home one evening in somewhat of a confused state having been asked to use logarithmic tables to do some mathematical calculations. This exposed my lack of general education as most people would have used them at school but luckily Carol could give her own explanation and help me through that and similar problems because of her grammar school background. We also decided that Carol should commence her own studies now to make up for the fact that she had also left school before she could take formal qualifications. She therefore started a GCE O' level course in English Literature so we were both now able to make progress academically. This process certainly helped to cement our relationship as we both naturally had an interest in seeing the other succeed for the benefit of all of us.

I was immensely enjoying studying with my class as we were small in number (only about 12 altogether) and the nature of our work was so interesting to us. We often worked with oscilloscopes and other electronic equipment doing various laboratory experiments. We also carried out fault finding on receivers by inserting signals into various sections of their circuits to determine if there was an output and therefore where the fault was located. I remember also enjoying working with another close classmate who was affectionately called 'Spud' Murphy. Most people in the Navy had nicknames and anyone with the name of Murphy was referred to as 'Spud' because of the link with Ireland (and therefore potatoes). I wish I could remember his real name as the name 'Spud' does not reflect his warm personality, friendliness and intelligence. There was nothing more enjoyable than to have coffee during our stand easy outside the N.A.A.F.I. rooms, and chat together with the two Steves and Spud about how our experiments had turned out as well as life in general. We were all working up the ladder of our careers and liked to learn from each other in such discussions. We studied all aspects of radio and radar theory and also did specialist courses on various pieces of equipment we would be expected to work on in our future drafts. I don't remember there being one bad word spoken among us as a class and I was happy that I could go home each evening to Carol and Lisa, which was in stark contrast to being on board a ship away for long periods of time. I know Carol found it quite difficult at times to be constantly entertaining Lisa on her own, but that left room for me to play with Lisa and try to make her less 'clingy' towards Carol when I returned home each evening.

Steve Marsh and I also met up in each other's homes with our wives so we could practise playing the guitar and learning new tunes and guitar riffs. I especially remember that Steve was left handed, and like so many left-handed people he had some unique 'gifts' when it comes to music (or sport). He showed me how to play the introduction to the song 'You've got a friend' by James Taylor (Carole King, 1971) which I was very impressed with as it involved some fairly tricky finger picking. We also learnt some well-known songs by the Beatles and Simon and Garfunkel but our focus was on developing a style similar to the likes of Paul Simon, James Taylor and Cat Stevens.

Most of my letters to my parents over this period were about how Lisa was progressing and planning trips to Yorkshire at Christmas, or for weddings and so on. My parents also came down to visit and also enjoyed spending time with us at the seaside. In a letter on the 14th October, I wrote:

Lisa is walking now and Carol and I are very proud of her. Tonight a fast song came on the radio and we started dancing with her – she became so excited she fell on the floor. She also plays football with me – I kick the ball to her and even if I am at the other side of the room she kicks the ball back to me. She really knows how clever she is as she screams out as she walks around the flat.

We were also pleased to find that, living close to us, was my friend from *Bulwark*, Dave Catton and his wife, Lynn, and their son, Michael. My good friend from *Ganges*, Pete Kerley, also soon arrived in *Collingwood* to do his LOEM's course so life in the Navy was rather like being a member of a large family of brothers (and sisters) in many ways and I would continue to renew old acquaintances as my career unfolded.

LREM's course was 32 weeks in length so it wasn't long before we were considering what our next draft would be, but just before Christmas in 1972 I received some interesting news from my Divisional Officer regarding one very attractive option, as I explained in a letter to my parents in November:

I haven't actually got the draft order yet but my D.O. called me in and told me I could have a (married-accompanied) draft to Mauritius if I asked for it. Anyway, Carol and I both agreed to it because it means we can be together for another two years and I went back and told him 'yes.' Well, how is Barbara keeping? Has she got a date to go into hospital yet? It would be nice if she could come out to Mauritius so she can recover in all that sun. Anyway, you'll have to let me know what is happening.

It is interesting to reflect that Carol and I actually considered not accepting Mauritius because of things like bugs and snakes that were there in abundance. However, we clearly saw it as a potentially wonderful time in what was commonly termed 'Paradise Island.' I would also be working on some interesting equipment under the general heading of 'shore wireless.' HMS *Mauritius* was part of the Defence Communications Network (DCN), which provided worldwide communications for Royal Navy ships through long-range high frequency (HF) equipment based in various parts of the globe. We soon became excited at the prospect of two years in the sun and an opportunity for us to progress our education and my career. It was about this time that we decided to try for another child so that Lisa would have a brother or sister with a reasonable gap between them. We both agreed that wherever possible, children should ideally have siblings with whom to play and grow up with. Mauritius would be an ideal place to bring a new baby into our family.

The problem with my younger sister, Barbara, was that she had been diagnosed with scoliosis (curvature) of the spine and was a candidate for major surgery called a 'spinal rod fusion,' aimed at correcting the curvature. As she had been growing up I could remember my mother often saying to Barbara that she should "stop standing like that." Her right hip was always protruding but it was, in reality, nothing to do with her 'deliberately lazy' posture. Eventually she had been seen by a specialist and once she reached almost her full height she would be operated on at a specialist unit at King Edward VII Orthopaedic Hospital in Rivelin Valley, Sheffield. Barbara was 15 years old at this time and the doctors had agreed she should continue until she was 16 before they operated. It would be the case, therefore, that I would be in Mauritius by the time she would be hospitalised and then go through a year-long recovery period in a special bed that could be rotated. It would be a worrying time for all her family members.

My draft to Mauritius was confirmed in due course. I would also be required to do some additional training on the transmitters I would be working on in Mauritius before I left *Collingwood*. I had done well in my exams and finished LREM's course on the 9th March with a course average of 83%. This meant that another piece of my career jigsaw had been put into place as I was now qualified for Radio Mechanician selection in due course if my work performance warranted recommendation, and I could pass my P.P.E. for POREL. This would give me the option of either remaining in the mechanic stream or transferring to a route that offered more qualifications, rapid promotions and greater opportunities.

In due course I attended a specialist unit at *Collingwood* until the 14th April on some of the most impressive, if not elderly, transmitters I had ever seen. They came in three sizes and power ratings: HS 31 (low power), HS 61 (medium power) and HS 81 (high power) and got progressively larger in size according to their power output capacity. The course was a very relaxed experience – the transmitters were so large that one could open a door to them and walk around inside to undertake maintenance. We also studied and learnt about the drive units that were used to relay the signals from the Communications Centre to the transmitters themselves. The thermionic valves that formed the main power amplifiers of the transmitters were absolutely enormous, with large brass contacts that were literally bolted into place on the anodes of the valves. Being inside them would obviously be a potentially dangerous experience as any electric shock would come along with high current levels – the factor that produced lethal electric shocks. However, our training was very thorough and I would be supervised by POs and CPOs with experience of working on these 'beasts' once in Mauritius. I learned that the station I would be working at was called *Bigara*, which was on the top of a hill on the island, some way from the Married Quarters and Communications Centre at Vacoas. I knew I was extremely lucky to be given such a job and also that Carol and Lisa would be there and hopefully enjoy the type of life only the Royal Navy could offer in Mauritius. We were scheduled to fly out on the 5th May, exactly one year after joining *Collingwood* to complete my LREM's course.

While we were visiting Yorkshire and staying with Carol's parents in the New Year we also had confirmation that Carol was expecting our second child, which is something we welcomed as we could also plan our family as well as career and educational studies. Carol would have to terminate her studies in English literature but luckily she had completed enough of her course to take the exam in Mauritius. We therefore corresponded with the headmaster at the local school in HMS *Mauritius* and Carol was permitted to register as an unattached candidate and take her three 'O' levels very shortly after our arrival in Mauritius.

Just before leaving for Mauritius my mother came down to stay with us for one week so she could spend more time with us and especially Lisa as she wouldn't be seeing her for more than two years. I am sure our parents felt this would be a wrench as Lisa was now about 18 months old and at an interesting stage of life for parents and grandparents. There would also be a new child everyone would miss the birth of, so these things played on our minds to one degree or another but the adventure and stability of Mauritius focussed our minds in a positive rather than negative manner. In many ways it would be good to be out of the country as this was an era of increasing trouble caused by mainland bombings by the Irish Republican Army (IRA).

On the evening of the 6th May, 1973, we arrived at Heathrow and checked in ready for the 13-hour flight ahead of us. On board the British Oversees Aircraft Corporation (BOAC) DC10 we were welcomed by very smart and pleasant air stewardesses; Lisa was given a cot to sleep in and Carol and I were given blankets and pillows. All was set fair for a very long but hopefully pleasant flight.

I hadn't flown for more than 17 years so it was somewhat of a thrill when the plane taxied to the end of the runway, waited a few seconds and then went to full thrust as we were pushed back in our seats and rapidly accelerated until reaching take-off speed. As we rose up into the sky, the bright lights of London panned out below a dark blue horizon that was panning out ahead of the plane, and into the distance. We then turned south and headed into the night sky for a new life and adventure that we hoped would be unforgettable.

****

We landed in Cairo for our first re-fuelling stop at 3 O'clock in the morning, with only the city lights visible below us. As the plane took off again the sun was rising as we rose above the clouds to 37,000 feet where the views from the windows were spectacular. Breakfast was served just before our next scheduled brief stop in Nairobi. I had some flashbacks to my life in Rhodesia as I saw the many Africans that were involved in re-fuelling and replenishing the aircraft as we remained on the runway. In my first letter back home from Mauritius I described the last leg of the journey:

We kept passing over little islands and the sea looked blue and fresh. The plane was thrown about a bit just before landing in Mauritius because we had to fly through a lot of cloud which caused air turbulence. We landed safely and were met by the person I am relieving out here.

The first thing that hit us when we disembarked the plane was the almost unbearable heat of Mauritius – possibly because of the air conditioned cabin of the plane. The first question we asked ourselves on the runway as we walked towards the terminal was 'how will we get used to this?' Waiting for us and to help us along for the first two weeks was the family we were relieving, LREM Joe Miller, his wife, Sylvia, and their 2 year-old son. They gave us a warm welcome and immediately I could see that our 'English' clothes and pale complexions made us feel the heat more as Joe and his family all wore light cotton materials, shorts and sandals. They also had good sun tans which we quickly learned was an effective way of keeping away the mosquitos. Unfortunately, mosquitos seemed to love pale skins so we were to be bitten quite badly in the early period of our time in Mauritius.

We eventually got into a Royal Navy Land Rover, which was driven by a friendly Mauritian attached to the Navy, and drove up the hot road to the town of Vacoas. All families arriving at HMS *Mauritius* spent the first few months living away from the married quarters in nearby bungalows and houses. Our new home was situated in a narrow secluded lane called Granham Road about a mile from the married quarters, which were built on the same land as the main Communications Centre (affectionately known as the 'Comcen'). Joe and his family showed us around our new home and had kindly bought some extra things to complement the standard package of groceries that were delivered by the N.A.A.F.I. shop at the married quarters. The fridge was therefore filled with everyday things we would need before finding our way to the N.A.A.F.I. and other local shops in Vacoas. There were many new smells, sights and experiences around us as we settled down for the first night in our new whitewashed bungalow with its polished veranda floor, which again reminded me of the bungalow I had lived in as a child in Rhodesia.

While Carol and I took a while to 'warm' to our new environment for various reasons, Lisa was immediately at home. In my first letter to my parents I wrote:

We took Lisa to the swimming pool yesterday and she wouldn't keep out of the paddling pool. She kept swallowing water and going under the surface but it didn't bother her a bit – in fact I had to fight to keep her out of the big pool because she kept trying to dive in. I don't think she knew it would have covered her!

We quickly realised how privileged we were because on our doorstep we had so many facilities such as the swimming pool and the Navy's own beach retreat with a restaurant, tennis courts and chalets at 'Chaland,' which families and other Navy personnel usually travelled to using the Navy's bus shuttle between Chaland and the married quarters.

After a few weeks we also decided to call into the local MSPCA to rescue a small puppy, which Lisa would become attached to and get up to all kinds of mischief with. An additional reason for owning a dog, however, was to guard our home as intruders would often enter the garden soon after I left home for work when on night duty. This was naturally of concern to us as we had some broken blinds so people could see through the windows, and the property had very weak locks on the doors. We also experienced many an evening in candlelight as the island suffered from regular power cuts. There were therefore some early challenges for us when living in the local community, although the good points clearly outweighed the bad ones. The puppy, which we called Candy, would turn out to be one of the best dogs I would ever have as she grew up to be unbelievably fast, agile and intelligent. She was probably the reason Lisa became such a strong dog lover as the two of them were inseparable, although I recall getting up in the mornings on many occasions to face the consequences of all kinds of 'collusions' between the two of them.

Photo 46 - Lisa and new puppy in the front garden

Source: *author*

Although families living out in the local areas were a little isolated from the main hub of activity, we were soon joined by a classmate from my LREM's course. His name was Chris Sluman, and his wife was a very bubbly and bright lady called Elizabeth. Fortunately, they lived only a few hundred metres away in a similar property. We quickly became close friends and supported one another through various minor crises and would spend many a warm evening on the veranda debating some issue or other. While Chris was very quiet by nature, Elizabeth was a well-read individual with a very strong character and was not slow to put forward her opinions in a forthright manner. I do recall one discussion, which reflected my own naive opinions at the time, although I have to take into consideration I was still only 20 years old. The discussion was on the topic of which was the superior sex – male or female. I thought I clinched it by saying that while men and women were of similar intelligence, men were superior because they were physically stronger. Elizabeth didn't agree and she was arguably the 'stronger' one between her and Chris - she always rode at the front of the tiny Honda motor scooter they owned. However, it was certainly great fun to debate with her.

In Mauritius we also had our own maid, Nicola, and a gardener, who provided useful help as Carol was quickly becoming more advanced in her pregnancy. Between the two of us, however, we tidied up the garden, which had its own banana trees among many other tropical plants, and as I noted in a letter home we planted over 300 shrubs and bushes as well as cutting the grass in the front and back gardens. Whilst it was beneficial to have help around the home, Nicola did find Lisa difficult at times as she went about her work as Lisa was incredibly mischievous by nature. For example, despite warnings from Carol about Lisa's track record in England, she would regularly tip over the bucket of water being used to wash the floor. Lisa also liked to put on Nicola's shoes and copy the way she polished the floor with the coconut brush. Although Carol and I thought she looked cute when doing this, Nicola was not impressed from the look she sometimes had on her face. However, life was full of excitement for all of us on such a beautiful island and within our new and interesting home life.

On the appointed day for Carol to take her first 'O' level in English Literature at the HMS *Mauritius* school I recall wishing her well as she said goodbye to me and Lisa outside the bungalow. She was wearing sandals and a light-coloured cotton maternity dress – now seven months pregnant - and had a pencil case and notes in her hand. There was some doubt about the exam papers arriving in time and Carol had to report to the school in the hope that they had arrived that day. Holding Lisa, who didn't want her mother to leave, we gave her a kiss for good luck and waved her off on her mission and continued playing in the garden with Candy. After about half an hour I heard the phone ringing and on answering it I found myself talking to the school headmaster, who was in a bit of a panic. He explained that the papers had not arrived when Carol reported, and she had left the school in the belief that her opportunity had passed her by and was walking home along the road. However, he frantically explained that the exam paper had arrived a few minutes after she had left and requested that I find her as quickly as possible and ask her to return to the school. I therefore got hold of some extra pencils, pens and a rubber and, leaving Lisa with Nicola set off sprinting towards the school. Fortunately I spotted Carol walking along the road and ran across a large field to intercept her. I passed on the news, gave her another quick hug and wished her good luck. She immediately set off as fast as she could back to the school.

Later she told me that her mind had initially gone blank on sitting down to start the exam. However, she fortunately completed it in good time. I must say I was both impressed by her tenacity and confident she would do well despite her shortened course in England. In three or four months' time we would receive the news that she had passed with considerable merit as she received a grade B pass. Although we naturally celebrated and valued this first academic achievement, it crossed my mind that it was a great pity her school teachers at Hemsworth Grammar School could not see the fruits of her schooling. There would be more exams to come in the future as we both juggled with our work, home life and academic studies.

****

In the early days, when we first walked down to Vacoas on a typically bright and sunny day to do our shopping, it was somewhat of a culture shock as the place looked rather run down and frankly 'scruffy.' In spite of this, it was surprisingly efficient and always full of colourful things and people to see. The smells from one fish stall in the market, however, as I remarked in one of my letters home, nearly made Carol physically sick one morning but it was always quite an event to walk down the road with Lisa in her pushchair or on my back to explore the shops in Vacoas. This was in contrast to the 'safer' but more expensive shopping available in the N.A.A.F.I. In local shops it was also necessary to learn how to barter on the price of anything we wished to buy as the cost of most goods was not openly displayed. Some people were much better at this art form than me and I imagine I usually paid inflated prices compared with more persistent barterers and the local residents.

Everywhere we went shopping the locals, who were people of either Indian or African heritage, or 'Creoles,' who were of mixed race and formed the majority of the population, desperately wanted to touch Lisa's white skin and her golden hair. This was quite a shock for Carol and I when it first happened, but we quickly realised there was simply a strong fascination with Lisa because of her less-common physical and seemingly angelic features.

While this formed the backdrop to our 'home' life, I was busy learning my new job and settling down to the routine at Bigara transmitter station. As this was situated about five miles outside Vacoas on the top of a hill, I met the other members of 'E' watch at the Comcen and we were driven to Bigara in a large blue Navy Land Rover – always driven by one of the local employees of HMS' – the term which we were collectively known by among us and the local population. One member of my watch, Steve Greenough, who was also an LREM, had a sports car and occasionally collected or dropped me off at the bungalow as we followed a strict work pattern, which I described in my second letter from Mauritius to my parents:

I start my work cycle by doing the afternoon watch from 12.00 to 7.00 pm and then come home until the next morning when I am at Bigara until 12.00. I then have the afternoon off and return for the night watch from 7.00 pm until 7.00 am. I usually get dropped off at Vacoas and walk home, which gets me in the house for 8.00. I then have two and a half days off watch before the cycle repeats.

I would soon be known as a bit of a 'sleepy head' as a lot of my colleagues were up before me and out with their families while I was still recovering. Carol and Lisa were often ready for a trip to Chaland or somewhere similar by the time I dragged myself out of bed to join them in whatever they had planned together.

My main task at work during this early period was to learn how to tune up and maintain the transmitters. In the control room we had a teleprinter that was linked to the Comcen and from which we received coded 'engineering' messages to manage the equipment. I quickly had to learn how to interpret instructions like 'QSY VAAD 8s to 15s,' which in plain English meant 'change frequency on the transmitter used to link Mauritius (VA for Vacoas) with the UK (AD for Admiralty) from its 8 MHz frequency to its 15 MHz designated frequency. This had to be done regularly with short wave communications networks as the ionosphere changed with sunlight over the period of a day and without following these changes we would lose contact. Once this was determined the PO of the watch, in my case the infamous 'Bob Mitchell,' set the drive units to the correct frequency before we went through a 15-minute process of rotating large tuning wheels while looking closely at tuning metres as we progressed through each stage of the transmitter's power amplifiers. It was somewhat of an art form and the best people could do it quickly and accurately the first time. If we had problems, Bob or the Chief of the Watch – initially Chief 'Spike' Hughes and later Steve Chivers - would come and fix problems before giving a signal to the person manning the teleprinter.

The transmitter halls were enormous in size and had banks of large switches at either end to control the selection of an array of aerials we could select for any transmitter. The station itself was separated into the 'West wing' and 'East wing,' with the transmitters in each zone being looked after by one member of the watch.

Bob Mitchell was quite tall and a highly intelligent individual with curly blonde hair and a wicked sense of humour – I'm sure some may have regarded him as being a little arrogant or a 'big head,' but he was intensely interested in the welfare of the watch, wanted us to be the best, and was never slow to offer advice or help. He was as sharp as a razor at his job and was one of the most decisive people I had ever come across in the Navy. I use the term 'infamous' to describe him because he did love to drink copious amounts of tea when we were on watch, and even more copious amounts of alcohol when off watch. With his lovely wife, he was one of the strongest party goers in HMS, which I most certainly was not so we tended to move in different social circles outside of work.

This leads me to the issue of socialising as it fairly quickly raised its sometimes awkward head. One could easily identify, for example, a spectrum of behaviour and associations that ranged from the out-and-out anti-social couples, who wished to do their own thing and have a quiet life, to the wildest party goers on the island. As usual, my circle of close friends was mostly comprised of those I played sport with, which very quickly became the focal point of my life. Before settling down to a comfortable social pattern among like-minded colleagues who were friends, however, there were one or two challenges that Carol and I had to learn to deal with in terms of finding our own comfort zone.

The main issue could perhaps be encapsulated in the Biblical commandment of 'do not covet thy neighbour's wife' (Bible, 1995) (or husband). Most people were in the prime of their lives and the combination of sunshine, tropical clothes, alcohol, good food and plenty of spare time in tropical surroundings meant they were at the height of their attractiveness. Coupled with this was the social interaction of people of different ranks – namely junior ratings, senior ratings and one or two Warrant Officers. There was very little social interaction between ratings and the officers, except perhaps at some sporting or official occasions. The former was due to the relatively small population of Royal Navy personnel and their families and the fact that watch-keeping teams were very close because they spent so much time together, both on and off duty.

The first time this came home to me was one morning on a trip to Chaland where Carol, Lisa and I were sitting in the restaurant having a meal when we spotted a rather glum looking woman sitting on her own. It transpired that she had been having a relationship with someone other than her CPO husband and it had become known by the Navy's senior officers as well as among the families. We learned that she was being accommodated in Chaland before being flown back to the UK on the next available BOAC, and that her husband would continue his time as a 'single' draft. There was also an incident, which may or may not have been linked, whereby one of the married men had marched over to the single men's accommodation at the crack of dawn and started banging on the door with a sharp weapon (possibly an axe) while letting his wife know that she and her 'lover' were in serious danger if he could get hold of them.

There were also many stories going around about 'inappropriate behaviour' at parties and some clearly took advantage of a difference in rank to take liberties with other people's wives or husbands. Without going into any detail, this was something that potentially affected all of us but after a few months I began to realise that the best way to minimise this problem was to interact socially with people of our own status and interests as one could speak more frankly with them as 'equals' as and when necessary.

Photo 47 - The victorious Bigara swimming team

JN front left with Steve Greenough back left and Bob Mitchell centre back row. **Source:** *author*

In July I had been busy for some time with work and sporting activities. I was involved in competitive swimming matches between Bigara, the Comcen and Tombeau Bay, which was the receiver station close to the capital of Mauritius, Port Louis. I had also started playing football and rugby regularly for HMS'. Because of this busy period for me, I asked Carol to write home on our behalf and luckily that letter survived to the time of writing this book. I say lucky as Carol wrote a long and detailed letter that has filled in some gaps in my own letters, and reminded me of the closeness we were able to achieve as a young family in a small island thousands of miles away from home:

We are all quite settled down now to the idea of spending the next two years here but we'll feel better once we are in married quarters. I shall feel twice better once the baby is born, but there is less than 9 weeks left now so that isn't too bad. At the moment we are overloaded with bananas and have given away at least 15 pounds and will be looking like bananas if we eat any more. Lisa is coming along well now with her speaking and is now a proper Daddy's girl....when John was on days and came home for lunch she was heart-broken when he went back to work without her. John also swam for HMS Mauritius in a national competition and our team were the overall winners. He got three prizes, a towel, after shave and six glasses plus his photo in the local paper. He is also studying maths and preparing for his P.P.E. for P.O. in his spare time, playing football and he also started badminton on Sunday evenings but I said I would divorce him for neglect because the only time I see him is when he is sleeping. Anyway, when the baby is born we are both going to play badminton and I shall start going to football matches again.

Reflecting now on this letter I can see that indeed I was spending too much of my precious time playing sport, but did keep my promise to teach Carol to play badminton and we spent many an afternoon swimming in the pool at HMS as we waited for the baby to arrive. We stayed in our bungalow in Granham Road until November, when we were pleased to move to a very comfortable flat in the married quarters, again with white washed walls.

As I had missed the birth of Lisa I was pleased to know that I would be able to be with Carol on this occasion. Carol had been attending the maternity clinic at the hospital in HMS since we arrived and was doing well, although the baby had had to be turned physically a few weeks before the birth date because of being in the breech position. I vividly remember Carol emerging from the clinic to re-join Lisa and me looking rather concerned as it had not been the most pleasant of experiences. The baby had clearly not enjoyed it either because Carol had felt lots of kicking and the doctor had noted a rise in the baby's heartbeat. She therefore had to remain lying down until it returned to a more normal 104 beats per minute. As I noted in my letter home of the 21st September, things settled down well and the situation was monitored at further ante-natal clinic visits to the hospital at HMS'.

Time progressed in the same vein until the second week of November, when it became clear that Carol had gone into labour. At about 4.00 pm we called the hospital as Carol's pains were increasing in strength and frequency. We left Lisa in the safe hands of our close friends Brenda and Steve Chivers, who kindly took her to Chaland with them. As we were about to ring the hospital, however, Elizabeth Sluman came round and invited us to her bungalow to look at some slides Chris had taken of Lisa. Although there was some urgency in our plans we gladly accepted the invitation to view (on a slide projector) some of the best photos we had seen of Lisa. However, while we were there, Chris and Elizabeth were totally unaware that Carol was having contractions until we said we would have to go, and why! They naturally reacted with surprise and concern, and Elizabeth said with her characteristic chuckle and big smile, "Yes, well you'd better be off now - and good luck!"

On arrival at the hospital Carol and I were placed in the delivery room and the Naval midwife (a Sister of officer status), dressed in her impressive evening navy blue and maroon uniform with a white hat, came in to check on progress at about 7.00 pm. We also had our own nurse to hand and the evening progressed with the labour pains increasing in intensity. Carol, as usual, took the pain and discomfort with little fuss but did hold onto my hand very strongly at times as the pains became stronger. At about 9.30 pm the Sister said the baby was almost ready to be born and things intensified somewhat until Carol was told to hold back when the head of the baby was visible.

What happened next remains for me one of the most awe-inspiring experiences of my entire life. As the baby's head emerged I fixed my attention on a perfectly-formed ear on a tiny head. The complexity and mystery of the birth process rose me to new spiritual heights, which was even more enhanced as I knew this was my own child that was about to enter the world and into our care. Suddenly the baby shot out into the hands of the Sister and I could see it was a boy. He was a fine specimen with blonde hair and blue eyes. It was also obvious from the start that he was a calm baby at ease with his new surroundings, and was soon wrapped up and next to his mother with me looking on in dumb-founded amazement.

Carol and the baby were then moved to the main maternity ward, which was very comfortable and full of those very distinctive mother and baby smells that would become familiar to me over the coming days when I visited them. When I left at about 1.00 am I walked alone down the road that was adjacent to the married quarters with the wind rocking the tall trees that lined the road. I looked up at one of the incredibly clear night skies that we enjoyed in Mauritius and could see the 'Southern Cross' constellation that I would often gaze at in the coming year or two as it is not visible in the northern hemisphere, and felt something I had never felt before. I think that my belief in God was confirmed that evening as I knew the miracle of life I had just witnessed could not, in my opinion, have evolved by chance. Amid the haste and stresses of everyday life, a small oasis of spiritual tranquillity came over me as I walked back to the bungalow, and went to bed.

Photo 48 - The spirit of Mauritius, November 1973

Source: author

The next week involved me looking after Lisa and visiting Carol and our new son in the maternity unit. We went through some interesting times during my visits as we deliberated on a name for our new child. The first name we agreed on was Stuart John, which we mentioned to the Sister who had delivered him the day before. The next morning the Sister appeared while I was in the ward and said in a cheerful and jolly voice, "Well, how is young Stuart this morning, Mrs Nixon?" To which we replied, "He isn't Stuart any more, Sister, we've settled on Graham Alexander." "Oh, how lovely," replied the Sister and continued on her rounds. The following morning Sister appeared and said in her usual manner, "How is baby Graham this morning?" to which we replied, "He isn't Graham any more, Sister, we've finally decided on Philip but kept Graham as a second name." With a wry smile on her face she replied, "Oh how lovely, he does suit that name but I hope this really is the final choice." I think the issue was that some babies clearly suit some names more than others and Carol and I kept trying to call Philip 'Stuart' or 'Graham' but they just didn't seem right for him. The main concern, as with all parents, is that their baby is healthy and well, which Philip thankfully clearly was. After a day or two Carol and Philip returned home and Lisa quickly became Philip's second mother with the support of Candy the dog. Philip, indeed, was a contented baby who quickly flourished in the sunshine and freedom of a life on a tropical island. In a letter to my parents from Carol on the 15th November, which was written in the maternity unit, she graciously acknowledged my support and our shared joy, which I had not seen until the writing of this book.

He looked quite comical when he was first born but I've really taken to him and John is delighted with him, especially as he was able to see him being born. We feel like we have shared in the birth of him and John really helped me while I was in labour. He was really marvellous; there is no comparison to how much better I felt for his company.

When we moved to the married quarters very shortly after Philip's arrival, our new maid there, Teresa, became another second mother and would dearly love to show Philip off to the other maids, and looked after him with an enormous amount of willingness, warmth and pride. She clearly thought 'her baby' was the best. Carol has always acknowledged this as probably the happiest time of her life as she wrote to her parents, saying that 'there may be someone on this earth as happy as me, but I don't believe anyone is happier.' She expressed to me that she was actually worried about being so happy, and didn't believe it could last. Clearly, for both of us, life was at its peak and perhaps we both knew that our future family life, within the Navy, would not live up to what we had, there and then.

Because I had plenty of time during tuning transmitters at Bigara I settled down to a pattern of study for my P.P.E. for POREL. I had only just turned 21 years of age and knew that if I wished to be selected for Mechanician's course while in Mauritius I would need to pass my P.P.E. as soon as feasible and also to have a recommendation from the Officer In Charge (OIC) at Bigara. I had received four months advancement for further promotion from LREM's course as my average mark was above 80%. This meant I could take the exam in December, about seven months after we arrived in Mauritius. I therefore became very well organised with my book of exam questions, a notebook and my LREM's course notes. I sat for hours through the night at a table in one of the wings of Bigara, which were half the size of a football field and had spacious and highly-polished floors. I was therefore able to do this in some isolation from the rest of the Watch because I had a teleprinter on my table that showed communications traffic between us and the Comcen, so I would know if one of my transmitters were to be re-tuned. My time was spent drawing circuit diagrams and writing up other technical material in preparation for the written exam.

Photo 49 - Carol, Lisa and Philip at Chaland

Source: author

Photo 50 - Philip outside on a sunny Mauritius day

Source: author

My friend and colleague in E Watch, Steve Greenough, was studying for his P.P.E. at this time so we often studied together to compare notes and help each other. The music I recall at this time, which I often heard either in the Junior Ratings' Mess before going on evening watch or at the HMS' cinema where Carol and I would meet up with our friends in the evenings, came from Cat Stevens and his 'Teaser and the Firecat' album. The song I especially liked was 'Moonshadow' (Stevens, 1971) with words that struck a chord with my view of life and created the atmosphere of that era:

I'm being followed by a moon shadow, moon shadow moon shadow
Leaping and hopping on a moon shadow, moon shadow moon shadow
And if I ever lose my hands, lose my plough, lose my land
Oh, if I ever lose my hands - oh, if...I won't have to work no more
And if I ever lose my eyes, if my colours all run dry
And if I ever lose my eyes - oh, I won't have to cry no more........

[109]

Carol had bought me a new guitar for my 21st birthday in a shop in Port Louis, and I would spend many an hour learning to play the songs of Cat Stevens. I was further pleased to re-commence my friendship with Brian Moverley from my time at *Collingwood* on REM's course, who had joined Mauritius just after me and was now also an LREM, married to a WREN RO called Barbara. They lived in a married quarter only about 50 metres from our own so we regularly met up to have a guitar jamming session and we also both played football for HMS'. Carol and I also became close friends with Tony and Yvonne Lewis, who had a young daughter called Tracy and lived upstairs in the same block of flats as us. Tony was already a fully qualified POREL and would go on to be an inspirational friend and role model for me as my career developed. He was a few years older, and we were also close as two young families with similar interests and values. Tony, like me, was a keen sportsman with rugby and cricket as his main interests, but under some encouragement and guidance from me he would go on to be the goalkeeper for the 1st XI football team.

In a letter to my parents just after Christmas I recounted the results of my P.P.E. exam, which I took on the 18th December. The outcome caused me some mixed emotions.

I took my written first and then an oral exam with the Commander, my boss and another officer. In the written exam I got 86% but was the only one out of three to pass the oral, so the other two failed and will have to take it again later. I was disappointed about Steve failing because he is in my Watch at work so he is a friend of mine and it took away my pleasure when I found out he had failed. Anyway, I've got another eight months to wait before I actually become a PO so I'll still be 21 and until some new rules came out this couldn't happen until the age of twenty two and a half.

Looking back, my disappointment about Steve was probably worsened as I was concerned about him feeling that he had been unfairly treated compared with me. Steve was a little older than me and had been in Bigara when I arrived so I could understand how he might have felt, and I tried not to be too vitriolic in my celebrations. In the same letter home I also thanked my mother for the Rosary beads she had given me on joining the Navy, and informed her that I had taken them into the exam with me. Indeed the oral exam was a nerve-racking experience as I recall feeling so tense I might be unable to speak once I entered the room. Although I was christened as a child within the Church of England, my mother's Catholic upbringing under her father's influence had remained with her and therefore me and my siblings as we were growing up. Taking my rosary beads around the world therefore gave me a constant link back to my parents, and my mother in particular, as she had always been faithful to her upbringing and school days at the Catholic Church in Hemsworth.

The news of my pending promotion was welcome news as it would come with a substantial pay increase, which we would need with a growing family to look after. To continue working on my general education I also studied for G.C.E.'s in English and Maths, which I fortunately passed, and I also enrolled on a correspondence course to work towards a City and Guilds (C & G) qualification in electronics and telecommunications from an Education Department in HMS *Collingwood*. This was run by two or three retired Instructor Officers who I had been to visit in Howe Division at *Collingwood* before leaving for Mauritius. The reason this was important is that the route followed by Mechanics (Figure 1 on page 82) did not lead to any formal qualifications as the focus was on 'training people to do their jobs' rather than 'educating' them. In contrast, Mechanician's course did lead to nationally-recognised academic and professional qualifications that were valuable in terms of employment prospects after leaving the Navy.

Photo 51 - HMS *Mauritius* first XI football team

JN back row (right) next to Tony Lewis and then Brian Moverley. **Source:** *author*

Photo 52 - HMS *Mauritius* first XV rugby team

JN front row next to Tony Lewis (middle front), Toby Tyler, front left. **Source:** *author*

However, uppermost in my mind was working out a career path that would minimise separation time in sea-going ships, so I was very happy to do this correspondence course so that if I did choose to leave at the earliest opportunity at the age of 27, I would have more-or-less the same qualifications I would expect to gain from completing Radio Mechanician's course. The drawback of Mechanician's course was that I would be required to give at least five years return of service after qualifying, and this may well mean two consecutive sea-going drafts. I would then be in the infamous and well-known 'pension trap' of my early thirties.

The pension trap arose because once someone's career had gone into their thirties they usually stayed until the age of 40 to gain a pension and gratuity, and the Navy often used this time to draft people to sea-going jobs without much compassion as they knew people would usually grin and bear the consequences for them and their families.

With these thoughts in mind, it is clear from another letter home to my father that I also had other plans in mind to become professionally qualified and avoid the hazards of long periods of separation. My alternative plan involved transferring to the R.A.F. and I wrote to them with a reply letter to be sent to my father, which would then be relayed to me in Mauritius. I'm not sure why I took this clandestine route to contact the R.A.F. but it may have involved me not wishing to let the Navy know of my interests and intentions. Transferring to the R.A.F. would turn out to be problematic, however, as it was not a simple process. I would have to leave the Navy first and then apply to join the R.A.F., so it came with a number of brave decisions and risks that would eventually defeat my willingness to proceed along that path. In this regard, I also knew that promotion was much faster in the Navy and the security of income and accommodation that the Navy provided was guaranteed so long as my family and I could deal with the drawbacks. However, these topics would often dominate in discussions with friends such as Steve Greenough, Brian Moverley and Tony Lewis. One of the officers I later worked with, however, would play a big role in my future career – he was the only officer (Lieutenant) that played for the first XI football team, pictured second from right in the front row of the photograph above, and his name was Brian Welch.

While our life in Mauritius was panning out well and we were probably as happy a family as we could be, there were some developments at home that caused us considerable concern. Firstly, we heard the sad news from Carol's mother that her mother had died. As Carol had been very close to her grandmother, this loss caused some sadness, especially as I was very fond of Carol's grandparents. Carol's grandfather had become very distressed on losing her as they were inseparable as a couple. He had apparently reported seeing his wife several times in their home after she had died, and was clearly greatly affected by her departure from this life. The other major matter that emerged on my side of the family was the news that my sister, Barbara, had been admitted to hospital for the major surgery she needed on her spine due to scoliosis. I don't think anyone in the family had realised just how drastic and risky the procedure Barbara was about to have would be. She had been seen by a specialist in December (1973) and would have a steel rod fused to her spine using bone from her hip, and would have to be confined to a special rotating bed for many months. As it would transpire, the operation did not go as well as the surgeons had hoped, and we would soon receive some alarming correspondence from my parents as recorded in my letter home of the 9th April, 1974:

You must have been through a lot, all of you, since our Barbara was taken into hospital. We were very worried after reading your last letter because we didn't realise how big this operation was ourselves, and everyone seemed to be very upset. But since that we have received a letter from Barbara herself saying she is on the road to recovery, which put our mind at rest. There is a girl of about 20 out here and she looks as if she has scoliosis which hasn't been treated and Barbara may be grateful when she grows up as this girl walks very slowly and it looks as if one of her legs is shorter than the other, which makes her walk with a pronounced limp.

I asked for us to be kept informed but in fact Barbara had to be re-admitted due to an infection and we received a telegram with the worrying phrase, 'Barbara out of surgery and doing as well as can be expected.'

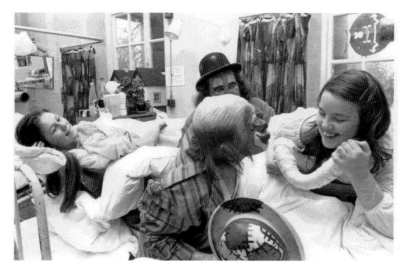

Photo 53 - Sister Barbara (left) recovering in hospital, 1974

Source: author

The last part of the message created much concern so it was with some relief that Barbara slowly started to recover, but would need to spend the coming year in hospital. We received a photograph of this recovery, which was rather difficult for me personally as I could see on her face that she was clearly keeping up her spirits in the face of what had obviously been a severe trauma. The good news was that Barbara was being cared for in one of the country's top hospitals for spinal surgery. There were thus mixed blessings about being on the 'paradise island' of Mauritius as there was no opportunity to visit or support relatives going through such ordeals.

****

Many developments with the children were occurring now as Lisa and Philip progressed in the unique freedoms and pleasant environment they were growing up in. We had started to teach Lisa to read from a book we acquired that used large word recognition techniques. In one of my letters home in August, 1974, I related Lisa's progress and the natural mothering approach she had towards Philip (and me).

Lisa and Philip are both coming along fine. Lisa really surprises me with some of the things she does. When I come home after working all night she sometimes tucks me into bed. The other morning she had just tucked me in and one of Philip's nappies was lying on the floor next to the bed. I said to her, "Aren't you going to give me a goodnight kiss then?" She looked at me and answered, "I'll be back in a minute, Daddy, I'm just taking Philip's nappy to be washed then I'll give you a kiss, orwight?"

Philip's character was also beginning to emerge as he behaved in stark contrast to Tony and Yvonne's daughter, Tracy, who was the same age as Philip. In the same letter I explained.

Philip is standing with the furniture now, but he doesn't seem really bothered about pushing himself on and walking, unlike Tracy as she struggles and goes red in the face trying to do different things. Philip is calm and quiet and does things when he is ready but he is not behind in anything – about average but he is as good as gold. His hair is golden blonde now– you can tell he has a hint of my hair but the sun is making it more blonde.

In the evenings when off duty I spent most of my time on my correspondence course and learning to read music using two self-instruction books I had asked my father to send me from England. My music interests came in useful with the children too as we would often teach them to sing songs like 'Daisy, Daisy' and 'Twinkle, Twinkle little star' to the accompaniment of my guitar. Fortunately, I had also been recommended for Mechanician's course by now and therefore my thoughts were often on trying to weigh the benefits and costs of taking that route in due course.

Just after my 22nd birthday on the 4th October, 1974, I was promoted to Petty Officer and as a consequence moved from Bigara to the Comcen, where I was to be in charge of one of the Engineering Watches. I related some of the perks of moving to a non-commissioned officer in a letter home dated the 14th October.

I have been given a new job, which I am pleased about, and the uniform looks a lot smarter. I've noticed improvements already – for instance when you go into the Senior Ratings mess in the morning there is a cup of tea waiting for you and other people seem to treat you with more respect. I need to close now as I must do my correspondence course and send off my latest assignments before tomorrow morning.

The issue of my new uniform was an interesting one because in Mauritius there was a small band of locals who provided various services to Navy personnel. For example, most of us had our shoes made by hand by a cobbler in Vacoas – the care this gentle spirited local man took in drawing out the shape of our feet using a pencil on card was almost hypnotic and although they took some time to produce, they were worth every penny and fit like a glove. Similarly, we had a colourful Mauritian tailor who was given the nickname 'Iceage.'

Photo 54 - POREL Tony Lewis and JN ready for divisions

Source: *author*

When I enquired about this choice of nickname I was told it was because he physically looked like a throwback to the Ice Age. He would visit our home to measure me up for shirts, trousers and eventually my PO's uniform. This is because we did not have immediate access to naval uniforms in the same way that one would have at home. Iceage also had that personal touch when measuring people up for cloths and uniforms, taking his time and smiling constantly as he went about his job, clearly with an immense amount of pride. My uniform was ready for my 22nd birthday and I have to confess that I wore it with some pride as I would make the transition from 'square rig' to the suit and peaked cap of a PO.

My new job in the Comcen involved working with a PO who was just about to return to England to complete POREL's course. I thus spent about two weeks shadowing him and starting to work with other members of my watch – an LREM and an REM. Our job was to monitor all the circuits to and from Mauritius and control the changes of frequency at the receiver site at Tombeau Bay and the transmitters at Bigara. To do this we had teleprinters for each circuit and worked with charts for each link that showed the 'Maximum Usable Frequency (MUF)' and 'Lowest Usable Frequency (LUF)' for each link over a 24-hour period. We also referred to lights above the teleprinters that flashed when the link was becoming unreliable, which triggered action from us to initiate changes of frequency. Once a circuit was up and running again we would return it to the ROs who manned each link. The main person in charge of this for the operators was the Radio Supervisor (RS) of the watch. In charge of all of the watch-keeping staff was an officer, who sat in an office between Engineering and the main communicators' area. I found my new work enjoyable and took pride in keeping as many circuits live as possible – there were some weather and ionospheric conditions that meant we lost circuits for a time (logged as 'E' time in the case of an error) so we honed our skills in working out the most reliable frequencies to retain links with stations in South Africa, Admiralty, Gan, Sri Lanka and many more across the globe.

Photo 55 - Admiral Lewin visiting the Comcen

Source: *author*

In the Comcen we had regular VIP visitors who, as PO of the Watch, I had to show round and explain the mechanics of how we operated. Two such visitors were Admiral Lewin and the Labour Government's Secretary of Defence, Roy Mason. The reason the latter came to Mauritius was because of the sceptre of cuts to the defence budget, and HMS *Mauritius* was in this firing line for closure. Because Roy Mason was also the MP for my home town of Barnsley, I was selected as one of the naval personnel to meet him and put forward a case for retaining HMS'. The photo below records this visit and shows some of the teleprinters we used at that time in the background.

[115]

Photo 56 - Meeting the Secretary of State for Defence, Roy Mason

Source: author

Unfortunately, none of us was successful in persuading him to exclude our idyllic naval outpost, which provided a vital cog as part of the Defence Communications Network (DCN), and the closure of HMS *Mauritius* was announced for a date about one year after we were due to leave the island.

The photo below illustrates the kind of projects we engaged ourselves in while doing what was referred to as 'day routine.' This occurred for each watch in turn and gave us an opportunity to carry out planned maintenance of the equipment we worked on but there was always spare time so the Chief Tiffy (pictured left below) came up with a plan to build a dalek.

Photo 57 - the Day Watch Team and the Dalek they built

JN back right, and friend from HMS Bulwark, Geoff Anderson, is front left. **Source:** *author*

[116]

I recall that my job was to build a circuit that would make the main light bulb at the end of the dalek's 'arm' flash on and off. Although this might sound like a waste of naval resources, there was always an educational objective as the light had to flash at a specified frequency. About this time two episodes unfolded that revealed the mixed blessings of friendship, comradeship, naval discipline and some of the negative influences of alcohol consumption in the Navy. The first incident is rather humorous in hindsight although it was definitely a great source of irritation for one of my best friends and his WREN wife.

They both worked on the same watch-keeping cycle to maximise their time together when off duty. They therefore usually said their goodbyes outside the Comcen before going to their respective places of work. As they were married they naturally gave one another a brief hug/kiss before departing, which was a natural thing to do. However, this was strictly against naval discipline regulations, which clearly state something along the lines that 'naval personnel in uniform should not show outward signs of affection to each other' whilst on duty in public places.

While the majority of people above my friend's rank would turn a blind eye to this, there was an exception in that the one of the senior WRENs clearly wanted to take steps to stop this behaviour. Therefore one evening when my friend and his wife were saying their goodnights to each other, she jumped out from behind a wall and promptly put them both on a charge. Although I do not recall the details of what happened at the subsequent investigation I suspect there may have been a reprimand handed out to both of them, or even a fine. I think this incident showed the degree to which some people would go in order to show they were faithfully implementing the rules of the Royal Navy. However, it gave some food for thought and humorous discussion when we met each other in the N.A.A.F.I. shop one sunny afternoon while queuing up to be served.

The second event was a little more challenging for both me and the friend that it affected but it illustrates some specific 'trials, triumphs and tribulations' that had a common theme. To put this story in context I had been helping one or two REMs to prepare for their own P.P.E. examinations for LREM, which meant spending time working with them on electronic theory and considering likely questions and solutions in the oral exam. These exams, as I had found out from my own studies and preparation time, were very important to anyone seeking promotion.

In due course one friend passed his exam and was eventually promoted to A/LREM, which we could both take some comfort and pride in as it meant more money for him and his wife and a first step on the ladder of a career. However, a few months later he got himself into trouble one evening following some over-indulgence in whisky consumption, which led to him punching a fellow Killick over a verbal exchange and disagreement between them. The episode became worse when the duty PO arrived to sort the situation out as my friend then decided the duty PO needed to be punched as well. Naturally this was a serious offence and led to the confinement in cells for the night and a charge of striking a superior officer. I remember visiting my friend in cells the following day and was a little taken aback as he had worked so hard to achieve his promotion, and now he was sitting on the edge of the bed in cells facing a serious charge. In due course he went before the Captain to explain his actions and, quite predictably, was demoted back to REM.

This account illustrates the dangers that many succumbed to in a community that had a high degree of partying and access to almost unlimited alcohol when off duty. Luckily, in due course and through good behaviour my friend re-gained his promotion and went on to complete his LREM's course and be recommended for Mechanician and one has to recognise that people did recover from such setbacks.

After working in the Comcen for a number of months my association with Lt Welch had developed more for several reasons. First of all, Brian's wife was one of the teachers in the playschool at HMS' and therefore Carol and I both had close contact with her. Lisa enjoyed her lessons immensely and Brian's wife was always talking to us in positive tones about Lisa's progress. Secondly, Brian and I both played for the first XI football team and therefore did a degree of socialising together as well as playing on the field. Thirdly, Brian was often duty Officer in the Comcen when I was on watch and I reported to him on day-to-day management issues concerning Engineering duties, for which he had the final say on any decisions we had to make on communications circuits. Therefore, although he was not my Divisional Officer, he knew me well and we had what one might call a friendly but professional relationship. One morning after the busy period of the day had elapsed, he called me into the office and said, "Petty Officer Nixon, I've been thinking about your career options and want you to consider applying to be a Weapons Electrical Officer via the Upper Yardman route." When I had drawn my career paths on *Bulwark* (Figure 1 on page 82) this had been one possible option. I was naturally pleased and felt an enormous amount of gratitude that Brian had apparently seen in me potential officer material, and agreed to discuss it more with him, although I knew quite strongly that my thoughts were on developing my career as a Radio Mechanician rather than a Weapons Electrical Officer. I also knew that my focus was on my family and it seemed that the steps to becoming an officer were beyond my ambitions as it would mean going into unfamiliar territory at a time when I was working rapidly to lay the foundations of family life and my present endeavours with my City & Guilds qualifications. Any moves into the 'Wardroom' or officers' mess, would also involve many social changes and challenges, and I clearly came from a working class background, as did Carol, and would probably encounter some difficulties in that regard if I did pursue the Upper Yardman route.

Over the coming months I spoke to Brian at some length, but in the end decided, after discussions with Carol, that I would put myself forward for Mechanician's course and that we would return to England for two years to follow that route, although constantly at the back of my mind was the question of long periods of separation while I was at sea after the 'honeymoon' period at *Collingwood* undergoing training. For now, we simply wanted to enjoy our life in Mauritius and see the children growing up. Carol was especially happy as she could dedicate all her time and effort to the children. She had developed a powerful bond with them, partly because of the advantage of having a maid to do most of the chores in the home. We also had sufficient money as we did not have a car and our lives were spent on low cost trips to the beach and socialising with our close circle of friends. This circle had grown to include POREL Gary Taylor and his wife, Frances, and their daughters Trina and Louise. I recall one evening when Tony, Gary and I plus our wives were returning home from a meal in Chaland on one of the Navy's blue buses, thinking that life was full of pleasant surprises and experiences, and that we were all in good company. Gary had a very quick and witty sense of humour which was full of 'double entendre' jokes that most, but not all, around him appreciated. However, a shock was just around the corner, which would affect all of our family, but particularly Carol as we were soon to discover that another baby was on the way.

****

Carol becoming pregnant again was somewhat of a challenge as we had not planned for another child. She had already carried Philip for several months in the hot weather and the prospect of doing this for another nine months was rather daunting, and caused her a great deal of anguish to say the least. Also, with two very young children already, it would add to the workload and this would increase dramatically once we left Mauritius and lost the support of a maid.

However, pregnancy in Mauritius was a common experience for many wives as families were together for longer and the combination of sunshine and youth meant that couples were highly productive. After reflecting on this new development we both reconciled ourselves to the advantages of another child in that Lisa and Philip would have another sibling to play with and they would all be close in age. This was reflected in a letter home on the 18ᵗʰ December, 1974, when I wrote that, 'We have been blessed with yet another addition to this family.' The new baby would be born in April, which was only six weeks before we were due to return to England, so we would literally 'have our hands full' with the journey home. We had already decided to return by sea in a ship of the Union Castle line from South Africa, as I had done as a child when returning home from Rhodesia. We both thought it would be a good opportunity for all of us to experience a cruise and the cost would not be an issue as we were able to transfer the money assigned to us for the flight to the sea route. Once we clarified that Carol would not in fact feel the burden of carrying another child until she was about five months pregnant we decided to increase the number of family trips and hired a car to do some sight-seeing around the island with our good friends Tony and Yvonne.

Many of my letters home between now and the major new event of the birth of our new child relate to every-day matters such as birthday parties, the sending of parcels to and from home, watching Tottenham Hotspur (Spurs) play Mauritius on a tour of the island – when I had the good fortune to train with international players like Steve Perryman, Cyril Knowles, Pat Jennings, Mike England, Martin Peters and Alan Gilzean on the training ground at HMS'. I remember being asked by them if I was new to the island because of my 'un-tanned' body. Indeed, being fair-skinned I generally kept out of the mid-day sun and wore a towel over my head when on the beach at Chaland. Reporting developments concerning Lisa and Philip and our close friends also naturally dominated in my letters home. We were enjoying what might be considered a British colonial life although the island was in fact independent and had been so since 1968; the year I had joined the Navy. We had access to amazing facilities such as our own cinema, which we would watch films in regularly while sitting in a spacious area on a comfortable chair and chatting to friends with an ice cream or coffee to hand. We also had concerts with performances from various talented people among us – I remember Brian Moverley singing two songs and playing guitar at one event and one or two of the rugby team doing comic sketches.

Life in Mauritius had many perks and benefits but I can see from my letters home that I did miss some things such as Christmas in England with snow on the ground rather than a hot sun beaming down on us. Carol's view, in stark contrast, was that we were all far better off in Mauritius. To partially deal with my feelings of disconnection from 'home' I asked one of my good friends, Gordon Selby, who was one of the few MEMs in HMS' with his wife Sue, who would become a close friend of Carol's once we returned to England, to help in addressing this issue. Gordon was in charge of the 'fire engine' we had in HMS' and I asked him if he could drive it over and hoist up the ladder so I could climb up onto the roof of our block and run a long aerial wire across it and down to our flat on the bottom floor. Once connected to the short-wave receiver I had bought, I could tune into the BBC World Service and listen to the football match commentaries from home and the results so I could monitor the progress of Rotherham and Leeds United. Saturday afternoons were always relaxing and fun as Tony would come down from his flat and join me to listen and follow his own team, which was possibly Plymouth Argyle as he was from that part of the world.

[119]

Our time was ticking by and a new chapter would unfold in the coming year, but a severe storm was brewing on the horizon that had some challenges and devastating effects for the community we lived in and the island more widely.

****

On Wednesday the 5th February I went to bed at 1.00 pm in preparation for the night watch in the Comcen that evening. We had been told that a cyclone was heading roughly in the direction of Mauritius and the eye of the storm was expected to pass 100 miles to the north of us. However, when I woke up three hours later we were in what was classified as 'class two' warning state and families were gathering outside the N.A.A.F.I. shop and elsewhere discussing how the warnings might develop. Flags flying over the Comcen were used to relay warning states and people were looking at them at regular intervals. By 6.00 pm the warning rose to 'class three,' which meant the island was expected to be hit within twelve hours. Therefore, when I left Carol and the children that evening to go on watch at 7.00 pm we didn't know when I would be returning and so we had taken some precautions such as filling the bath with water, getting hold of extra food from the N.A.A.F.I. - as all families had been doing that afternoon - and following instructions given to us by the Navy.

When I reported to work it transpired that the watch I was relieving would also remain in the Comcen and that between us we would work an eight hours on and eight hours off routine until the situation returned to normal. In due course 'intense cyclone' *Gervaise* approached and went directly over the island with winds gusting up to 154 mph; wreaking havoc and damage to the island and our communications equipment. I knew that Carol and the children would basically have to fend for themselves in the flat, which naturally made me worry although I knew that our friends and neighbours, Tony and Yvonne, would help in any way they could. Inside the Comcen, there was a hive of activity as we struggled to keep circuits alive in the face of aerials going down at Bigara and Tombeau Bay and flooding causing damage to equipment. In a letter to my parents on the 10th February I noted that I spent '96 hours in the Comcen over the period of the cyclone and its immediate aftermath, of which 56 hours was spent on watch with my team.'

My vivid memory of this episode was looking out at times to see unbelievably powerful and horizontal winds and rain blowing trees down and throwing all types of debris around the married quarters. Incredibly, the eye of the storm passed directly over the island and I remember we were allowed to go for a short stroll in the early hours of the second night while this was happening. The stillness and tranquillity were pronounced and palpable, with an almost eerie atmosphere all around – made even more remarkable by the knowledge that the 154 mph winds would soon start passing in the opposite direction. It was also difficult for me personally as I knew Carol and the children were literally a few hundred yards away in our home, but I was not allowed to go over to check if they were safe. I did, however, manage to phone a neighbour to find out how things were going and it seemed that Carol was coping as well as could be expected. When I returned home briefly on the Friday afternoon I could see and hear how the ordeal had gone for my family, as related in my letter of the 10th February.

All the time I was on watch I didn't really know how Carol was managing at home. As it was she had no electricity, the house got quite flooded and she was constantly mopping up water. When I got home she had lifted the carpet from the lounge and carried it into the bedroom as it was wet. She had a small primus stove which was difficult to start up, but I still got a hot drink and some dinner when I got in! I was speaking to Tony upstairs and he said it was murder trying to keep all the water out and he had Yvonne to help him and only one child to look after. Carol said the wind had scared Lisa and Philip, so she let them sleep with her, so all in all I think she had quite a rough time. Little Lisa was apparently helping her to mop up the water!

Although the Naval personnel, including my team, received a commendation from Whitehall for keeping our systems going through the cyclone, I think this paled into insignificance when I consider, as I do now, the bravery and strength of Carol as at least half of the wives would have had their husbands at home to take the strain. It is even more astounding to realise that, in February 1975, Carol was almost seven months pregnant and I hope I afforded her the credit she deserved at that time. It is perhaps worth noting also that cyclone *Gervaise* turned out to be the biggest intense cyclone to hit the island since records began in 1892, and had not been surpassed in intensity to the time of writing this account. Most cyclones have winds that gust up to 110-220 km/h, but *Gervaise* produced winds that reached an incredible 280 km/h (Mauritius Meteorological Office, 2012).

The damage to the island was extensive and eight people lost their lives. Our maid, Teresa, told us that she had had 15 relatives staying with her and the airport was damaged such that aircraft could not land on the island. We also had 400 'refugees' living in our cinema who were holiday makers from various parts of the world. One of our most popular and talented CPOs, Ted Ledger, went with a small team to repair all the electronics at the airport – putting himself in some danger by climbing to the top of a very high mast to reach some essential equipment. The French and British governments both gave extensive amounts of aid to bring the island back to normal, and after two or three days we once again had electricity and running water in our flat and normal life could resume.

As I re-commenced playing for HMS' in football and rugby matches, Carol resumed swimming in the pool to help keep her fit as the arrival of the new baby approached, I recall Chief PTI 'Bagsy' Baker, coming out of the PTI's office next to the pool one sunny morning and calling out in his normal authoritative and witty manner, "Mrs Nixon, what *are* you doing swimming in my pool – aren't you 38 weeks pregnant?!" His inference was that if any emergency happened he would be responsible for sorting it out. In spite of our new challenges at home and at work, including battles with the cyclone, Carol had decided to take two more G.C.E. 'O' levels – in Maths and English. She had seen the school headmaster to confirm this was feasible as her preparation had not involved any formal tuition. Her efforts were based purely on the studies we did together on my own earlier Maths and English 'O' level preparations at the school. She had to wait for confirmation that this was feasible from the examination board back in the UK. The planned exam date was very close in time to when our new baby was due and there was a risk that Carol would not get out of hospital soon enough to take her exams. As it transpired, she passed both Maths and English 'O' Levels, getting a grade A pass in Maths and only taking half the required time in the exam itself. I recall that my first attempt at Maths 'O' level – back in the UK at the end of LREM's course – had been a complete disaster as I had only attended a couple of lectures and, not surprisingly, failed miserably. Therefore, our academic collaborations whilst in Mauritius had been beneficial for both of us in more ways than one.

On our stereo system around this time in our flat, the songs of Joni Mitchell ('Brand new key'), Demis Rousos ('For ever and ever'), Elton John ('My song') and Melanie could be heard as everyone went about their tasks or played. One tune of Melanie ('Tell me why') (Parish, Edwards, & Spaeth, 1971) has remained with me over the years as I quickly learned to play it on my guitar. It expresses something magical and elementary about the human spirit, endeavours to improve ourselves both professionally and academically, and the 'miracle of life,' which was strongly in evidence at this time.

Tell me why the stars do shine/ Tell me why the ivy twines
Tell me why the ocean's blue/ And I will tell you just why I love you

Because God made the stars to shine/ Because God made the ivy twine
Because God made the oceans blue/ Because God made you, that's why I love you
Because God made you, that's why I love you

****

At just after midnight in the latter half of April, 1975, Carol and I went to the familiar maternity unit of the hospital and prepared for the arrival of our new baby as her labour had started earlier the previous day. However, it seemed that the actual birth would be some way off so we decided that I would return home to look after Lisa and Philip and be telephoned when the birth was imminent. I received the call at 6.00 am and rushed down to the delivery ward but arrived a few minutes after the birth of our new son, who we would name – only once in this case - Christopher Michael. My first reaction was one of relief that all had gone well in my absence and that both Carol and our new son were fine. Later that day I wrote home to my parents to fill in the details.

The new baby is the image of me (poor thing) although I did see Carol in him as well but expressions more than anything. He weighed 7lb 4oz so it was just right and Carol had a fairly easy time. She was asleep until 4.00 am so she only had one and a half hours of pain (only!). I couldn't stay long as I had to return home to look after the other two as the people who were looking after Lisa and Philip have gone to the beach for a week.

After a few days Carol and Christopher returned home, when Lisa and Philip immediately started to take an interest in checking out and looking after their new brother, as shown in the photograph below. Life with three children under the age of four was clearly going to require a lot of organisation and energy, and it is true to say that Carol became quite run down as the time for our departure from Mauritius approached. Lisa, as if to compensate, expanded her mothering instincts and clearly started to co-ordinate interactions between the three of them.

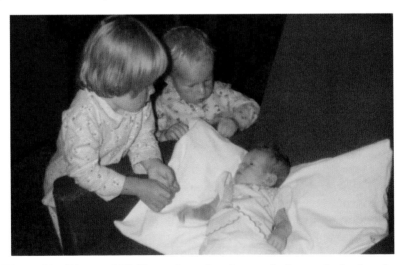

Photo 58 - Lisa and Philip welcoming home their new baby brother

*Source: **author***

[122]

Carol and I also made as much effort as possible to ensure Philip was not marginalised by the increased demands on our time. I noted his nature as being 'quiet with a bad temper' in a previous letter home but he clearly 'was his own man' even though he was still only a young toddler. Lisa's personality and sense of humour were also blossoming as I recounted in a letter of the 19th April, just before Christopher was born.

Lisa has also got a lovely nature – very deep thinking and sensible - but is getting a bit cheeky now and comes out with some unbelievable things. Yesterday, the egg man came to the door and because he comes every week Lisa knows him well. She was in the kitchen with us and when the egg man went out to get our eggs from his basket, Lisa walked out and in a casual sort of voice said: "Hello, chuckie-egg man." Carol and I couldn't stop laughing and Teresa our maid was also laughing in amazement.

Luckily, we had Teresa, who was a kind and gentle spirited lady in her 50s, and good friends Tony and Yvonne, among many others, to help and encourage us as we only had three months to consolidate our new situation and finalise our journey back to England, which needed a great deal of effort as we had confirmed our booking on the *Windsor Castle*, which was the flag ship of the Union Castle line. Although we – less so for Carol - were looking forward to returning home, the lifestyle, sport, isolation from realities in the UK, and the general freedoms we experienced in Mauritius were something we would all miss. It was true, however, that there were many aspects of the behaviour and dilapidated buildings associated with the locals that attracted some criticisms from me in particular, and as Carol noted in her diary I was often in a 'bad mood' about this aspect of our life in Mauritius.

In one letter home to my sister, Valerie, I did express my perceptions quite strongly and mentioned things that aggrieved me, such as Carol going shopping in the local markets every week and having to pay very much more for the same goods as locals because there were never any prices on display, so bartering was always necessary, and the fact that one national airline operating out of Mauritius had recently reduced its fares, but not to Europeans. When one considers the employment HMS *Mauritius* provided for locals, the international aid and cyclone relief monies provided by the UK government, among numerous additional and on-going initiatives, it was somewhat difficult to comprehend at times although I have to acknowledge that various levels of poverty were in evidence in the local population and we could, in reality, afford to pay more.

The time quickly passed now as we made preparations to pack and leave our paradise island. This was a significant task as we would be travelling with four suitcases and three children of three years old or under, plus a formidable amount of toddler and baby equipment. We also had to pack some crates a few weeks before we departed, containing the small amount of furniture we had, which would go on ahead of us. I recall also that we had some 'cold weather' clothes made for the children as it would be winter in South Africa and that Philip in particular had taken a dislike to them. Iceage the tailor had made a beautiful blue corduroy duffle coat with a matching cap for him, but Philip saw them as being too restrictive as he was used to being in a Tee shirt, shorts and sandals. To express his dislike, being only 17 months old, he was naturally limited in his way of expressing this so he repeatedly used the word 'dirty' in conjunction with a disapproving look as we encouraged him to try them on. Lisa was more amenable to change as she knew, among other things, that she would be meeting grandparents and several cousins, and Christopher was naturally too young as a three-month old baby.

So it was, then, that on a sunny morning on the 5th July, 1975, we boarded a Navy mini-bus outside our flat and looked through the windows rather sadly at Tony, Yvonne,

Tracy and Teresa. With hand waves, smiles, and a few tears, we were driven out of HMS *Mauritius* and along the familiar roads that led to the airport. Our time in Mauritius had come to a close. As I looked out of the window I reflected on the enormous progress and change that had taken place over the period of two years – we had arrived with one child and were leaving with three, we had enjoyed a privileged lifestyle in the tropical climate of the island, and I had made much progress in my career. Despite being pregnant twice, Carol had also made her own progress and passed three O'levels and experienced many other things that she cherished. For all of us, the changes that lay ahead would be difficult at times, but for now the challenges of our journey home would hopefully be pleasant too as we looked forward to a three-week cruise that would return us back to our roots and family.

The first challenge that met us was the walk we had to make to the South African Airways Boeing 707 that we were about to board. I was carrying Christopher in his cot and holding Lisa's hand, while Carol was holding Philip's hand and carrying bags in her other hand. The engines of the plane were extremely loud and Philip became rather concerned as he had never seen a plane up close before. Probably at this point Carol and I realised we had one too few arms between us but somehow we managed to pick Philip up, perhaps with the help of another passenger, and boarded the plane successfully. We settled into our seats and just after the take-off a young woman who was sitting next to us began to help and take an interest in us and the children. She turned out to be Australian and would be staying in South Africa on holiday, but she became a big help in keeping Lisa and Philip amused and generally assisting us. We would be helped on many occasions through our journey by people like her who were sympathetic to our situation.

After landing in Durban, we quickly had another major hurdle ahead of us in getting to the ship, and took a large taxi which was driven by a friendly and helpful South African lady. The challenge came, however, when she dropped us off at the end of the jetty at 8.30 pm - several hundred metres from the *Windsor Castle* itself. The problem was that we could clearly not carry or escort our children and the incidental luggage, as well as four large and heavy suitcases, in a constant forward motion. The system we therefore worked out was to repeatedly carry or escort the children and luggage about 30 metres forward, and then I would return to carry two suitcases at a time back to Carol and the children.

Photo 59 - The R.M.S. *Windsor Castle* alongside in Durban

Source: *author*

Although I'm sure we found this manoeuvre amusing between us as it involved a lot of sweat and effort, we eventually made it to the jetty and saw our ship ahead of us. At this point we were helped aboard as our plight had become known by the crew.

In a letter dated the 11th July, written on board *Windsor Castle* on letter-headed paper, I described the first few days of our cruise.

> *Our cabin (B. 239) is very comfortable and everyone is happy with their bunks. Having said that, we have had a horrible trip up to now as all of us have been sick apart from Philip and Christopher. We are in Port Elizabeth now and have had very rough weather since leaving Durban. We went ashore with the kids to do some shopping and visit a beach, which everyone enjoyed as it's a nice place. We call into Cape Town and then set off for home on the 15th July. Give our love to everyone and we will see you soon!*

In this letter I go into some detail about how we all reacted to sea sickness, which in my case was due to my long period ashore and for everyone else it was there first time at sea. In fact Carol was to be the first one to be physically ill, followed by Lisa and then me. I mentioned that Philip was never in fact sick, but he did react to his ill feelings by throwing things around the cabin and kicking the cabin door a few times. I wrote 'I am no sailor, I don't mind admitting that!' At this point it should be noted that the *Windsor Castle* was 37,000 tonnes, and would dwarf all Royal Navy ships below that of the aircraft carriers we had at that time.

In Cape Town we hired a car and drove to the most southerly tip of the African continent where the Indian and Atlantic oceans meet – and that meeting is quite apparent from the way in which the waters of both oceans interact. We also experienced another turbulent meeting of two different systems when we inadvertently drove into a coloured area of Cape Town. Some rather hostile looking people came out to view what seemed to have been interpreted as an invasion by 'the wrong coloured people' so we promptly left without stopping to ask for directions. Also, around the nature reserve that led to the southern tip of Africa we could see several signs that said 'whites only' and this stood out compared with our experiences in Mauritius.

Photo 60 – Lisa, John and Philip at the southern tip of Africa

Source: *author*

Although there were some 'natural' associations based on culture and ethnicity, there were no explicit signs of this as we witnessed in South Africa and those not used to living there clearly had to be aware of the kind of risks apartheid was associated with.

Even though the sights of familiar landmarks like Table Mountain brought back fond memories of my time as a child in Southern Africa, I think we were all pleased to sail north from Cape Town, and the 'Cape Rollers,' into the warmer and calmer waters around the equator and both tropics. Extracts from the Ship's Log indicate that we departed from Cape Town on the 15th July and that it was cloudy/clear with a force 6 wind blowing. On board were 128 first class and 451 tourist class passengers and in the evening there was tombola and dancing for entertainment (Union Castle Line, 1975). The food and facilities on board were excellent and we soon settled down into a routine that involved a lot of time on deck playing games in the sunshine with the children. Lisa and Philip also went to a crèche every morning, which gave us some respite as Christopher spent much of his time sleeping in between feeds. There was also a regular cinema for the children and I recall sitting with Lisa and Philip on many occasions watching films together. This was also helpful as Carol needed some time to recover from her demanding run-up to our voyage and had to see the ship's doctor early in the trip to receive some antibiotics. Her time on the upper deck and the good food we enjoyed clearly helped her to make a recovery by the time we reached England.

Photo 61 - The sea voyage in R.M.S. *Windsor Castle*

Source: author

One of the highlights for the children was the crossing the line ceremony as we passed the Equator at 16.30 on the 20th July (Union Castle Line, 1975). Father Neptune and his team performed the usual tasks of catching people and children, performing mock ceremonies and pouring nasty looking substances over their heads. The Ship's Log shows there were 'few clouds and clear, slight haze, light variable winds.' and the entertainment included a cricket match between the passengers and the Ship's officers, a classical concert, cinema 'What's My Line' and 'Windsomnia.'

I think Carol and I were too busy to take part in most of the official functions, although we did attend a fancy dress night the following day, which had an international theme to it. I clearly remember us sitting in the cabin that day wondering how we could 'internationalise' ourselves, but we came up with an ingenious plan based on originality rather than 'official' costumes that others seemed to have access to. Using only crepe paper, we sewed coloured squares onto our black and white clothes, and I used a money cheque for a tie and we had 'Czech' and 'Czech mate' sewed onto our white tops. When asked by other passengers who were we said, "Cheque and Cheque Mate from Czechoslovakia." Well, it seemed funny at the time and the organisers awarded us first prize for originality! For Lisa we put her in red dress and a red crepe cloak and hood so she could be Little Red Riding Hood.

Photo 62 - Czech and Czech Mate

Source: author

Philip – much to his reluctance - had some bulky green clothing tucked into his shorts and a crepe Robin Hood hat and perhaps, unsurprisingly, cried when he realised everyone was staring at him which, for us, was an early indicator of his reserved personality. During the cruise we had observed southbound ships on many occasions, including the liner *Edinburgh Castle* on the 16th, and on the 23rd, with overcast weather and a 'haze horizon' we looked out onto the starboard side to see the mail ship *Pendennis Castle* steaming through a deep blue sea as we enjoyed the warm breeze blowing across the deck. Later in the afternoon, apart from the children's fancy dress parade and tea party (pictured above), in the evening 'Jack Clarke entertains' was among the entertainment on offer (Union Castle Line, 1975).

At 09.30 on the 25th July the ship anchored off Madeira and we joined a sight-seeing trip around the island. With three children to supervise this was a challenge but a bus came directly onto the jetty so this made our task much more manageable. I recall the many traders that appeared on the deck, selling all kinds of exotic things and creating a colourful scene for passengers to mingle amongst for a few enjoyable hours. At 13.00 the ship weighed anchor and sailed out on a flat and deep blue sea, following a wide sweeping arc with the island above us.

Photo 63 - Little Red Riding Hood and a reluctant Robin Hood

Source: author

On the 27th July the ship rounded Ushant and thus entered the English Channel. In the evening there was cinema, a classical concert and a farewell dance. Although the run-up to the voyage had required a lot of thought and management, we had become accustomed to going down to the dining room three times a day and to be woken up each morning with a cup of tea and a biscuit. Life at sea in *Windsor Castle* was quite different to that experienced in one of Her Majesty's warships, so I was grateful to have such an opportunity to be at sea with my family and relax for a few weeks. My experiences in the coming years at sea, I thought, may well be in stark contrast to what I was experiencing now.

Perhaps with this at the back of my mind I savoured the moment and ordered from the menu 'Darne of Salmon Amiral,' 'Baked York Ham Oporto,' 'Apple Strudel Apricot Sauce' and coffee to finish. The children had their own 'Snow White' menu with many healthy choices such as 'Poached Salmon Butter Sauce,' 'Roast Turkey with Cranberry Sauce,' 'Chipped or Mashed Potatoes,' 'French beans,' 'Fruit salad with Cream,' and 'Hot or Cold Milk, Tea or Orangeade.' We knew we were being 'spoilt' and that life in England was going to be harder work one way or another, but our thoughts were also on meeting our families after being away from home for so long.

The approach to the English Channel was familiar to me because of my previous voyage in the *Athlone Castle* as a child, and also in my many returns to the UK on board HMS *Bulwark*. The seas slowly changed from azure blue to murky grey and a colder chill filled the air, even though it was late summer in the UK. My parents had kindly agreed to hire a large car and drive down to collect us from Southampton and take us home to Yorkshire. It was emotional, therefore, after two years absence, to see my mother and father waving at us from the jetty as our ship came alongside. My parents had missed us a great deal during our time in Mauritius and 'Nana' was waving enthusiastically and in tears below us as we waited to dock properly and finally go down to greet them. I'm not sure how we would have managed with the five of us and our expanded luggage without my parents' help as we also made good use of the *Windsor Castle's* shops. It was good to be back in England in many ways although it was probably a shock in others; we clearly missed our good friends and the many advantages that were associated with the life we had enjoyed there.

Photo 64 - Our arrival in Southampton docks in late July, 1975

Source: author

Photo 65 - Fred with Christopher   **Photo 66 - Peg with Christopher**

Source: author

After spending a short time with my parents at their home we went to Selby to see Carol's parents and stayed with them for most of our leave until it was time for me to join HMS *Collingwood*. Looking after three very small children was certainly a demanding time, especially for Carol but we continued to work out our approach to managing our expanded family with the assistance of our parents but knowing that we would soon be moving south.

Therefore, in early August I hired a large Ford estate car and filled the back area with our luggage and a new washing machine. We all said our farewells once more and drove the 250 miles south that took us to the Rowner married quarter we had been allocated. Although we were comfortable and well looked after by Carol's parents in Yorkshire, life quickly seemed to be taking a greyer tone as our new home was a flat amidst what one would call a 'concrete jungle.' At least for the time being, my letters home would be limited as our new circumstances did not require written correspondence, but letters of a different sort would be my focus of attention in order to consolidate my progress and increase our income and stability as a family.

VI - HMS *Collingwood* & HMS *Falmouth* [1975-1979]

After settling into our new home, I joined *Collingwood* and became re-acquainted with my *alma mater,* now in the Petty officers' Mess that was situated along a new road adjacent to the parade ground. It had replaced the old wooden huts that I had worked in whilst on duty as an REM and had extensive bar, catering and new accommodation facilities.

My new classmates were all PORELs or A/PORELs with an age range of about ten years from 23 to the early thirties. As it transpired, I was the youngest in my class but a friend from Mauritius, Norman Cooper, was among our ranks and he was just a few months older than me so Norman and I would become close friends and 'allies' as our two-year course unfolded. As I was at the reception desk I was pleasantly surprised to bump into an old friend from *Bulwark* called Gerry Stone, who had been an LREM on *Bulwark* and was now a POREL – also joining *Collingwood* to complete Mechanician's course. He had always been a straight-talking and witty person and he greeted me, perhaps surprised to see me in the PO's Mess at such a young age. When I explained that I was also in *Collingwood* to complete Mechanician's course, he wryly remarked, "(expletive removed) are they giving away Mech's course places with Cornflake tokens these days!?"

As I would discover and was already familiar with to one degree or another, there was an acute sensitivity among my new cohorts regarding why and when various people got promotion or were recommended for courses that led to more qualifications, and therefore further promotion. It would be something that some of us would need to get used to as, among the members of my class, there be a good deal of enquiring and commenting on such matters from those with more experience. Time served in the Royal Navy was signified by 'long service' stripes on the left arms of our uniforms – each stripe representing four years' service up to a maximum of three stripes. The term used for this, however, was 'badges,' and people were given titles such as 'three badge PO' or 'one badge LREM' and so on. A derogatory term, or even a desired title by some, was to be a 'three-badge AB,' meaning that the individual in question had not achieved any significant promotion in his twelve-years of service, although it signified 'good conduct' during his service.

Despite my relative inexperience – especially in a sea-going role at my present level, which I was always aware of as my last sea time had been as a 'lowly' REM - my additional studies in Mauritius to acquire C & G qualifications in Electronics and Radio theory, plus the associated mathematics, would give me a good start as the main challenges ahead of us would be academic, and in particular our efficiency in studying and passing exams. As usual, there would be a great deal of competitiveness among class members when it came to exam results. Indeed, over the two-year period of formal instruction, the list of subjects we would study, as my Service records indicate, was formidable. These included Naval general Training (NGT), maths, electro-technology, electronics, communications, radar, workshop (precision engineering), power distribution and generation, engineering drawing, control engineering, electrical machines, Defence Philosophy and General Studies, NGT Power of Command, NGT self-expression, and any number of modules on specific Royal Navy communications and radar equipment. The task ahead was therefore daunting, but success would lead to 'BTEC Diploma' which, in conjunction with additional studies with the C & G Department, would lead to a 'Full Technological Certificate' (FTC) and be equivalent to a Higher National Certificate (HNC) in our chosen subjects. However, I was relishing the challenge and quickly assimilated into the training schedule with my new electronic calculator and a vast array of study aids. The principal of Radio Mechanician's training was to turn us into 'artisans' or specialists who had a wide range of skills that could be brought to bear in solving any problem. For example, if a piece of equipment we were responsible for became defective and there were no suitable spare parts on board ship, and we were in a conflict zone, the expectation was that Mechanicians (and also Artificers, who started their training on entering the Navy) could 'build a new one' or improvise using their skills in engineering and electronics. This is why our training period was two years as we had to learn and practise these skills as well as pass academic exams.

In my class was also someone I would work closely with over the coming two years, one Michael (Mick) Westwood, who would go on to become the football manager for *Collingwood* - and I would also be a regular player for the first XI. We would go on to win the Navy Cup with Mick as our manager. He was also quite an outspoken and assertive individual by nature, and although we were to be close friends in many ways there was always an edge between us as we would turn out to have strong and sometimes opposing views over a wide range of topics – there was also an unspoken north-south divide between us as he was from London and a staunch Chelsea supporter.

Mick also instigated what was to become known as the 'Dit' book, which was a record of 'ill-informed' observations on theory or general knowledge made by classmates. During lessons Mick and others were always alert to something 'silly' being said and it would immediately go into the Dit book as a running record. I recall the most memorable of my entries emerged during one of our numerous 'stand easy' discussions. I had been reading about the Norman invasion of England at the Battle of Hastings in 1066 by William the Conqueror, and had learnt that many of William's soldiers were in fact Nordic people – in effect 'Vikings.' I had been surprised by this fact as I naturally assumed most of them would have been southern European French people so I was keen to discuss this with my classmates over coffee. However, when it came to my explanation I mistakenly said, "Did you realise that Norman the Conqueror was a Viking." This caused an eruption of laughter as, although I had intended to say 'William' instead of 'Norman,' I think it is fair to say that William, in any event, was actually French. However, Mick and the others placed me in the Dit book – I think this resulted in a minor fee being due, which went into our 'coffee boat' fund. Although making a *faux pas* like this caused some embarrassment as well as hilarity among us, it did have a positive effect in sharpening our minds and made us think more before we spoke. The Naval expression commonly used in this scenario was:

Engage brain before opening (your) mouth

A number of friends from previous ships were also among the other Mechanician classes, including Mick Ross and Kenny Everett from *Bulwark* and Steve Marsh from LREM's course. What I quickly realised was that there was a slightly uncomfortable uniformity going on among the Royal Navy personnel and their families. This is because, every day a large number of people would get up in their married quarters, which all had the same furniture and range of crockery in them (although to be fair it could have been either blue, yellow or tan coloured), get into the same uniforms, say goodbye to their wives and young children, and drive from Rowner to *Collingwood* – often sharing transport together. This brought with it a certain amount of community spirit, but it seemed to go against my natural instinct for individuality. This aspect of my nature would indeed lead to difficult situations in the future for me as might be expected in an organisation like the Royal Navy with its plethora of rules, regulations and rigidity.

During our first three months at Rowner I had been applying for a move to another married quarter as there were some more 'leafy' areas within the Fareham district that we felt would be better for the children. This is because our married quarter, whilst comfortable and adequate inside, was part of a quadrangle with flats on three sides and a tiny back garden of only paving stones. This meant that Carol and I had to take the children to close-by areas such as Stokes Bay or Lee-on-Solent to find large playing areas for them to be in. I think we all felt the contrast with life in Mauritius as I vividly recall rather gloomy days when I was watching breakfast television – we never owned a television in Mauritius as the children were always out and about – and looking out at Lisa and Philip in the tiny back garden and realising it was unforgiving if one of them took a tumble. Carol and I were both adamant that we needed to do better for all of us, but especially our young children. As part of this thinking, we wanted to move to an unfurnished married quarter so that we could build up our own possessions – leading to when we could buy our own house.

Just around this time we bought a small car, a white Hillman Imp, with the intention of getting out into the countryside more and in the hope that Carol would eventually be able to pass her driving test, which would have some long-term benefits when the time came for me to go to sea. It was clear to us that Carol would not be able to get far on her own with three young children and these thoughts were captured in a now rare letter back to my parents on the 6th December, 1975. As well as commenting on how pleased I was that my sister, Barbara, had now recovered enough from her back surgery to be starting a new job, I flagged up the 'perils' that many men encounter when teaching their wives to drive.

The car seems to be a reasonable buy up to now. It has a new engine and dropped suspension at the front. Carol is learning to drive in it under my expert tuition! Things are going smoother now compared with the first time I tried to teach her – I've taken a different attitude this time as I just sit back and enjoy the ride (eyes closed!). Actually, she's doing very well because last week she drove all the way from Wickham to Fareham with no problems. We want her to learn because we've applied for a new home in Peak Lane.

In fact Carol had started some 'proper lessons' with a learner driver company but had made only little progress. We therefore decided to go out regularly for her to practise but as one might expect, there were a few sticking points and one or two close scrapes. I remember one incident in particular when we were driving through Gosport near to the harbour when a bus stopped unexpectedly in front of us. The issue was whether or not to stop behind it and wait, or move out and overtake it. Quite rightly, Carol pulled up behind the bus and was waiting for my clear instruction but I was more focussed on the inconvenience the bus had caused us and uttered a mild expletive. Unfortunately, Carol interpreted this comment as disapproval of her decision to stop and that she should have proceeded to overtake the bus, which is what she then commenced doing. All the children were in the back as usual and produced many of their own distractions for a budding learner. The eventual outcome is that we got rather close to the bus before swerving past it at the last minute to perform the overtaking manoeuvre with warnings of, "Look out, Mummy, there's a lorry!" coming from the back seat. As we passed the back of the bus I heard a distinctive scraping noise before we roared off down the road. We were convinced we had come into contact with the bus so when we got home, safe and sound, we looked down the left-hand side of the car and saw a wonderful green stripe going along the whole length of our Imp! We were so concerned about a 'hit and run' claim from Gosport Transport Corporation, however, that I called them and asked if they had received a report from their drivers that a white Imp had scraped them in Gosport. We breathed a sigh of relief when no such incident had been reported!

To be fair to Carol, the Imp was quite tricky to drive and had a technical defect that made changes from third to second gear difficult as, when the torque of the engine took hold when releasing the clutch, the car would pop out of gear and the lever would fly forward into neutral. This meant we had some problems with my 'teaching skills' and patience as Carol – understandably - then formed the habit of not letting her foot off the clutch when slowing down using second gear. I remember we had some long conversations at the side of the road as I explained that she would fail because the car was effectively out of control if either the break wasn't engaged or the clutch wasn't fully released while in a gear. With three hungry and boisterous toddlers in the back, me holding my head in the front passenger seat, and Carol trying to explain her situation we had some very interesting rides! However, to her credit, my fortitude, and some good behaviour from the 'three in the back,' she passed her test – in the Imp with its popping gears – on the second time of asking. Our several months of driving in and around the local town and to and from our favourite spot at the forest of Bere near Wickham had done the trick. Among other benefits, it helped us in our steps to survive the demands of future separation. In the New Year we were fortunate enough to move to 36, Harcourt Road, in the Peak Lane area of Fareham. Although not enormous, we had a grassed back garden in a more residential area and were generally more comfortable in our home and environment.

Photo 67 - Carol, children and our Hillman Imp in the Forest of Bere

Source: *author*

Even though we had no furniture to start with apart from a three piece suite, we quickly bought two single beds that we all slept in until the double bed arrived – only to find I had ordered a four-foot bed, which was cosy if a little cramped. Family life therefore settled into a pattern whereby I cycled to *Collingwood* each morning, was one of the duty POs about once a fortnight, and studied in the evenings for exams – often with other members of my class who lived close by such as Geoff Harvey. After a year or so two issues that would impact on my future began to surface more and more. The first one was that of the familiar and potential problems of future separation, which caused me to consider my options. The second one was much less subtle but related to the qualifications of some of our instructor officers in the subjects they were required to teach.

With regard to the first of these, I was doing well in my course exams and often came top of my class or thereabouts, and the comradeship among me and my classmates was very positive. We were developing our academic knowledge in order to make us more professional and capable in our future jobs in the Navy, and on leaving, but I knew the path I was on would tie me to five years return of service as a minimum after Mechanicians course and take me into 'pension trap' territory. I therefore discussed the possibility of withdrawing from Mechanicians course and returning to the mechanics' career path as a POREL, with the option of leaving quite soon at the age of 27. After many discussions with Carol at home and other close friends such as Norman Cooper, I signed an official request to do just this. This was a sensitive issue for me and I would have preferred to have kept it from my class mates. Unfortunately, our Divisional Officer, who was teaching one of our academic modules, suddenly, and without warning, announced my request in front of everyone. Many of my friends and classmates had 'wise heads' and opinions on this matter as most of them were grappling with the 'costs and benefits' of a career in the Navy and the impact it had on their personal and family lives. Therefore in many coffee breaks over the following weeks I listened patiently to the many perspectives that were put forward. The question was focussed on the comfort of security of employment and income in the Navy versus the dangers and challenges of separation and sea time. In due course, and almost certainly against my natural instincts, and against Carol's strong advice, I took the option of 'kicking the can down the road' and settled on the benefits of continuing with Mechanicians course and withdrew my request. After this, I simply put my efforts into passing my exams, spending time with the family, and enjoying playing football for *Collingwood*.

The second issue related to the way in which the Navy used direct-entry graduates within the Instructor Officer branch, which was sometimes in contrast to the teaching we received from technical experts such as CPOs. In the latter, these instructors had worked on the equipment they were teaching for many years and we naturally had a great deal of respect for them as we were basically following in their footsteps. In the case of Instructor Officers there was a mixed bag of permutations. I recall, for example, that we had a Lt Cdr 'Schooly' who taught us mechanics and physics. He had a Master's degree in Physics and was highly intelligent with superb teaching skills. He was able to teach our class with consummate ease as we grappled with learning, and remembering, a vast array of formulae that we applied in problem solving. In my class we were always looking for ways to help us remember various formulae. Some of us came up with mnemonics for magnetic flux calculations and how to calculate the inductance in an electrical circuit. When looking at the letters and Greek symbols that made up three important formulae we had to remember for exams, we came up with 'Bill' 'Bah' 'Lamu' - without reproducing all the associated formulae the first was B = IL in that magnetic flux (B) is dependent of the size of the electrical current (I) multiplied by the inductance (L). A few classmates naturally got these wrong at times, and their confusions were duly recorded in the Dit book. However, this experience for all of us showed some degree of imagination.

Problems occurred for Instructor Officers, however, when they taught subjects outside of their degrees or professional qualifications. This was the case for electronics in particular. For all of us in the class, this was our main subject and we had been studying it for up to ten years or more, so we were already experts to one degree or another apart from the academic rigour that we were now applying to it. The course involved studying the atomic structure and functioning of various electronic components such as, for example, thyristers, and we needed to know how to analyse their function and operation within complicated electronic circuits. This often involved drawing various graphs and waveforms of voltage and current changes to explain how amplification or other waveform production was achieved. Our academic instructor in fact had a degree in mathematics and his knowledge had to come from reading around the subject to apply his graduate skills to learn the topic sufficiently well to explain it to us. It isn't difficult to see that this would be a recipe for conflict and disagreement as everyone in the class was capable of asking a question to 'catch our instructor out.' I remember having a certain amount of arrogance myself about this situation, as did most of us in the class, and some of our discussions got rather heated at times as we weren't always satisfied with the answer, "I'll do some more reading and we'll come back to that question tomorrow." The situation was further exacerbated by the rank differences between us – one Lt Cdr versus 15 self-opinionated POs – and it came to an unsavoury end when one of our instructor officers offered one of our more vocal members to a 'fight in the park after school!' Although this was a source of great amusement at the time, I don't think I realised that this scenario could be imposed on any of us in the future and that we could be in our teacher's predicament although his reaction was well outside what one would expect in the circumstances.

Life in Harcourt Road continued and as I can observe in a letter home to my younger brother, David, on the 4th May 1977, we often had visits from my family and some from Carol's sister, Sandra, and her husband, Keith, and family. I noted now that we had all taken an interest in wildlife and walks on the South Downs, which were only an hour's drive away. It was during this period that we could see that Philip, in particular, had been affected by our move back to the UK. Carol and I observed that he had become more withdrawn and wouldn't tolerate being left at a local playschool when he was about three years old. There were some similarities with my own experiences as a child in moving back to England from Rhodesia, but Philip would eventually settle down in local schools and do equally well as his brother and sister. As the time drew closer for me to be drafted back to sea, I constantly reflected on the potential impacts this would have for all of us. Our youngest child, Christopher, was now developing into a toddler and revealing a very unique and strong personality with an iron will. I recall how he could, even before the age of two, deliberately keep a straight face and ignore the actions and words of adults who were trying to get his attention. He seemed to have the attitude that he wasn't going to be manipulated by older people and his lack of response always generated a good deal of laughter and astonishment. When the time came for me to be drafted to sea I had a strong desire to be given a job in the area of telecommunications or radar, but there was to be a sting in this tail that took me in another direction.

When my class reached the end its formal teaching to pass out as a Radio Mechanician Third Class (RMech 3) we all awaited receipt of the famous 'chit' that would inform us to report to the drafting section of the Administration block in *Collingwood*. I remember receiving mine and duly walking over to see the relevant CPO, who handed me some papers that indicated I was to join HMS *Falmouth* as the maintainer in charge of the gunnery control radar system, known as 903 radar. I would also be in charge of maintaining the radio elements of the gunnery direction system, known as GDS5, and the radio equipment that controlled the Seacat missile system. I was disappointed with this news principally because my new role would move me away from my favourite types of radio and radar equipment to gunnery and missile systems. These would be totally unfamiliar to me and my working environment would be much less independent in comparison with my previous work. HMS *Falmouth* was also a small frigate, which meant life would be much more cramped and the ship, which was only 2,800 tonnes and therefore classified as a 'small ship,' would not behave as well in rough waters compared with my first ship, the 22,000 tonne commando carrier, HMS *Bulwark*. It was therefore with a certain amount of trepidation that I told Carol of what was about to happen.

Just before this news we had taken the step to buy our first house and move out of married quarters. This was a significant step as it required me to 'sign on' to complete 22 years in the Navy as that action created the possibility of me taking out a 'long service advance of pay' (LSAOP), which would generate enough money for the deposit required by mortgage lenders and furnish our new home. I would pay this off over a number of years through deductions from my pay. We eventually moved to the more select area of Hill Head and bought a fairly modest three-bedroomed terraced house, which was in the safe cul-de-sac of Elsfred Road about 400 metres from the beach. I recall that our choice of area had caused somewhat of a reaction among one or two of my classmates as there was the suggestion I was snobbish in some way. I think this response was partly my own doing as I expressed the view that 'I could always improve the modest house we were buying but I could never change the area,' and implied that some local areas were less desirable than others.

Photo 68 - Lisa, Christopher and Philip in Elsfred Road, Hill Head

Source: author

This generated some antagonism towards me as many of my classmates lived in the areas I was alluding to as being less desirable. It was also the case that many officers lived in areas such as Hill Head, and there was a view that I would be better off in a lower cost area. However, I was adamant in my views and accepted the judgements of my peers but was re-assured by the fact that some of them also shared my perspective. Therefore, we were now in a new home, I was committed to remaining in the Navy until I was 40 years old or at least until the age of 30 if I were to give notice after my five years return of service, and the challenges of a new mode of 'separated' family life lay ahead. After completing Mechanicians course, which I did with an average of 74%, I went on to do the additional equipment-specific training I needed to complete before joining HMS *Falmouth*. This involved learning all about the 903 radar system, GDS5 and Seacat missile system. I continued to feel out of my comfort zone in spite of learning about interesting new techniques such as 'conical scanning,' which the radar system used to generate control signals for the 4.5-inch gun turrets to move as targets were tracked. In between the gun turrets and the radar system I would be responsible for, was a large electro-mechanical computer, which modified the signals coming from the gun director according to many factors such as wind direction and speed, to create a reliable point of aim for the 4.5-inch guns.

In early March I visited HMS *Falmouth* in Portsmouth harbour ahead of my official draft date to meet the person I would relieve and get to know other colleagues I would be working with. In terms of its history, *Falmouth* was commissioned in 1961 and took part in the Third Cod War between Iceland and the UK. Her role then was to protect the British fishing fleet from Icelandic gunboats that were trying to cut their gear. She famously engaged the Icelandic vessel *Tyr*, ramming her at speed when she was attempting to cut the gear of the trawler *Carlisle*. Ironically for me personally, *Falmouth* was also one of the Beira patrol ships that undertook the oil embargo of Rhodesia in 1966 as a sanction against the Smith Government that my family had left behind us in Africa.

As the overall system I was working on, known as 'MRS 3,' was new in its design and installation in Royal Navy ships, there was also a civilian expert working alongside my new colleague, CPO 'Grifth' Griffiths, who was a Control Mechanician. My LREM, who would work with me on the radar and gunnery control systems, was a very amiable, humorous and competent Scot. Like my friend from Mauritius, he was also called Gary ('Buck') Taylor. I was to be accommodated in the 'Aft PO's Mess,' and briefly got to know the president, POMEM Paul Hankins, and some of my new messmates. When I first entered my new accommodation I was a little taken aback as to how cramped it was, and someone in the Mess clearly had a liking for reading material I didn't particularly welcome, which was piled around the seating area. On first entering the Mess the sleeping area was immediately ahead and contained 18 bunk beds within an area no bigger than that of a kitchen in an average home. Being fit and slim I was given the first top bunk on the right of the sleeping area. When I first examined it I saw that there was a large fan trunking with a brass lever partly blocking my access to the bunk. To get into my bunk, therefore, I had to hoist myself up to a height of more than six feet using two bars that were welded to the deck head (ceiling). The gap for me to scramble through was not much more that the depth of my chest so I decided I would use a sleeping bag on my bunk rather than sheets and blankets as there wasn't much room to move around up there. I was therefore making preparations on board *Falmouth* and at home for my departure from Carol and the children, and moving my personal belongings onto the ship - conscious of the stark differences between my two homes.

During these occasional visits I remember the first person to greet me in the PO's Mess was a Petty Officer Marine Engineering Mechanician (MEMN2) called 'Ginge' Poucher. He was about 25 years old and I could immediately see he was a genuinely warm and thoughtful person as he was the first one to offer me a cup of tea, which he made in the small bar we had in the 'lounge' area of the Mess. By the way he enquired about my role and background he was clearly aware of, and sensitive to, how I might be feeling about joining *Falmouth* after five years ashore and the wrenches involved with leaving a wife and three small children on their own, away from extended family, during periods at sea on exercises and visits to foreign ports. I did realise at this point, that although life was going to be difficult in many ways over the coming years, I would be in the company of some excellent people such as my new friend and other colleagues. In addition to Paul Hankins, who looked and behaved very much like the 'Fonz' (Arthur Fonzarelli; played by actor Henry Winkler) in the TV sitcom 'Happy Days,' there was a Petty Officer Marine Engineering Artificer (MEA2), who would become somewhat of a 'guardian angel' in my future struggles. He was called Nigel Butterworth and among us, affectionately known as 'Nidge.' Reflecting back on those days now, I can see that my engineering friends in particular were exceptional individuals with big personalities and a strong awareness of what was happening both to them and to others.

The time soon came for me to join *Falmouth* officially. March the 28th, 1978, would be a day I would never forget as it would mark a time of mixed blessings and struggles in the coming two years. Having gone to my children in turn as they slept in their beds, I said my goodbyes to Carol at 6.30 am on the doorstep of our home and made the journey across to Portsmouth. While passing through the coastal road of Lee-on-Solent I noticed with some dread the grey skies, rain, turbulent seas and strong winds that were sweeping across the Solent and creating white caps on large waves.

Photo 69 - The Type 12 Frigate, HMS *Falmouth*

Source: *Barry Pearce, R.N. by permission of MaritimeQuest: www.marinequest.com/warships*

I arrived on the jetty at 7.15 pm and after reporting to the gangway staff and Officer of the Day I went across the small flight deck, down the ladder to the quarterdeck and then turned right next to the mortars and into the red and white tiled passageway that led to the metal door of the Aft PO's Mess. All around me was a hive of activity with people in overalls and caps, or No. 8 uniforms, making ready for us leaving harbour at 8.30 that morning. After placing my possessions in my modestly-sized locker I reported to the 'WE Admin' office and was told that I should report to the WEO, Lt Cdr Neil, in his cabin at 9.30 am for a joining briefing once we had left harbour. I then went across the passageway into the 4.5-inch Transmitter Station (TS) Annexe to let Grifth and Buck know that I had arrived and that I was due to see the WEO at 9.30. The activity through the passageways was increasing in intensity and several pipes were made over the tannoy regarding leaving harbour routine. In due course, movement of the ship occurred and I heard several pipes and announcements being made as the ship slipped out of Portsmouth harbour and into the Solent. Almost immediately the ship started to lurch, pitch and roll quite markedly and movement up and down the ladder to the operations room alternated between climbing without any effort and feeling 10 kilogrammes heavier depending on where the ship was in its pitch and roll cycle. My body detected this with some mild discomfort to begin with but as we traversed the Isle of Wight and went into the open seas of the English Channel the movements became much more violent and continued to intensify as we picked up speed. I would soon learn that the design of frigates that makes them fast and manoeuvrable adds to the effect waves have on them. Captains of these vessels were required to drive them 'like sports cars' to gain tactical advantages when in action, but for those with motion sickness this was an added burden.

Very rapidly my surroundings seemed to become more hostile and the movement of the ship intensified my senses of smell, sight and hearing in a negative way. The smell of diesel and rubber-insulated mats became more pungent, the creaking of the ship as it corkscrewed through the rough seas became like the worst funfair ride one could ever imagine being on, and looking at technical documents and complicated equipment became hard on the brain as my attention was on my stomach and the violent churning and cramps that were emerging, and intensifying. The sights in the operations room were a sickly mix of red and ultraviolet light, made worse by people with either glum or determined looks on their faces gathered around radar displays and writing in white chinograph pen on their displays. Everywhere I went electrical and electronic machinery was buzzing and whirring with lights flashing. My colleagues were looking at me with expectation about my duties but with some recognition of how I was feeling as some of them clearly weren't having any fun either.

After about 30 minutes my digestive system gave way and I dashed down the passageway to the CPO and PO's Heads (toilets). I rushed into a cubicle and was immediately and violently ill. As I looked down into the toilet I could hear loud influxes of air and churning sea water within the plumbing as the waves pushed and pulled at outlets along the sides of the ship. I was not able to control my reaction and continued to reach over and over again – eventually I was on the floor with my head permanently at the ready and had no option other than to stay there and wait for the next convulsion of my stomach. By now it had passed 9.30 and I knew I was late for my joining talk with the WEO. At about 9.45 there was a knock on the toilet door. From behind it I heard the voice of Buck Taylor, my LREM, saying, "Are you in there, John?" I confirmed I was and Buck replied, as predicted, "The WEO has asked me to find out where you are and why you didn't turn up at 9.30." I anticipated this would happen and asked Buck to explain I was unable to attend due to sea sickness and that I would try and make it for 10.30. Buck gave me a few words of sympathy and left me to my plight. I returned across the passageway to the Mess once or twice and some colleagues there could see that I was in difficulty.

None of them looked very happy and most had resigned looks on their faces but Ginge Poucher gave me some water as he said that something like tea or coffee would make matters worse. After short periods attempting respite like this, I repeatedly returned to the toilets and continued being violently sick. At 10.30 I made my way down the pitching and rolling main passageway to the WEO's cabin but after a very brief introduction I had to apologise and dash back to the toilets. By lunch time I had completely evacuated every trace of the contents of my stomach and was now producing diminishing amounts of green bile. I missed lunch and only grabbed some water from the coolers in the passageway when I could. By mid-afternoon I was becoming seriously ill and Ginge Poucher said, "Come on, mate, we've got to get you to the Sick Bay." He said I should return to the toilets, where I felt 'safe,' while he went to find the ship's Leading Medical Assistant (LMA).

Small ships like *Falmouth* didn't carry a doctor and all our medical treatment was provided by the LMA in the small Sick Bay, which was situated at the aft end of the ship. After repeatedly being sick again I happened to notice my reflection in the mirror. My face looked like I had been in a boxing match as my eyes and cheeks were swollen and my complexion was devoid of any colour. I thought to myself, 'how can I possibly stand such an existence and work on highly technical equipment while feeling like this?' I looked out of the sea-sprayed porthole in the toilet and scanned the stormy conditions that were bringing me such misery. I had never felt as dejected or 'defeated' in all my life.

I eventually saw the LMA in the Sick Bay at about 4.00 in the afternoon. On entering the calm and quiet atmosphere of the Sick Bay the LMA listened to my situation and asked me if I had taken precautionary medication, which was the drug cinnizarine (Stugeron). This 'duty' was apparently laid out in the ship's standing orders and in spite of its limited effectiveness, people suffering sea sickness who were unable to work could be charged under the Naval Discipline Act if they hadn't taken it 2-3 hours before going to sea. This was not what I wanted to hear at such a time but I explained that I had only joined the ship that morning and had no opportunity to take Stugeron.

Fortunately, after examining me and prodding my stomach he could see how unwell I was and decided to give me an injection to stop me being 'physically' sick. After this I returned to the Mess and managed to scramble up into my bunk – the ship was still moving violently but I was able to get some respite and felt better when lying down. I stayed there until the ship thankfully anchored in a sheltered bay at about 5.30 pm. Ginge Poucher, Nidge Butterworth and Paul Hankins gave some welcome support and after a shower they showed me to Chief's and PO's dining room. Queuing up in the passageway with my new friends and other messmates would become a pleasant part of the day as time went by as we had an opportunity to exchange ideas and converse together. On this first day, they all had their own way of trying to make light of my experience by saying things like, "That'll teach you to have a greasy bacon sandwich for breakfast, matey," or "get up on the upper deck as quickly as possible if you feel sick as you can see the horizon," "carry a bucket around with you as well as a screwdriver," "eat dried bread when you feel sick and remember to take your Stugeron," and any number of similar pieces of advice. Paul Hankins cheered everyone up further by saying, "We're in luck – the chefs put on babies' heads." 'Babies' heads' were a favourite among us as that was the nickname for steak and kidney puddings, which of course we had with chips, vegetables and gravy. Food like that also helped in settling people's stomachs after being in rough weather.

At this point I realised that I hadn't spoken properly to the WEO and could also be in trouble because of that, so after supper I returned to his cabin to discuss my responsibilities and duties. He was a fresh-faced man in his early 30s with wispy blonde hair and a slightly uncomfortable air about him. He did have some words of assurance for me as he felt I would eventually get used to being at sea again. As I sat listening to him I noticed that his cabin was about the same size as the sleeping area of the PO's Mess and had a single bed at one end. His highly-polished wooden desk was in the middle, which is where he was sitting with my service record in front of him. The cabin was decorated with high quality drapes and bedding, and his bunk was made of a rich-coloured hardwood. He explained that the main concern of any WEO was to ensure all the equipment they were responsible for was working well and properly maintained so that the ship could operate at full level of readiness and defend itself when required, or engage other targets. If this wasn't the case the Captain would be asking some very pressing questions about when it would be available again, and pressure would be applied down through the section Charge Chief. As I was in charge of the 903 radar and Seacat missile's guidance systems, which were vital in this primary purpose, I was one of the ship's 'key personnel' and needed to be on top of my responsibilities. I was confident in my technical abilities, but the question of how I could work in small windows of time when the ship was in calm seas or in harbour sent a chill down my spine. Indeed, this was to become my primary strategy in dealing with sea sickness and would mean me working 'unsociable' hours on many occasions – but in the Navy everyone, not only me, was required to work as and when needed and especially when our equipment required repairing or maintaining.

My return to sea after five years away, and in a small ship, was indeed a trial of some magnitude and one that quickly made me feel like a prisoner in a place that was capable of inflicting torment, and away from my wife and children, who were now coping for themselves at home without my immediate help. I hoped and prayed that they would be safe and could manage, and was grateful for having such good companions and friends around me who could encourage me through the ordeals that by now were looking all too familiar – not only to me but to some of them. From now on I would be a slave to the BBC's daily shipping forecast and often thought, "Why me, Lord" when I regularly heard there would be gale force 8 or 10 winds in our area of operation for the days we put to sea.

In spite of my ordeals with motion sickness, in the early weeks and months in HMS *Falmouth* I developed a good working relationship with Grifth and Buck in particular as we were part of an interdisciplinary team. Our programme in the first few months was partly 'day running' out of Portsmouth and then weeks at a time at sea doing post-refit sea trials, leading up to a full workup at Portland, which would last for about five weeks. After that we would be spending several weeks away at a time making official visits to Gavle in Sweden, Esbjerg in Denmark, Middlesbrough, and the Isle of Wight during Cowes Week. Following this a Far East deployment was planned during 1979, which would last more than six months.

In these early days the MRS3 system would be tested and fine-tuned through numerous tracking exercises and target practises with towed targets from aircraft and tugs. Our daily routine always started early with System Operator Checks (SOCs) at about 8.30 am, which meant that people in my section had to check the proper working of the equipment through various tests and procedures, and where necessary repairs, before the operators of the system arrived to actually take the equipment through its functional tests. Our Chief GI, Chief Rose, was always standing in the middle of the darkened TS with a black microphone in his hand and holding on to a support bar coming down from the deck head above him. He was therefore on the intercom to the Principal War Officer (PWO), who was sitting at the radar system and direction system I was responsible for in the operations room. Chief Rose barked out commands and gave instructions to the operators manning the consoles in front of him, who looked at green radar traces and operated what were known as 'slew' and 'trim' levers to acquire targets. Maintainers like me usually stood in corners of the TS observing what was happening and looking for clues of any technical difficulties that they needed to deal with.

I quickly realised Chief Rose was not particularly fond of 'Greenies' and 'Pinkies' like me as he probably thought we had a relatively easy life and got promoted too quickly. As technical specialists we also received additional pay. Promotion in the Seaman Branch, which he belonged to, took much more time compared with what we enjoyed and I don't think he was particularly sympathetic to those who were prone to sea sickness – especially as the PO Seamen's Mess was right at the front end of the ship and therefore much more affected by pitching and rolling of the ship in bad weather. However, he may have given me some credit for having my bucket close to hand as well as my screw driver. When a fault developed, Buck and I had to investigate and repair it as soon as possible, and Chief Rose was not short of the odd expletive and derogatory comment about our radar system if it wasn't fixed within a very short space of time, or if he thought it wasn't performing properly. Indeed, the 'operator-technician' conflict was regularly in evidence as there was always some opportunity for one camp to blame problems or errors on the other when things went wrong. However, Buck and I soon became a good working partnership and enjoyed many a laugh as we went around the ship visiting the several compartments we had equipment in, or chatting on the upper deck. I remember he told me that 'the best way to avoid being given extra jobs by the Section Chief was to walk around the ship with an important looking piece of paper in your hand.' He had two young children and his family lived in a married quarter in Portsmouth. Like me, he was concerned for their welfare while away at sea and we discussed these matters on many occasions over a cup of coffee while working on the equipment together.

Being on the upper deck in the fresh air quickly became a source of relief that helped with my prevailing sea sickness as I could see the horizon – sea sickness is known to be related to balance problems and conflicts, and its minimisation depends on co-ordination in the brain between the inner ears and sight. The 903 radar was located in the 4.5-inch director behind and above the gun, and was easily recognised by its small dish-shaped aerial. The director was also manned during exercises or action stations so that tracking of targets could be achieved either automatically through the 903 radar or manually using hand controls and a viewing sight. Below the director was the 903 maintenance room, which was exclusively used by my small team as it contained a spare radar unit and various test equipment that we used. We could hoist the spare unit up to the director using a manual lift and replace the whole unit if necessary. We would then work in our small compartment to repair and maintain the second unit – there were some dangerous voltages very close to where we had to tune the system so having two of us was both useful and safe.

An enjoyable part of our work was carrying out 'balloon runs,' which involved us inflating a balloon with hydrogen, releasing it and then locking onto the balloon such that we could test the radar's ability to track real targets. The balloons we used were surrounded with a radar-reflective net, so they were ideal for tracking over long distances. At the same time, Grifth would do his checks of the computer and analyse the results that could be recorded in the TS. We were supported and supervised in all of this by a very talented, considerate and intelligent Charge Chief Control Artificer (whose name I have sadly forgotten), although Buck and I generally had a free hand in looking after the 'radio' elements of the system.

For those of us who were married, our main mission was to get home for every week-end we could and after crossing the Gosport Ferry on a Friday afternoon once the ship docked, I would sit on a small wall next to the ferry terminal waiting for Carol to arrive to collect me in the car. At week-ends we would do things together with the children, who were now settled in local schools or play groups in the case of Christopher, but what Carol and I came to hate were Sunday afternoons. This is because the time quickly came after lunch and I had watched some football on the television – something I couldn't do when I was at sea – that I had to go upstairs to pack my bag and be taken by Carol and the children back to the Gosport ferry, where we would say numerous goodbyes in the coming months and years. The music of ABBA was now becoming popular, and I often recall some of their songs being played both at home and on board ship. One song that perhaps captured my thoughts at that time was 'Chiquitita,' (Andersson & Ulvaeus, 1979), which I liked very much but some of the words were somewhat prophetic when I look at them now with the wisdom of hindsight.

Chiquitita, you and I know how the heartaches come and they go and the scars they're leaving;
You'll be dancing once again and the pain will end, you will have no time for grieving

Although we perhaps weren't aware of it at the time, there were some subtle changes occurring in our family life as I was struggling with my life at sea and was often lonely and also sea sick, and Carol was having to learn to cope on her own and often had to make important decisions to do with the house, our finances, the children and neighbours among many others. It was also clearly challenging for her to have mostly children to talk to, although they were all bright and capable for their ages. We both had to be strong in our own ways, but this development was laying the foundation for future friction, and there was nothing that could be done about it as all our reactions were 'normal' for most human beings in our predicament.

****

Some typical implications of separation and the conditions people experienced at sea emerged a few months later when *Falmouth* was at Portland doing trials. Workup involved many exercises and long periods at action stations with simulated aircraft bombings or missile attacks - with accompanying sound effects - early morning starts to the day with SOCs, gun and Seacat missile firings and many late nights working to repair defective equipment. Other departments had similar challenges specific to their own equipment or responsibilities. There were pleasant moments among this too, such as early morning checks on the upper deck in calm waters and the sun rising on the horizon with a cup of milky coffee in our hands. However, we were basically working under war conditions and inspectors – 'Portland Staff' –

would arrive each morning by launch to set up some scenarios that would require various individuals or teams to respond. One difficult aspect for me was that, as a regular 'duty senior electrical rating,' I would be required to take charge of starting up the ship's diesel generators and performing a procedure known as 'paralleling,' whereby a shore supply would be connected in parallel with the ship's generators so that we could either connect or disconnect one of these sources. It was not the kind of thing I did every day but among many other responsibilities as the 903 maintainer, but it was something I was required to demonstrate my competence in to the Staff. I remember practising this on several evenings with friends and colleagues from the PO's Mess who did this as part of their daily work. Needless to say, people were under pressure and worked long hours.

At this time one of my closest friends started to learn that his wife was unwell and I could see, and hear from him over chats in the evening at supper that he was extremely worried but there was little time at week-ends for him to help her. It obviously became critical to him but he was refused any compassionate leave to stay at home and look after her. It was particularly difficult to get Departmental Officers and the Captain to agree to a senior rating to be given leave whilst undergoing sea trials, even if concerns about family members were badly affecting that person's ability to be effective in their job. In times such as this, the Navy usually came first but there was variation depending on the ship's programme and the details of the case.

However, the matter progressed and on one Monday morning my friend failed to return to the ship. We all wondered what had happened to him but it turned out that he had simply stayed at home and the Naval Police had gone to his home where they basically arrested him and returned him to the ship. As a consequence he was punished by loss of leave and a fine, which made him feel worse as he knew he would have to remain on board and not be able to return home at the weekends. That evening I saw him sitting in the Mess and slowly getting himself more and more drunk and distraught. Although I, and others, attempted to reconcile his situation with him, he clearly felt it was hopeless. He therefore started to protest to various people in his department and clearly got deeper into trouble. In my opinion, this was most definitely against his nature but of course there are always gaps in people's knowledge and recollections over such matters.

The next progression regarding my friend's predicament was that he was taken away from the Mess and placed in 'cells' in the ship. This involved being locked up in a small compartment in the bowels of the ship whilst under the supervision of the Master at Arms. I felt unbelievably sad about this development; not only because I knew he was in a difficult situation caused by the conflicts between family and service life, but because he had regularly recognised my own concerns and was always one of the first to offer a hand of friendship and support. I felt helpless in not being able to reciprocate as the 'unyielding cogs of naval discipline' had been set in motion.

Over the coming weeks as the ship got further into our Workup he got himself deeper into trouble. As a result, a 'warrant' was taken out against him, which was about as serious as things can get except for a court martial. The day that this event took place is etched in my mind as it seemed to be an occasion deliberately aimed at humiliating the 'guilty' – a personal friend - in front of his peers and close friends, such that they might learn not to emulate his behaviour. All 50 senior ratings were ordered to gather in the Junior Ratings' dining room and various officers and regulators were lined up at one end of the room. We all stood there in orderly silence, observing and listening. After a delay my friend appeared at the entrance to the dining room with the Master at Arms and was marched into the room and ordered to halt in front of the presiding officer. The Master at Arms called out "off caps!" and another senior rating removed his cap – usually this is done by the 'offender' himself but the action of someone else doing it was intended to add to the humiliation. A list of charges was then read out that recorded his repeated absences from the ship without leave and drunken and disorderly behaviour on board one of her Majesty's warships. After this the punishment was read out, my friend had his cap replaced and he was marched out of the room. To add to the humiliation, however, the officers realised that the punishment given – a suspended sentence of detention - had been 'incorrect' due to a mis-interpretation of the warrant by one of the officers, and my friend was marched back into the room and the procedure repeated. This time the sentence of Detention Quarters (DQs) was given and not suspended – which meant he was destined for a long period in 'jail.' Among the ranks I was in this was greeted with muted disbelief as, among other things, it seemed to go against the legal principle of 'double jeopardy.'

I found it painful to see this happening to such a decent person as my good friend, who could have been my brother, and many of us returned to the Mess to ponder in disbelief at what we had witnessed happening. It made me realise that we were all living on a knife-edge that could tip us from being compliant in our duties, and thus be able to sustain our lives and those of our families, and being punished harshly in front of our friends with subsequent loss of status, freedom and income. As I reflect now, I am more aware of the loss of basic human rights, such as freedom of movement and association, that we had to endure in the Services and that are taken for granted by the majority in society. Sadly, I never saw my good friend again.

****

Life, however, was not all bad and the negative experiences I was feeling or observing were compensated for, as always in my naval career, by my close friends. In the PO's Mess we had the N.A.A.F.I. manager – known as the 'Canteen Manager' or 'Can-man' - and he was fond of arranging quizzes that were always held between the 'Greenies' and the 'Engineers' as there were roughly the same numbers in each camp. These were held in the lounge/bar area and the Can-man had also concocted up our own 'cocktail' know as a 'gin-fizz,' which was mixed up in a large metal tea pot with the help of a soda machine and orange juice as well as the gin. These evenings were so popular that we had our own sweat shirt produced that we wore on each quiz night. On it was a picture of the pot (with a large spout) and the inscription 'Aft PO's Mess – Gin Fizz Pot – HMS *Falmouth*' (which I still have to this day). Competition between the Greenies and Engineers was always fierce and we naturally kept a running record of the results – I believe we had a marginal lead but I'm sure this might be disputed.

These evenings usually took place during 'up channel' nights or when we had just finished an exercise, and I was the resident accompanist on my faithful guitar for the singing we always enjoyed. By now I had moved on to a 12-string Echo guitar which I played using a finger-picking folk/classical style – although strumming was essential when the noise increased. Among the Greenies were two close friends – POREL Wright ('Shiner') and CEMN2 George Norrie, who was the maintainer for the mortars. Both of them were Scottish and like most of my friends from north of the border, were larger than life characters. Shiner was fiercely patriotic as a Scot, especially when watching Scotland playing football and was also a keen fan of the Beatles so he was forever saying to me, "Come on, John - get the old guitar out, mate!" Combined with several glasses of Gin Fizz and a Beatles' songbook we had a healthy way of getting rid of our daily frustrations and the difficult life we sometimes endured on board a Royal Navy frigate. Our sleeping quarters, however, were cramped and there was very little opportunity of getting any privacy – I often took my guitar to one of the compartments I worked in and played songs I was fond of and wrote letters home.

All of my children, under Carol's guidance, wrote to me and as I look at them now I can see they were all aware of how much I disliked being away from them and how much I suffered at times. They always started their letters with:

Dear Daddy, I hope you are okay and not feeling too sea sick at the moment.............

To her credit, I heard Carol on many occasions saying to the children that, as a family we had to recognise the hard work and sacrifices I personally made to give us all a good standard of living in a comfortable and safe home in a good area. Indeed, in these times of separation and striving to meet the needs of our young family we both made some considerable and damaging sacrifices, and had to face the rigidity of the Royal Navy in its requirements for my services - at equal magnitude to some others.

By now I was taking Stugeron before going to sea but its main effect was to make me very drowsy so concentration was quite difficult. It didn't stop me being physically sick when we were in rough seas, but as I mentioned previously, I was perhaps lucky enough to be able to work in the evenings or week-ends when in harbour or when the sea was calm to make sure I got well ahead of myself. My technical knowledge and skills as a maintainer and diagnostician were probably close to my full potential. However, there were many times when I had to retire to my bunk for long periods and hope for calmer waters. This is why the loss of my right-hand man, Buck Taylor, in the middle of Workup was quite a blow as I did not get a replacement LREM and had to do the work of two under the most demanding circumstances we would normally face. For several weeks, therefore, I was regularly getting to bed in the early hours of the morning and then rising again at 5.30 am to start preparing for SOCs. I still managed to get home for some weekends by sharing the driving with other colleagues and friends. I recall we used to return in the early hours of the Monday morning and regularly stopped in Dorset at an all-night eating place, which meant we could possibly skip breakfast as the ship was invariably putting to sea early and exercises were usually planned to happen very soon after leaving harbour. There were week-ends when the ship was either docked in Portsmouth or Plymouth, and it was during one of these brief visits that another development took place regarding the perils of separation and family issues.

One evening after supper a knock came at the door of the PO's Mess and someone opened the door. The call came out from Paul Hankins, "Petty Officer Nixon, visitor!" When I went to the door a close friend of mine said to me, "John, would you be able to drive me to a street in Portsmouth tomorrow morning? I've got something I need to attend to and wondered if you could help me." I naturally said I would be happy to do that as I could see he was concerned and it was clearly important to him.

The next morning we met on the jetty and got into my car and set off towards the city. I had known for some time that he was having problems at home but wasn't aware of all the details. However, he started to open up and provide detail as we drove along towards the street he had asked me to take him to. He explained that while we had been away in Portland, his wife had called a gas engineer to fix an appliance, and to cut a long story short a relationship had developed between them. In spite of having two very young children, this had progressed to the point whereby a divorce had been agreed and, to make things more stable for his children, the gas man and my friend's wife had agreed that adoption of the children would be the best thing for them. I was naturally saddened to hear this but by the time my friend had explained all of this we had arrived at the required destination. My friend said, "Can you wait here for a few minutes, John, and we can then get back to the ship." I said he should take his time, but looked on in some disbelief as he walked towards his wife and their two small children.

His wife remained in her position and the children ran forward about 10 metres to greet their father. He stooped down to put his arms around them and said some words of re-assurance to them and patted them on their shoulders. After a few minutes, he gave them a final hug and ushered his children back towards his wife, and returned to my car. He didn't seem as upset as I would have anticipated, but I could nevertheless tell it was a difficult ordeal for him and he was putting on a brave face. We drove back to the ship to resume our duties for the day – my perspective was not to blame anyone in particular but it probably re-enforced my view that human beings all have needs, both physical and mental, and the long periods of separation both husbands and wives endured came with enormous risks for their marriages.

It was difficult to see anything positive in this situation and the sense of being out of control in one's life when connected to sea-going periods within the Royal Navy became more etched in my psyche. I realised my own family life was also at risk, even though I knew Carol and I were strong and loyal to one another, and that our first concerns were for the welfare of our children.

****

Once we had completed sea trials and Workup the ship went on a series of visits that meant me being away from home for about six weeks at a time. For most of my colleagues and friends, life was often about killing time with our work until we could get back home. I was always looking for opportunities to call Carol to find out how everyone was and I recall one such time in Finland, when we were visiting Helsinki. One afternoon I jogged, as I often did at the end of a working day when we were alongside, to a small town which had a large post office where it was possible to make long-distance calls. These were not possible on board for various reasons – only in an emergency at sea could we arrange a call via one of the ship's HF transmitters and receivers. After registering my requirements with one of the staff, I sat down in a large waiting area for my turn to enter one of the phone booths and remember thinking, 'what are you doing in this place, John?' Whilst people were generally friendly, I had absolutely no connection to any of them or the local area. These realisations, which occurred quite often in my periods away from home, always made me feel isolated in the world. However, it was reassuring to finally get to enter the small sound-proofed booth and pick up the phone and have time to talk in person with Carol and the children, although it accentuated the sense of isolation when I finished the call and had to jog back to the ship.

One of my close friends was REMN1 Gordon McDermott, who worked with another good friend – a Chief Radio Electrician - on the 993 radar system. Being fellow 'Pinkies' we often had chats over a cup of coffee in the 993 Office as I sometimes needed to borrow some specialist test equipment from them. Gordon and I had got to know each other because our daughters, both called Lisa, went to the same school in Stubbington where Gordon lived. We often shared lifts to and from Portsmouth dockyard and conversations about the ship's programme and how our daughters were doing at school. I recall that Gordon experienced a mishap whilst working on a defective television as it suddenly started producing a strobing effect at a particular frequency that caused Gordon to experience a fit. This kind of event, although rare and no reflection on what Gordon was actually doing, illustrated the many hazards of working with electronic equipment. This danger would be something that affected me through the experience of another colleague in the coming year.

In early September, *Falmouth* sailed up the eastern side of the British mainland to join a NATO exercise in the North Atlantic off Iceland. This voyage was to be one of the worst experiences of my career and would match my first day in *Falmouth*, but extend over a period of three weeks. I recall sitting on the quarterdeck with a cup of coffee after supper as we sailed north at speed past some spectacular scenery off Scotland, where we briefly paused for some exercises. However, as the ship continued north we hit some of the worst sea conditions that one could ever imagine. I resigned myself to the fact that I would have to face down some difficulties in my working arrangements during this period in order to get by.

The weather system that caused such mountainous waves was the work of 'Hurricane Ella,' which was initially anticipated to make landfall in the United States. What happened, however, was that Ella turned out to sea and combined with a frontal system over the North Atlantic. By the 4th September, Ella was classified as a 'category 4' hurricane with winds reaching 140 mph at storm force 12 on the Beaufort scale. RMS *Queen Elizabeth 2* was in close proximity to us and even a vessel of 80,000 tonnes, as we heard from various communications between ships, was badly tossed around such that a number of people were physically injured, including broken bones. Waves were recorded as reaching a height of 50 feet and as I looked out of the porthole in the PO's Mess the imagery before me was indeed discouraging – it was difficult to know how such a small vessel of 2,800 tonnes could stay afloat in those conditions. Clearly, the Officer of the Watch was choosing the right path to avoid 'broadside' waves hitting the ship, which could have been catastrophic. One minute we were in a deep valley and all we saw to the side of us was a wall of sea as the ship lurched, shuddered and banged violently from side to side. A few seconds later the view out of the porthole was that of being on a hill top and looking down 80 feet to the trough of the wave we had just risen out of. One second, therefore, my body felt like it was twice my actual weight, and the next I felt almost weightless. The effect on my stomach (and head) was as expected and I was confined to my bunk or in the toilets for days on end. In between time I swayed through the main passageway to check my equipment and made running repairs with my bucket alongside me. The ship was sustaining upper-deck damage and when lying on my bunk, the movements were so violent that bottles of various liquids were regularly smashing 'inside' our lockers. I remember lying on my bunk, not being able to attend meals, and literally praying to die over and over again. For someone who loved nature, pottering around at home and playing with my children in the back garden, the environment I was now confined within was an anathema.

This is when Nigel Butterworth came to my rescue and I can only hope that one day he will read this book and see my acknowledgement of his help. He wasn't being as badly affected as I was and could stumble his way to the dining room for meals. However, he realised that I couldn't manage it so he collected some soup in a cup and picked up some dry bread from the dining room as he knew this was about all I could manage. He then stumbled back down the passageway, carefully holding the cup no doubt, to appear next to my bunk with some typical words of comfort you'd expect from an engineer; "Here you are, mate, see if you can keep this down – you're all the same, you Greenies!" To the average person in the street this might not seem like a big deal, but in my predicament it was a life-line. I think this principle is something everyone should know – the smallest acts of kindness we offer in our lives often have the greatest impact on others.

However, things were to get worse for me on the trip. Because I had been confined, unofficially, to my bunk there were defects building up with my equipment and it was clear that I would need to change the radar unit in the 903 director once an opportunity arose. This opportunity came a few days later when the ship was forced to enter a bay off Iceland so that repairs to the ship's steering system could be carried out. I knew that I would have only about 12-18 hours to work on my radar, get it fixed, and retire to my bunk once we returned back to the hellish conditions we were in amongst. Therefore, once we had anchored in the designated bay and the ship became still, I went to the 4.5 TS to start preparing for the radar change and testing I desperately needed to do. At this point, however, one of the departmental Chiefs came into the office and said to me, "Petty Officer Nixon, I'm allocating you the task of doing a book of reference (BR) muster and you'll have to do it before the end of the day."

This routine task, that all departments had to do every six months, involved someone – me in this case – walking around all the sections in our department and identifying BRs and then recording their presence and making sure they were up to date with modifications and amendments. This unexpected development made me see red as I wouldn't have enough time spare to do this task before we sailed again. At that point, whilst sitting in my chair, I calmly but firmly explained that I had urgent repairs to make and that I could do the BR muster once we were heading back from our exercise. However, he suddenly slammed the door behind him and threatened me with disciplinary action in an aggressive manner. I immediately stood up and squared up to him and we shared some frank words with each other to put it mildly. Luckily for both of us, he stomped out of the room and I didn't do the BR muster and managed to complete the repairs successfully on my radar system. Although my reaction was understandable, and my work priorities were based on a sound and defensible rationale, I had come within a cat's whisker of being charged with disobeying a direct order and facing some very serious consequences.

I had stuck to my guns and faced the situation down, but there would be one sting in the tail to come later in the year as a result of my defiance, when this Chief called me to be reprimanded by the WEO in his cabin for a minor technical mistake that I made while preparing for a practise 4.5-inch gun shoot with a towed aircraft target. Luckily, however, I was given what one might term a 'slap on the wrist' as the fault was cleared well before the aircraft arrived. Although I was permitted to personally remove my cap before receiving my reprimand, the event was designed to bring some level of humiliation to me personally.

The exercise off Iceland continued in the same vein, although the sea conditions improved a little over the next two weeks. However, I recall the ship going into a 'pre-wetting' simulated nuclear fallout environment exercise when all the hatches were closed such that the upper deck could be sprinkled with a wall of water. The poor air quality – which smelt like stale food - that we experienced within the ship due to internal circulation, and the degradation in the quality of food due to our long period at sea added to the misery and I really longed for a time when I could walk along the beach in the fresh air at our home in Hill Head.

The NATO exercise finished with a beard growing competition among the senior ratings. Once in calmer waters as we sailed south in the Irish Sea, an award was given to my good friend George Norrie on the flight deck for having the best beard and there was the usual singing and quiz nights in the PO's Mess for up-channel night.

Although I was young and strong enough to recover from these experiences, my general health was gradually deteriorating and it was about this time in my life that I first started experiencing bouts of what might count as clinical depression. I often pondered on how to escape from the life that I, and uncertain circumstances, had manufactured for myself and my family. However, for now I was only interested in sitting on the small wall outside the Gosport ferry terminal, and seeing Carol driving round the corner in our new Morris 1100 Estate to pick me up and take me home.

****

As we entered 1979 the ship's programme was confirmed and we were indeed scheduled to go on a Far East deployment that would last for more than six months. This was something that filled me with dread as I would be absent for so long, miss important developments in the children and naturally be away from Carol for such a long time. She was strong, loyal and highly competent as a wife, but having witnessed the episodes I had with my two close friends I clearly thought something similar could easily happen to me. However, in spite of chronic sea sickness, my career was progressing well and after sitting my Professional Qualifying Examination (P.Q.E.) for REMN1 I was awarded a very good pass and promoted to Chief Petty Officer on the 12th March, 1979 – less than a year after joining *Falmouth*. I was 26 years old and had reached this milestone just about as fast as possible with my background.

I was therefore moved to the CPO's Mess just along the passageway from the PO's Mess, which brought with it some extra living space in the lounge area, and a less cramped sleeping section. It was about this time that Carol and I decided that we should have a family portrait produced while the children were young and we were 'in our prime.' As the time approached for our long deployment I remember being ashore in uniform on the Isle of Wight during Cowes week, when it was suggested by one of the 'yachties' there that life on board a Royal Navy ship must be exciting and lots of fun. Overall, this wasn't such a bad description in the right environment and circumstances, but my experiences over the previous year had left me run down both physically and mentally. My answer, therefore, was more of a description of how difficult it was to work on complicated equipment while being sea sick for a large part of the time.

Photo 70 - Family portrait taken while at Elsfred Road in 1979

Source: author

In late March the event that would affect my capacity to complete the deployment to the Far East started to emerge. In the days leading up to Easter week-end I noticed some discomfort in two or three of my front teeth. The first feelings were of slight pain and numbness. As I was not fond of visiting dentists I called into the Sick Bay and asked for some pain killers in the expectation that it would soon go away. Unfortunately, over the week-end my symptoms became more intense and I had no alternative other than to visit the dentist in HMS *Nelson* on the Monday morning. I explained what I was feeling – my teeth had become more painful and the numbness had increased – and the dentist gave me an X-ray. After placing a card behind my front teeth while the machine clicked and whirred, he showed me there was an oblong-shaped lesion clearly visible at the level of the top of my teeth and that he thought it was probably a cyst. As it would require specialist attention I would have to visit a dental surgeon at the Navy's Haslar hospital in Gosport and have more tests done. I was given an appointment, which was about three weeks away and returned to my duties. Whilst at home every evening in the week, however, my pain levels started to increase significantly and my face began to swell up quite dramatically.

It was so bad that the Sick Bay at HMS *Collingwood* delivered some more powerful pain killers to my home during the early hours of the morning as sleeping was impossible. Carol said to me, "Your face is so swollen now you are beginning to look like Pooh Bear!" I therefore called the dentist and told them what was happening and was given an appointment to see the specialist the following day. I remember visiting the oral surgery department at Haslar and being met by the tall, dark-haired, and quite imposing Surgeon Commander Keeble in a crisp white coat, accompanied by one of his colleagues. They could see my face was swollen and immediately started doing some tests that involved passing electrical currents through my teeth. As I lay in the green leather chair and looked at the light above me, he touched a probe onto my teeth in turn and turned up the current until I could feel it. For the three teeth at the front/right, however, I answered, "No, Sir" when he asked me if I could feel anything. I then had a 360 degree x-ray done of my head, which involved sitting in a chair with a circular cage around my skull that rotated whilst taking the x-rays. After analysing the results with his colleague, the Surgeon said, "You definitely have got a cyst growing in your jaw that is basically destroying the roots of your teeth and surrounding tissue. It will need to be removed surgically under general anaesthetic as soon as possible before it does much more damage."

I was a bit shocked about how serious my condition appeared to be and asked him if I would lose these teeth. He said they would do their best to save them but if the cyst wasn't removed completely it would spread and do more damage to my jaw and teeth. Because of the seriousness of my condition he said, "We will schedule your surgery for this Thursday and you need to come into hospital on Wednesday morning." When I returned to the waiting room, Carol listened with concern to my summary but was surprised about how well I had taken the news of possibly losing three teeth. We soon returned home and started getting my clothes and other essential items ready. The next day she dropped me off at Haslar hospital.

Haslar itself could take up a chapter of its own in my story as it had one of the richest histories of any hospital, military or otherwise, in the whole country. Built in the reign of George I, it was the biggest brick-built hospital in England and opened as a Royal Navy hospital in 1753. It provided medical care to service personnel both in peacetime and in war. One of its most famous physicians, Dr James Lind – who practiced there from 1758 until 1785 - played a major role in discovering a cure for scurvy, not least through his pioneering use of a double blind methodology with Vitamin C supplements (limes) (BBC, 2008). Because Haslar also had a history of providing an asylum for treating sailors with psychiatric conditions, in conjunction with the many service men and women who died there, it always had associated stories of ghosts from bygone days remaining in some parts of the hospital and was affectionately known as the 'boneyard' by many of its nursing staff. Unlike the typical hospital of today, however, it had expansive gardens and grounds with benches and trees, so recovering patients could often be seen strolling around the grounds being escorted by a nurse or MA. It certainly was an impressive institution.

After walking along its highly polished floors and passageways, I was admitted to the oral surgery ward in B Block. Although I was naturally apprehensive, I was quickly made to feel at home by the wonderful nurses of the QARNNS and male MAs that the Navy had. The nurses all wore light blue dresses with a white hat and apron, and many had a watch pinned to their dresses for taking patients' pulses. The MAs wore blue serge trousers and a white high-necked top with short sleeves. I was in a large 'Florence Nightingale' open ward and could see all the other patients – some were sitting up recovering in bed and some were clearly awaiting surgery or to be seen by Surgeon Commander Keeble or other doctors. I quickly got to know one Able Seaman (AB) in the bed next to me. He had blonde hair and a friendly demeanour, and we started exchanging stories about why we, and others, were in hospital. It seemed that the majority were either having wisdom teeth removed or had suffered things like broken jaws – which was his case and he, like me, was due for surgery the next day.

As was often the case, colleagues in the Navy often made witty comments or joked about their predicaments to lessen their stress levels and those of others. In this vein, with a wry smile on his face and his mouth more or less closed permanently because of the pain he was in, my new friend said, "Apparently they wire up your jaw to keep it in place until the bones knit together, and the one thing you have to avoid is 'throwing up' otherwise they have to get a pair of wire cutters to you 'asap' - otherwise you choke!" I said, "I'm in here to have a cyst removed as my wife's had enough of me looking like Pooh Bear!" We both chuckled while holding our jaws and watching the nurses checking us out for finding agony to be a humorous subject! One of the MAs laughed and suggested, "You two need an injection to keep you quiet," or words to that effect. After settling down for a few hours the surgeon came to my bed with his staff to examine me.

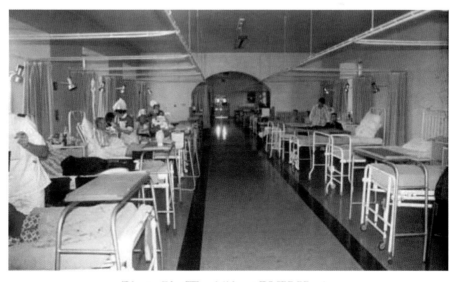

Photo 71 - Ward life at RNH Haslar

Source: RNH Haslar Heritage Group (photo taken in the 1960s), by kind permission

He immediately looked concerned about the swelling of my face, which had increased rapidly to the point that it was almost level with the tip of my nose. Turning to his colleague he authoritatively said, "We need to see Chief Nixon later this afternoon in our office to drain the cyst. It's growing rapidly and we can't bring forward his surgery." Indeed I was in tremendous pain and getting more concerned every time I saw myself in the mirror. At 2.00 pm, in pyjamas, I went down to the outpatient clinic where I had been seen the day before, and sat in the green chair once more. The experience I was just about to have would probably be the most painful of my entire life.

The surgeon said, "Unfortunately we can't give you an anaesthetic and we have to insert two needles into the cyst – one to pump in and one to drain the fluid. However, I will put some cream on your gum to try and numb it." I lay back and let out loud hissing noises as first one needle and then another was pushed deep into the cyst. The pain and my hissing intensified through the pushing and pulling of the needles to remove the fluid and the surgeon said, "Grip the seat with your hands – I know this is painful but we have to do it." The procedure only lasted a few minutes but I returned to the ward feeling like a tortured animal, and went immediately to bed to 'lick my wounds.' I glanced at my diary and noted the date – it was March 28th - my anniversary for joining *Falmouth*. Perhaps the soothsayer's warning message to Julius Caesar concerning his welfare, "Beware the Ides of March," (Shakespeare, 1599) was beginning to apply to me although the precise date referred to in the Roman calendar for the 'Ides' was the 15th March. Nevertheless, this month was turning out to be a bad omen in my life and has always remained my least favourite time of the year.

My new friend cheered me up a bit later after tea when he thoughtfully said, "Hey, I didn't realise you were a Chief Petty Officer – you look too young to be one!" We were both given a sign on our beds saying 'nil by mouth' after supper by one of the nurses, who had a certain reassuring manner as she moved away and walked around the ward checking on other patients. During the early hours the lights were turned off and the nursing staff used torches to move around the ward checking patients and administering to their needs. At the end of the ward on the left-hand side was a large desk where they regularly gathered to discuss cases, and could therefore immediately see anyone who needed their attention. On reflection I have to say that this method of nursing is in stark contrast to modern-day nursing and procedures on hospital wards, where sleeping is almost impossible because of constant noises, lights being on and sectioned-off areas for patients, which mean that nurses are not readily visible to patients. In our case, all we had to do was put up a hand or call out and the nurses would be at our bed sides in seconds.

The next morning two nurses came to my bed and my neighbour's bed too and gave us a pre-med injection to calm us down. We were both moved onto wheeled beds and then to an area near the end of the ward where the nurses placed curtains around our beds and we were told to relax and wait to be taken to theatre. We carried on talking to each other through the curtains despite the effects of the pre-med, but the jokes and exchanges diminished until we were wheeled down to the preparation room. One of the anaesthetists came out and checked my details, and after inserting a small needle into my wrist I was quickly asleep.

The next thing I remember was starting to gain consciousness in the ward itself rather than the recovery room. I felt the hand of one of the nurses gently stroking my left arm and calling my name, and saying to her colleague, "I'm not sure why it always happens to those with red hair." Once I had come round a little more I could see her angelic face and that I was in the bed next to the nurses' desk. I was receiving quite a lot of fuss and monitoring from them and being asked, "Are you okay now – how are you feeling?" I have always remembered this moment in my life and the care of that particular nurse who held my arm, to whom I am eternally grateful. Such small acts of kindness can have a significant impact on a patient's recovery and remain with them for the rest of their lives. At the time of writing this book I would find out, through contact with former nurses and MAs at Haslar, the name of my staff nurse so I could pass on my thanks to her.

The following day I was moved back to the bed next to my friend, who had returned to the ward before me the day before. It was good to hear him as we settled down to resting and recovering. By now I could feel the extent of my surgery as I had lost three of my teeth and could feel stiches intertwining my gums and teeth, and there was now a large gap. The stiches went from the middle left-hand side to the middle of the right side of my upper gums. It felt serious – and it was. Nevertheless, my friend and I quickly began making light of what had happened and made comments to cheer ourselves up. We would both have to be in hospital for more than a week to recover.

Later that day I was seen first by the surgeon, who came and sat on my bed and examined his handy work. For some reason I knew that my surgery had not been without incident and the impression in my mind was that something had gone wrong and it had had to be cut short. I therefore said, "Did it all go to plan, Sir?" He assured me that it had been a surgical success and that an infection had started to attack the cyst, which had made the swelling worse. However, the cyst had been removed as planned. Indeed, I had been given very large doses of antibiotics before the surgery – which continued now on the ward. He explained that my gums and jaw would need three months or more to recover and after that I could then have a denture made for me. Luckily the swelling was already beginning to come down slightly. The first time I saw myself in the mirror and smiled I was rather shocked as there was a large gap with black stitches and I spoke in that familiar and 'floppy' way people do with missing teeth.

Over the coming week my friend in the next bed and I began to talk about our post-surgery conditions as day-to-day activity continued around the ward. I could see that his jaw was well and truly wired up and that talking was difficult for him. As the days went by I was pleased to be visited by Carol and the children. I was concerned that my surgery had 'ruined my good looks' but Carol, as always, took everything in her stride and mostly focussed her comments on encouraging me to get better so I could go home and get back to normal.

Every evening before bed time, the patients who were recovered enough to do some 'chores' gathered in the ward's kitchen to make hot drinks for the patients who were confined to bed. This was always a fun event as two or three patients in pyjamas – the walking wounded so to speak - came round pushing the famous trolley, stopping at each bed and saying, "Hot chocolate, Horlicks, coffee or tea, mate?" They would then prepare the required drink while the nurses and MAs went about their own tasks. I always had Horlicks and while relaxing my neighbour and I would play some card games or Scrabble. Playing Scrabble was something I was good at because we played it a lot at home with the children, and consequently he lost almost every game. He rather graciously remarked one evening, however, that he could see why I was a Chief Petty Officer at such a young age, and no wonder he couldn't win a game. I was never much of a card player though so he definitely had the upper hand on that score. My young friend was indeed good company whilst I was in Haslar.

Despite the trauma of my surgery I did return to full health quite quickly and played sport as usual. The 'blessing in disguise' my episode in hospital had brought about was that Surgeon Cdr Keeble issued instructions to the drafting authorities that I was to be posted to a local shore establishment for at least six months so I could have the necessary follow-up appointments and treatment. When I asked him to clarify my position about the Far East deployment before I left Haslar, he said, "You will not be going on any deployment so you can put that out of your mind." On the 24th April I received notification that I would be drafted back to HMS *Collingwood*.

Although I had been through a very painful ordeal I felt it had been worth it in some ways when compared with the reality of being away from my family for six months. Before I left the ship, a new Deputy WEO had kindly taken measures to have me classified as a 'big ships' rating due to chronic sea sickness. Despite my woes over the year I had been categorised as 'superior' in the way I conducted my work, but it was clear to my associates that I was too badly affected by motion sickness. I was therefore relieved of my duties whilst still on sick leave by someone I had briefly known in my earlier days in *Collingwood*, called REMN1 'Stan' Stanbridge. Unfortunately I did not meet him as I was still on sick leave until the 25th May, when I arrived back at HMS *Collingwood* to work as a radar instructor. I would be facing my first official instructing duties in due course – with three missing front teeth.

My life aboard HMS *Falmouth* had indeed been a mixed blessing with many challenges and difficult personal circumstances to observe and deal with – both for myself and for some of my closest friends. It is perhaps significant to recall that, despite being a footballer of some standing in the Navy, I had not represented *Falmouth* as there had been very little time for serious sporting recreation. My focus had been on surviving the challenges of my technical job and the impacts on my health and welfare, culminating in extensive surgery, a long recovery period and some very difficult personal challenges along the way. It is also relevant that Carol and the children were becoming more independent of me as a family, which they had to in order to manage their own situation when I was 'absent.' Six months in *Collingwood*, therefore, would provide some recovery time in more ways than one.

VII - HMS *Kent* & HMS *Falmouth* [1979-82]

My time in HMS *Collingwood* to recover from surgery and be a laboratory instructor for the 993 radar system lasted for the anticipated six months. I had a number of excellent friends and colleagues in my section, which was headed by Lt Farrow who ran the department with a great deal of consideration and balance. He was a Special Duties (SD) Officer and therefore had worked his way up through the non-commissioned officer ratings' route and, in general, officers like him were often more aware of the pressures and influences that affected people in my position at that time. Also among the staff was my good friend, POREL Gary Taylor, who we had known in Mauritius. Gary, his wife Frances, and their two children Terena and Louise, were now our neighbours in Elsfred Road. Also among the staff was a friendly POREL, whose name I have forgotten now, but he helped me a great deal with regard to what to expect when I finally got my first dentures from the dentist as he proudly wore his own set of 'partial uppers' and had any number of stories about how to 'live with them.'

I worked in my own laboratory, which had five complete radar sets and a radar aerial on the top of the building for when we were actually transmitting – most of the time we connected the system to what were known as 'dummy aerials' (which absorbed the signals) as there were always local restrictions on what we could transmit for training purposes. My classes were usually four or five JREMs under training, which brought me back to my own time at *Collingwood* as a 16 year-old. Despite the embarrassment I felt when talking to my classes because of my missing teeth, I did enjoy this experience as there was always a good deal of practical work after I had covered the theoretical aspects of the course. The trainees had a manual they worked from to complete their maintenance and repair tasks and my job at that point was to observe and supervise them and answer their questions. At the end of the course they completed a written and practical exam.

After about four months and several trips back to see the surgeon at Haslar, where I would be x-rayed to check the cyst had not returned, my gums were sufficiently healed for me to have my first set of dentures made by the dentist at *Collingwood*. Throughout this period I had felt uncomfortable about how I looked and sounded to my family, and Carol in particular, but when I finally arrived home at the end of the day in September with my new teeth 'installed' I smiled with the intention of showing them off and that I was 'back to normal' but Carol didn't notice the difference until I pointed it out. I grappled with the problems of eating, which will be familiar to anyone who has partial uppers (or lowers), but eventually got used to wearing them although I was always wary of being seen without them.

By this time my next draft had been decided. I was assigned the role of 903 radar maintainer for HMS *Kent*, a larger guided missile destroyer (GMD) at 6,200 tonnes – consistent with my 'big ships' category. These 'County Class' Destroyers (more accurately 'cruisers' because of their tonnage), had good sea-keeping abilities and long range with an impressive top speed of 32.5 knots. *Kent* was a Portsmouth-based ship that had been active as an escort warship for the aircraft carriers HMS *Victorious*, HMS *Eagle*, and HMS *Hermes* in the Atlantic, Indian, and Pacific Oceans during the 1960s.

As my responsibilities were essentially the same as those in HMS *Falmouth*, I did not require any further specialist training and arrived on board *Kent* on the 22nd October, 1979. My new 'home' was Number 2 CPO's Mess, which was situated along the spacious main corridor of the ship. *Kent* was impressive and full of high-tech equipment, as all the GMDs were, and had good seaworthiness compared with *Falmouth*.

Photo 72 - Guided Missile Destroyer HMS *Kent* leaving Singapore

*Source: Tony Lee by kind permission (picture taken in the late 1960s),
http://www,countyclassdestroyers.co.uk/photos.htm*

My first impression when I walked up the gangway was that she was a good looking ship and quickly noticed the large flight deck, the light-wooded upper decks with tar in between each segment, and long ladders with wooden hand rails that led from the flight deck to the quarterdeck. She was bristling with missile systems and associated aerials and directors, and also had twin 4.5-inch gun turrets – unlike later GMDs of her class, which only had one. Just behind and above the aft 4.5-inch gun turret were the 903 radar aerial and director, which I was to be responsible for.

It wasn't long before I made good friends with my colleagues in the Chief's Mess, some of whom had joined with me from *Collingwood* – including Chief Radio Mechanician Derek Kimber, who was a tall man with blonde hair who had taught me the GDS5 system at *Collingwood* before I joined *Falmouth*. He was a highly confident person with a strong personality and was now the Section Chief for the Sea Slug Sea to Air Missile (SAM) system. Among my new messmates there were many people of similarly high calibre who were at the top of their games and the senior 'middle managers' of the ship. The President of the Mess was a larger-than-life Charge Chief Petty Officer Engineer called Ted Hodges, who was in his late 30s and had a beard. He gave me a warm welcome and showed me to me new bunk and locker. At the age of 27 I was one of the younger and least experienced Chiefs with only six months' seniority. One of my closest friends that would emerge was an engineer called Tom Heath-Webb. He was short in stature with a beard and had an interest in squash, played the ukulele, was highly intelligent – which helped him to beat many seemingly bigger and more powerful opponents at squash – and was somewhat of a performer with his ukulele as he was brave enough to play, sing and tell jokes at various musical evenings. However, he had the ingredients to be a 'Napoleon' by nature and was not averse to cursing and gesticulating at other motorists if they had upset him one way or another when we shared lifts to and from the ship. He was certainly a character and one people messed with at their peril.

As I sat in the lounge for the first time I noticed a large electronic board hanging on one of the bulkheads (walls) with all of our names on it in neat rows and columns. When someone from outside wanted to speak to one of us, they pressed a small control panel next to the door with our name on and a buzzer sounded inside the Mess and the required person's name lit up on the board. This was a clever little system that had apparently been built and fitted by one of the 'Greenie' Chiefs and was another sign of the skills and initiative of senior non-commissioned officers that were my new peers. I fairly quickly settled down in my new accommodation but on the work front there was to be an early and 'fast ball' for me to deal with, and soon after that some unexpected news from one of my colleagues from HMS *Falmouth*.

****

The ship was still in harbour awaiting our first exercise in the English Channel. I had been down to find the 4.5-inch TS the night before my official start date to find my bearings, and had seen that the equipment was more or less identical to what I had worked on before. However, when I reported to the WEO I was told that there was a personnel problem within the Radar and Communications Section and that I was the most likely candidate to fill a vacant position. It was further explained to me that the Charge Chief Petty Officer of that section had been drafted elsewhere for compassionate reasons and that the section was now being run, temporarily, by a Petty Officer and there were no other CPOs in the section who could be given the task. Charge Chiefs were responsible for whole departments, not just sections as I had been expected to run. This new role for me, if it was agreed by various WE Section Officers, would involve me being promoted to a 'Local Acting' (L/A) Charge Chief and I would be responsible for all the senior and junior ratings who worked in the Radio and Communications Section – about 20 altogether.

I was therefore sent to discuss this with the WE Officer in charge, Lt Cdr Hall, and the Section Officer, Lt Samuel. Lt Cdr Hall was of medium build and in his 30s and had short and neat dark hair. He was a General List (GL) officer who had entered the Navy directly from University at Dartmouth College, and although I could quickly see that he had an endearing side to him, he did come across as being rather aloof and somewhat suspicious by nature. He obviously believed in maintaining differentials between officers and ratings and my instinct was that he could make life difficult for those under his charge although I did appreciate he would undoubtedly be under pressure from the WEO and Captain for the operational capability of the equipment. Lt Samuel, in contrast, was an SD officer who had worked his way up from the 'lower deck.' He was short and stocky in stature with a moderate Welsh accent and a warm and enthusiastic personality. He was clearly someone with a keen focus on doing things properly and I sensed he would be supportive of his staff. If I were to be given my new role, I would be working directly under Lt Samuel but my overall boss would be Lt Cdr Hall, who would lead weekly planning meetings I would attend to plan work and solve any issues in the department.

They both acknowledged that I was a newly-promoted CPO and that Charge Chiefs were usually much more experienced and in their mid-30s, so I would have to 'rise to the occasion,' so to speak. In addition, I had not been trained in the management tools and other administrative skills that regular Charge Chiefs were. On the plus side, I would be given all the privileges of a Charge Chief as well as a pay rise. After speaking to the person who was then in post, POREL Chris Russell, who clearly seemed keen to hand the task on to someone of CPO level, it was agreed that I would take on this new position. I could also see that PO Russell was somewhat troubled and didn't seem particularly happy about life in general – he was doing his duty very well but had some kind of burden on his shoulders. In some private conversations with him he explained the main reason why, although I believe it is too personal a matter to repeat in this book. Suffice it to say, as was usually the case for such a feeling of resignation that was so apparent in him, it was related to his family inasmuch as something untoward had occurred at home that he could have possibly prevented from happening if he were a 'free man.' In that sense, I was pleased to ease his burden somewhat as he would soon be able to return to his section responsibilities and not have the weight of the whole department on his shoulders in addition to his family difficulties.

Generally speaking, I relished this new challenge as it meant me moving back to 'mainstream' communications and radar work that I had been doing whilst serving in *Bulwark* and *Mauritius*. However, I would be in charge of several people and I was not familiar with at least some of the equipment that my new staff would be looking after. I would therefore be somewhat compromised in my new role.

The following morning at 8.00 am all members of my new section were mustered in the EMR - my new office – when Lt Cdr Hall and Lt Samuel walked in ahead of me to introduce me as their new Charge Chief. Standing in rows along the work benches of the EMR and into the large running machinery room adjoining the EMR were the Petty Officers and junior ratings that I would now be responsible for. I was pleased to see that they looked quite a friendly and amenable group but they all clearly gave me searching glances and muted smiles or nods as I stood there next to the two officers. We were both weighing each other up one way or another and they knew I was being 'parachuted' into my new position.

Although I was still in some shellshock about what had transpired, I knew that I wanted to speak to my new team 'alone' at the earliest opportunity and after the introductions and explanations were over, Lt Samuel asked me if I wanted to say anything at that point. I therefore moved one step forward and gave a brief speech on why I was drafted to the ship and that this new job, which I was very pleased to taking up, would be a challenge for me and I would need the support of everyone if we were to be an efficiently-run department. I also made it clear that I would like to meet everyone individually over the following days and also collectively in their respective sections so I could find out more about their equipment and responsibilities. I said that we would need to establish some ground rules which would help in the running of the department. When the meeting ended, everyone seemed to respond well, and with one or two smiles and some brief chit chat, they all returned to their relevant sections. I immediately started a hand-over process with POREL Russell. A new and exciting challenge was now before me but I had yet another steep learning curve to face.

A week later, whilst on week-end leave at home, I received a telephone call from Gordon McDermott. It was one of those calls no-one wants to receive, especially as I was settling down into my new and unexpected position in *Kent*. Gordon said, "I've got some bad news, John, I've just heard that your relief on *Falmouth*, Stan Stanbridge, died when the ship was on deployment off New Zealand." It turned out that Stephen, to give him his correct name, died of an electric shock on the 30th October while working on the GDS 5 equipment. Because of the high temperatures he had apparently been working without his shirt on, alone, and had leaned over one of the units he was working on and accidently touched a high voltage connector. This news sent a chill down my spine as I knew that Stephen was only serving on *Falmouth* because of my premature departure due to my surgery in Haslar. I felt a strong sense of guilt because he may not have died if I had not become ill, and his death badly affected me for a long time. However, looking back as I do now, I perhaps did not fully appreciate that I was now in a similar position myself having been given a new job because of someone else having to leave *Kent* early. This kind of substitution was extremely common for most service personnel, but I think it was because of my dread of the idea of being away for so long, and my wish to leave *Falmouth* before this happened, that left me feeling I had 'wished' it to happen in some way. It was another tribulation for me to endure as I turned my attention to the task ahead.

[158]

In the first few weeks we were on short exercises in the English Channel. When we first sailed out of Portsmouth Harbour I expected the ship to pitch and roll in the same manner that *Falmouth* had, but HMS *Kent* was very comfortable in even quite severe sea conditions and I quickly became more at ease with meeting my work commitments. There was also a great deal of room on the flight deck and upper deck so walking along the white and freshly-scrubbed wooden decks with a cup of coffee first thing in the morning was an enjoyable experience. The thing that really lifted me, however, was to discover in those early days what a tremendously talented and supportive staff I had inherited. The photograph below - one of my favourites with regard to my time at sea - shows us all together on the flight deck after about three months of me joining.

Photo 73 - The Radar and Radio Section, HMS *Kent*, 1980

Back row: LWEM(R) Grintner, R.Mech 2 Saunders, POREL Russell, Lt. Samuel, me, POREL Thorne, REA2 Michael Balding, LWEM(R) Butler; Front row: WEM(R) Bell, WEM(R) Park, LWEM(R) Hughes, WEM(R) Legg, WEM(R) McQueen, LWEM(R) Fudge, WEM(R) Holmes, WEM(R) Gray. **Source:** *author*

Because I valued equally the contributions of the section Petty Officers, who became my 'right-hand men,' I describe them now in alphabetical order, along with some of their staff. First of all, therefore, was REA2 Michael (Mick) Balding. He was an Artificer of about 24 years of age with a youthful appearance and an efficient, pleasant and relaxed air about him. He was one of the brightest and most intelligent among all of those I worked with in the Navy. However, he showed no sign of arrogance because of this, as was sometimes common among some Artificers, who, like Mick, generally had better educational backgrounds than other ratings. Whenever I needed a second opinion or advice on something I knew he would be familiar with, I stepped into the machinery room next to the EMR and found him working on the radar computer system he looked after. He would always pass the time of day with me as he passed through the EMR to his office, and never hesitated in offering his help. He did this in a manner that maintained his respect and appreciation of my position. Whenever he saw a situation that he felt I might be unsure about, he was at hand to chip in his sensible and logical observations.

[159]

His LWEM(R), 'Spike' Hughes, was tall with a slight beard and of a quiet, well-mannered and confident disposition. He was similarly supportive in taking charge of the younger WEM(R)s and matched very well the ethos Mick Balding established for his section. They also looked after the radar displays in the operations room just above the EMR and were an excellent team - there was never any concern from me that they were not on top of anything that came their way. I would often see them in the operations room working on one of the huge radar displays, with all kinds of dangerous voltages ever-present, and test equipment such as oscilloscopes illuminating the darkness around the display. We would chat about their thoughts on the problem to see if there was any help, support or advice I could offer. Indeed, one of my primary roles was to find out what my section Petty Officers needed to solve particular problems in terms of replacement parts or test equipment. We would first check if the required item was stored in the EMR, then the main Naval Stores, and if those options failed I would raise a signal with the Stores Department to have one flown to our next port of call. Alternatively, a helicopter could be flown to collect it from any ports we would be passing. Helping me in this task in the EMR was a very amiable and capable young man called WEM(R) (Sherlock) Holmes, and of course Lt Samuel, who I worked very closely with as he ultimately authorised signals and things like dockyard work requests prior to a maintenance period in harbour.

The next Petty Officer, who would go on to provide my children with their first 'rosetted' guinea pigs and be a close friend, was REMN2 'Sandy' Saunders. He was probably a little older than me and looked a 'real sailor' type with a respectable beer belly and a beard, which he would often twirl around his fingers when thinking or talking to others. I had known him from *Collingwood* and Mechanician's course, and he looked after the medium range 992 radar system with LWEM(R) Grintner and one of the WEM(R)s. They also made an excellent team and needed very little supervision from me personally. Sandy was particularly good at explaining problems and how he was going to solve them so that I never had any difficulty in explaining how long it would take to fix a fault when I briefed Lt Samuel at the end of the day in his office. He was also particularly talented when it came to teaching the staff something new in the EMR when we would muster at the start of the day or during stand easy. I remember LWEM(R)s Fudge, Grintner and Hughes and some others asking if they could re-arrange their duties as they all wanted to go to London to watch a *Genesis* concert, which of course the singer (and drummer) Phil Collins headed. I think they all appreciated my willingness to help them achieve this by getting various request forms and changes of duty roster signed by the Lt Samuel. I always felt a great sense of achievement when I could use my influence to do something to lift morale among those I was in charge of as the reciprocation from them was invaluable.

Petty Officer Henry Thorne, who maintained the long-range radar system, known as '965,' was one of the most loyal, capable and supportive colleagues one could wish to have. He had some very distinctive and reassuring mannerisms whenever he talked to me or others about the work that was going on in his section. He was of slim build with a slightly nervous temperament, and always had a wry smile on his face as he smoked one of the Navy's roll-up cigarettes. He often rolled his cigarettes next to my desk as we chatted over the day's work ahead and the planned maintenance forms I regularly passed on to all the section Petty Officers. His LWEM(R) was 'Rab' Butler, who, again, I could not speak too highly of. He was a senior LWEM(R) and always knew exactly how to get any problem fixed. He was always the first one to say, "Morning, Chief," and keep the WEM(R)s in line in his conciliatory manner of working. He was never hesitant in helping me personally to solve issues that affected me directly. The 965 Office was high up in the ship and it was necessary to climb some vertical ladders through deck hatches (in the main mast itself) to get to see them, as I often did on my rounds of the various sections. I can see from the photo (above) that Henry is standing next to me, and that tells me a lot about him as he was the type of 'familial' person who added to the sense of cohesion we enjoyed in the department.

What I appreciated about the working relationship I had with my staff is that it was never necessary for me to have harsh words with anyone as we were a co-operative group of people that worked well in supporting one another. The one person that caused me some minor difficulties, however, was a young man from Yorkshire, who I will refer to as WEM(R) Terref. He was about 18 years old, affectionately known by a nickname that reflected his slight build and wispy blonde hair. He was absolutely unique as an individual. This is because he stuck to his ways and hobbies in a manner that caused him some personal grief, which tended to make him a 'loner.' I feel it is worth spending some time on his story under my charge as it reflects many of the challenges some of us faced in a service that expected conformity in its various manifestations, and young Terref was having none of that – perhaps with a particular intention in his mind.

His main interest was rock and roll music of the 1950s, which immediately set him aside from others who preferred more contemporary pop music. However, he also took this to his clothes and always wore a black suit with tightly fitting trousers, pointed shoes, brightly coloured socks, a white shirt and a tie. When going ashore he changed to a 1950s Rockabilly hair style with a quiff that protruded out from his forehead. He tended to walk with a 1950s swagger and had possibly modelled himself on James Dean and his role in the film 'Rebel without a cause.' Although there was not a bad bone in his body, his behaviour was indeed that of a rebel without a cause and he was constantly being told off by various people for not having the right uniform on, being untidy in the mess deck, turning up a few minutes late for musters and generally responding to questions about his behaviour with comments like, "Sorry, Chief, I forgot all about that," or "I can't think what I've done with my cap," and so on. Rather cleverly on his part, he never fell into the category of being placed on a very serious charge but he kept accumulating various warnings from those of us above him as well as copious amounts of coaxing and coaching from the LWEM(R)s who lived in the Junior Ratings Mess with him.

We generally found WEM(R) Terref amusing and polite to work with as he was quite a comedian too. I remember one day in particular, when the ship was visiting Gibraltar, he came down to the EMR to collect something and I was working at my desk with Mick Balding and Henry Thorne discussing their work for the day. When he appeared in his full 1950s attire I said, "Very impressive, WEM(R) Terref – how about demonstrating one of your Rockabilly dances." I had heard about their fame from some of his messmates so I was keen to observe them for myself.

"Okay, Chief" came the confident reply and he duly put on some rock and roll music using a cassette player that he had with him. What we witnessed next was about the most impressive demonstration of rock and roll dancing I have ever seen. He performed his knee bends, arm shifts and swivels with such precision and timing, and without any outward sign of embarrassment, that he was given a loud round of applause by those present in the EMR. Having cheered everyone up, he went off on shore leave wearing a wide grin, presumably to seek out like-minded rock and rollers.

Rather than being punished severely for his numerous acts of rebellion, we adopted a strategy of giving him things to do to see if he would respond positively. The first thing I tried, with LWEM(R) Hughes, who as he was the Killick of the Junior Ratings' Mess, was to give him a full kit muster. This was an unusual test for someone like him while at sea as he was required to lay out all his kit on and around his bunk, and I was called to do the inspection - accompanied by LWEM(R) Hughes. As might have been anticipated it was quite poor and he produced a list of 'plausible' reasons why his kit wasn't up to standard. Indeed, it was difficult to do what was normally necessary in a shore establishment because of limited storage, laundry and ironing facilities. I said it wasn't good enough and he was given a repeat inspection for the following day. Although there was marginal improvement the result was more or less the same and he was given some advice about how to improve his appearance and kit – all to no avail. I discussed his case regularly with Lt Samuel and he received various warnings and minor punishments, but young Terref just continued in his ways. I suspected there was something more deep-rooted about his behaviour and had several personal discussions with him. However, the finale of his story was that he parted company with the Navy earlier than he might otherwise have done so.

I think he felt that the rigid discipline of the Navy wasn't for him and he wanted to do his own thing as a Rockabilly free spirit among his own kind, and he had embarked on a mission to 'work your ticket.' I often saw devout Christians struggling under similar conflicts as they also attracted attention and ridiculing from some of their peers – occasionally referring to them as 'Bible bashers.' However, I always admired people like WEM(R) Terref and sincerely hope he found his true way in life.

****

Although I was generally much happier serving in HMS *Kent* I did have some tribulations to deal with. The first one emerged about a month after I joined. We were scheduled to deploy for about three weeks and so Carol and the children would be left to their own devices once more. However, in the week before we sailed our car broke down and it quickly became apparent that the best remedy would be to have a new engine fitted. Carol relied totally on having a car while I was away so I frantically phoned various garages to find out which of them could replace an engine within two or three days. I found one garage in Portsmouth that said they could comply and so I took it there on the Wednesday, and was told to pick it up on the Friday evening. However, I was duty WE Senior Rating on the Friday and needed to find someone who could stand in for me. This 'sub' routine, as it was referred to, usually involved getting permission and sometimes a signature from one of the departmental officers, but because of the time pressure I was not able to follow that 'official' route and one of my friends agreed to do it for me on an informal basis. As it turned out I just about managed to get the car back and running properly for Carol before I left home.

The problem occurred because one particular influential officer had somehow found out about my unofficial duty swap and although I was not formally charged with anything, I was subjected to an ordeal that I could well have done without bearing in mind my last-minute rush to get the car fixed and also the negotiations regarding my Friday duty slot. The way he exacted his 'punishment' was to require me to undertake a joining examination that involved carrying out certain routines with running machinery and switching processes we might have to do as duty WE Senior Rating in an emergency. He knew that I should have been doing this preparation while I was attending to my broken-down car, and that I had not had the time to walk around the ship identifying all the necessary equipment and learning how to operate it. During my 'premature' test, he was sitting in a control room with another officer and saying to me, "For exercise, electrical supply to 'x' compartment down – set up emergency supply from 'y' point." I was then expected to go and perform this task so that he could see it had been done from his control position. Unfortunately, I had little idea of where to locate these supplies and returned to ask for clarification. Nevertheless, he repeatedly said, in a rather pompous manner, that I should have learned this by now and sent me out again to do 'my duty' and find out what to do and where to do it. After about half an hour of this charade, which I have to acknowledge was down to my lack of time and preparation, I saw red, glared at him, went through the hatch and slammed the door behind me as loudly as possible – the whole compartment reverberated with noise. I'm not sure what transpired immediately after that but I gave up playing his psychological game one way or another. This wasn't a good development, but luckily it was outside my mainstream work and didn't really affect me other than the details of this incident may have passed on to Lt Cdr Hall or Lt Samuel. It was another one of those family-service conflicts that quite often placed a tremendous amount of stress on me and others.

The second episode occurred when we were in Gibraltar. I had been playing football for the Chiefs and POs – scoring four of the best goals I have ever scored and in front of a reasonable crowd of locals who were lining the road above the pitch. It was one of those games in which everything I tried came off. I particularly remember one shot on the volley from about 25 yards that went flying straight into the top left-hand corner of the goal, which prompted cheering and clapping from those watching. This game was the one that got me back into playing football for my ship once more, as my playing days had lapsed on board *Falmouth* for the reasons noted in the previous chapter. The issue that emerged was my preference for playing sport and not drinking too much alcohol, which was in contrast to at least some of my colleagues in the Chief's Mess.

When I returned to the ship at about 4.00 pm there had been the usual Saturday afternoon drinking sessions going on and four or five of my fellow Chiefs were somewhat the worse for wear and laughing and joking as I entered the Mess. I could see what the atmosphere was like and jokingly said, "Have there been any fights going on yet?" One of the engineering Artificers, who I regarded as a friend in 'normal' circumstances, jumped to his feet and said, "No, but there is going to be one now!" He then came over to me and started prodding me in the chest and issuing some derogatory comments about 'Greenies.' If this had stopped after a few prods I would have laughed it off, but he persisted and became more threatening. I therefore moved out of the main lounge through the dividing curtain of the Mess and he followed me, continuing his prodding and pushing. I did this to move out of sight of the others - one being the Mess President - but once he passed through the curtain I forcefully grabbed him with both hands by his shirt, swung him round, lifted him into the air and then slammed him as hard as I could into the metal lockers in the accommodation area – which resulted in a loud bang that everyone heard. I then looked him straight in the face and said, "I'm ready when you are!" His face suddenly dropped and he sobered up very quickly – he declined my offer to continue and had a look of shock and horror on his face. He clearly had not anticipated my response. Our Mess President, Ted Hodges, called out, "Hey, you two pack it in!" This episode was a little unfortunate as I obviously had to live in very close proximity with my colleagues and although not much happened after this between me and my engineering friend, it highlighted some differences in social behaviour between us. However, my position on issues like this was that I would not compromise my principles no matter how much peer group pressure I received, and especially on excessive drinking, which I was now growing to loathe.

The service-family conflicts that most of us endured were illustrated further by a story told to me by another of my engineering friends in the Chief's Mess. After supper one evening I was sitting with this particular friend talking about issues that affected us at home. He said, "Yes, mate, it happens all the time. In my last ship we were in the States when I got news from my wife that she had been diagnosed with breast cancer and we have four children. Like all of us her parents were hundreds of miles away and I clearly needed to get home to help her and look after the children. However, when I asked the Engineer and Captain if I could be released for a few weeks they said I was a key person and refused to let me go. I was so desperate to get home that I got into my bunk, put my arm through the roll bars, and threw my body out of my bunk to deliberately break my arm. I reported sick and because of the seriousness of my break I was flown back to the UK and got back to my family to help out – albeit with a broken arm." This particular person was extremely responsible and sensible, but his story illustrated the means to which some people would go when they faced these matters – the Navy usually came first although, as I have already recounted, there was enormous variation depending on many factors – not least of which was how important you were considered to be regarding the fighting efficiency of the ship. We were also expected to operate as if we were at war regarding our presence on board the ships we served in.

When the ship was away at sea I always followed the same routine of having a nap after the mid-day meal. Before that in early December I read a letter dated 28th November, 1979 from Carol, which showed me what an impressively competent wife she was in looking after the home and the children while I was away. She describes the numerous DIY jobs she had been doing to keep herself occupied and to improve our home – including taking old cement bags to the tip and painting the kitchen after filling in cracks – supervising the children in swimming lessons and assisting them in writing a letter to me. Lisa, who was now nine years old, mentioned she could 'swim crawl with her head under the water' and play 'pees pudding hot, pees pudding cold' on her recorder; Philip mentioned he had 'had a cold and hoped that I was not sick' and that Christopher had been 'a naughty boy' (Lisa expanded on this as he had apparently put 'Vick vapour rub all over the washing'); Christopher, who was now four, wrote 'I hope you was well at Italy' and 'I helped mammy paint the wardrobe in my bedroom.' After reading these words and others I got into my bunk (another top one of three) to rest before our usual start of 1.30 pm. I had bought myself a cassette player and kept this with one particular tape I was fond of. As a form of escapism and meditation in dealing with separation and life aboard a warship at this time, I always listened to two ABBA tracks that captured my mood and thoughts – 'Eagle' (Andersson & Ulvaeus, Eagle, 1977) and 'Move On' (Andersson & Ulvaeus, Move on, 1978). The words that I focussed on while lying in my bunk were:

And I dream I'm an eagle, and I dream I can spread my wings/ flying high, high, like a bird in the sky; I'm an eagle that rides on the breeze.......

Like a roller in the ocean, life is motion - move on
Like a wind that's always blowing, life is flowing - move on
Like the sunrise in the morning, life is dawning - move on
How I treasure every minute, being part of it, being in it
With the urge to move on

I can see now that my love of nature, freedom of thought, expression and association, and the desire for time to pass by were at the heart of my choice of music at this time as I was often thinking about the safety and welfare of my family, and the comforts of home, which were all absent.

****

The deployments in HMS *Kent* were all enjoyable experiences if I ignore the influence of separation. We spent about six weeks in the blue seas and dolphin-rich waters of the Mediterranean with official visits to Gibraltar, Verona and Lisbon. Due to my footballing performance in Gibraltar I was selected by the ship's football team manager, a Petty Officer called Michael Upson, to represent the ship's team as a midfield player. I was pleased to be playing at a high level once more although equalling my footballing successes when playing for HMS *Bulwark*, *Collingwood* and *Mauritius* would not be realistic due to the size of the ship's company of *Kent*. I do recall with some amusement, however, the game we played in Verona against an Italian Navy side. I was expecting it to be a close game but in fact we were way above their standard and by the middle of the second half we were winning 10-0. At this point I noticed the Italian players had begun to lose interest, which was unusual for them with their footballing prowess as a nation. I think the final score was 11-1 and I can only assume they had put together a scratch team of reserves. Still, it was always good to beat the Italians even though they are such pleasant and colourful people by nature.

The next trip I remember with some affection was an official visit to the port of Esbjerg in Denmark. I always registered the fact that the people of Scandinavian countries invariably gave us an extra-special and warm welcome, despite their well-known reputation for being 'cool' as individuals. I was asked to raise and captain a water polo team to play a local sport's club and easily managed to get together about ten or more good swimmers/water polo players – including LWEM(R) Hughes from my department. We were met on the jetty by about 25 locals, with all the men wearing Viking helmets. Their wives or girlfriends were also wearing some Viking-type clothes and helmets. They took us in a bus to their club and we eventually jumped into the pool with our polo hats on and were ready for a good 'fight' with our Viking cousins. However, they were clearly novices and didn't even realise that players could not stand up in the pool while playing water polo. We stuck to the rules, ignored their 'transgressions' and won the game by a country mile. It was actually more of a 'skylark' than anything else and we were treated to a meal and some hospitality in the club after the game. I don't think I have ever met such warm and appreciative people, and we invited them back to the ship to show them round before they went home. Looking back, I think *Kent* and *Bulwark* were much better ships for me personally as the ship's programmes had a good balance of work and play, and we were mostly in blue sea areas. Although *Falmouth* provided some similar opportunities, it was more often like 'all work and no play,' and spent most of its time in northern, and therefore rough, waters. There were, indeed, many 'Royal Navies.'

As we moved into 1980 we were informed that the ship would be de-commissioning later in the year and that we would be spending time celebrating the ship's operational life with some official visits; one of which would be a visit to London up the Thames, where we would be tied up alongside the World War II cruiser, HMS *Belfast*. During this time we would be receiving an official visit from the Duchess of Kent. This was especially pertinent, of course, because her title and the name of the ship were the same. As part of this celebration the whole ship's company would have lunch with the Duchess and heads of departments, including those at my level, would be introduced to her. This was a trip that was difficult to beat as the ship looked so impressive just ahead of London Bridge tied up alongside *Belfast*, which we had to cross to get ashore, and both ships were floodlit at night time. There were also a number of official parties when the people of London came aboard to be entertained by the ship's company and in cocktail parties hosted by the Wardroom.

On the day the Duchess of Kent arrived, selected members of my department and I were lined up along the main passageway outside the Chief's Mess in our Number One uniforms. I had been growing a beard leading up to the visit and had wondered if I should shave it off as it was only partly grown, and I didn't want to look untidy for when I was introduced to her. However, my family in Yorkshire had visited the ship when we paid an official call to Hull, and my then brother-in-law, John Smith (husband of my sister, Barbara), had said I "looked like King George" in my uniform and beard – which my parents and others agreed with. I therefore decided to keep it. The Duchess was indeed a very refined and attractive lady to pass some time with, and we chatted briefly about our work as I introduced her to members of the Radio and Radar Section.

Photo 74 - Meeting the Duchess of Kent in HMS *Kent*, 1980

Source: *author*

She didn't seem to mind at all concerning my beard and from the photo (above) I had clearly amused her judging from the expression on the Captain's face – I was almost certainly excusing myself for my half-grown beard. It was one of those moments for posterity, but what I do vividly remember from the official lunch, held under canvas on the flight deck with bunting all around, is that I acquired a love of blackcurrant cheese cake, which we had for dessert and I had never eaten before – it wasn't the usual cuisine for Royal Navy ratings!

Photo 75 - HMS *Kent* passing under London Bridge, 1980

Source: *Tony Lee by kind permission, http://www,countyclassdestroyers.co.uk/photos.htm*

It was all a fitting end to the ship's service in the Royal Navy, and we soon returned to Portsmouth to await clarification regarding our fate. *Kent* was duly decommissioned in the summer of 1980 and became a static harbour accommodation and training ship at HMS *Excellent* on Whale Island, Portsmouth. A little while later we began to receive REMs under training from *Collingwood,* who spent about a month with us working more or less as they would be doing at sea under the supervision of me and the Section Senior Ratings. Being permanently alongside so close to home meant that Carol, the children and I could resume a normal family life and I probably had the best of all worlds during the coming 18-months.

I subsequently went on to be the captain of the football team and the ship competed in various competitions and leagues in the Portsmouth area. Our successes culminated in a game played under floodlights at (and against) Kettering Town, although my participation in this match was curtailed when the ball hit me in the nether regions from a point blank kick – from one of my team mates! Our team was fairly successful and it was always a welcome time in the week when, on Wednesday afternoon, I would leave work behind me and drive off to a local establishment, or football club, to play football and then go directly home.

It was during this period of time when an incident happened that gave me some assurance about how I approached my role as a manager of other people, and in this case the trainees that came into the department from *Collingwood.* My job was to welcome them into the department, allocate them to various sections and check on their progress by visiting them in their sections. I also assessed their performance and knowledge in various practical and theory tests. One of the trainees, however, became extremely distressed about something and the trainers from *Collingwood* were not able to uncover the source of his problem – he simply became too upset to talk about the matter when asked to explain. One morning after the trainees had been set to work in their sections one of the Senior Ratings from *Collingwood* came into the EMR to talk to me about this particular young man. He said, "We can't get this JWEM(R) to talk to any of us so we told him he could nominate anyone on the ship or anyone from *Collingwood* to talk to, and he said, 'I'll talk to Chief Nixon.'" This was somewhat of a surprise as I didn't think I had been very deeply involved in his training, but I was rather humbled as well as gratified that he would choose me to confide in. I therefore agreed and asked if one of the spare officer's cabins could be made available to discuss his problem with him.

When I entered the cabin later that afternoon he was sitting on a chair and I started by saying he could speak to me in confidence and that I would only pass on to others information that was necessary to get to a solution that would help everyone, and particularly him. He became rather upset as he explained that he had found out his mother had been diagnosed with a life-threatening illness (it may have been cancer) and that he couldn't be at home to look after her. As I knew from experience, many people in the Navy felt trapped and helpless at times like this and I suspect he knew I would understand his position. I reassured him that I did fully appreciate how he felt and asked him what he personally wanted to do – he could apply to leave the Navy or stay on and look after her from a distance as best he could although I believe she lived in the north of England. After listening to his preferences I asked him if I could talk to the teaching staff and that I would make a case for him to be granted some compassionate leave. This would allow him to spend time with his mother at home to discuss her options for medical care, including surgery, and how best he could help her to recover if she did actually need surgery. As a consequence of our discussions and my recommendations, he was allowed to go home on compassionate leave at the earliest opportunity. I can't remember the full details of how his story transpired as he returned to *Collingwood*, but these kinds of incidents made me feel that the pastoral care I could give to those I was in charge of was always at the top of my agenda, although ensuring discipline was actually part of this process. I think the influence of my instructor from HMS *Ganges*, Chief Jones, had a great bearing on me in these scenarios.

At home I had taken a keen interest in restoring an old Rover 75 car, which was built in 1954 and had a seized engine plus numerous problems with bodywork and its interior. I had developed a love of these particular cars, which were part of my growing up in Rhodesia and were also common in Mauritius. Looking back now I can see it had been a flawed idea and too ambitious for my mechanical engineering prowess, available time and budget. It had also led to the garage being non-usable for our regular car and it and had to be towed from the garage of a colleague's friend's home in Gosport and cost £150, which was a significant sum of money for our household budget. Carol had reluctantly agreed to me taking on this project and, despite some witty observations such as the Rover Club was going to remove it as it wasn't up to the required standard, she did, as always, lend a practical hand on more than one occasion in renovating various parts of the bodywork. In a way it was my pride and joy as a hobby as I used to look with fascination at the valve radio in the front console, the blue leather seats and small details like personal interior lights above the back seats, and the impressive sight of its V6 Rover engine. My father always referred to Rovers of this generation as the 'working man's Rolls Royce' and I had dreams of completing the task and driving the family, including my father, around in it. My son, Christopher, although only being five or six at this time, took a keen interest himself and was the start of the accomplished engineer he would go on to become later in his life.

As time went by I began, once more, to consider my future in the Navy and the issue of how I could minimise sea time and separation from my family. I once again looked seriously at my options as laid out in Figure 1 (page 82). I had reached more or less the top of the tree as a rating – the only future promotion could be to Fleet Chief - and the next 12 years until I was forty, when I could retire, could be expected to be divided equally between ships and shore time. In other words that meant at least another three ships for a two-year period at a time. The thought of that prospect filled me with dread. My other obvious option would be to apply for a commission as an SD officer and remain in my current branch doing the same job as my boss, Lt Samuel. The difficulty with this option was that I might have a similar amount of sea time to contend with, so I wasn't particularly attracted to that option. However, I did read a Defence Communication Instruction (DCI) one day in the EMR that was encouraging people with my educational background and status to apply to join the Instructor Officer (IO) branch. When I read the details I could immediately see it was probably what I was seeking as a career move because, if I were successful, I would be teaching artificers and mechanicians at establishments like HMS *Collingwood* and HMS *Sultan*. I also knew of one other person called Michael Jones, who was in a similar frame of mind, and we discussed this option at some length.

To be selected for the IO branch as a Supplementary List (SL) officer I would need to pass an Admiralty Interview Board (AIB) at HMS *Sultan*, which lasted for two days, and also have a provisional place at one of the country's teacher training colleges. This, once completed, would provide me with a Certificate in Education (Cert Ed) and, along with my higher national qualifications in electronics, I would return to the Navy with the equivalent of a Bachelor's degree – the main requirement of Instructor Officers who joined directly and went to Dartmouth. In my case, I would go to Greenwich College to complete officers training and undertake what was affectionately referred to as the 'knife and fork' course, which was undertaken by SD officers after gaining promotion from the 'lower deck.'

I spoke at some length with Carol about this and naturally we discussed the implications of me becoming an officer as making a transition from the lower deck to commissioned rank was not to be taken lightly. However, I persisted with my interest and my new boss, S/Lt David Hambrook, who was very supportive and encouraging in my endeavours, followed up the DCI requirements and sent my documents off for approval. At this time I also applied to attend Garnett College in London and in due course, after an interview plus a series of aptitude and I.Q. tests at the college, was given a provisional place for the following year. The Admiralty duly accepted my application and I just had to wait for my AIB date. It was all going smoothly – perhaps too smoothly - and I just had to wait for a date to attend, although I knew this would be the trickiest element in the process as I would have to compete with several other applicants and also demonstrate that I was 'officer material.'

In late 1981 I duly attended for my assessment at *Sultan*. Leading up to this I knew that I would need to take a greater interest in subjects such as politics, naval history, and expand on my 'credible and relevant' hobbies as the matter of my academic qualifications was not in question. Therefore I read quite extensively and ordered a broadsheet newspaper to be delivered to our home every day so I could more widely keep abreast of events in the news and politics. I had already started researching my family tree several years before so genealogy was one thing I could discuss, and I had, by now, taught myself to play classical guitar and had passed the first four grades. When I considered my background there were naturally some concerns as I clearly came from a working class family line, although my time in colonial Africa and travel abroad as a child brought me some advantages as I was used to having a maid and other servants in my home as a child. This was probably an advantage but in general, and under the influence of my parents, I never considered myself to be 'inferior' to anyone or any class of people – I acknowledged I was 'different' or hadn't achieved as much as some people – but never inferior. There were also relatives in my family who had been very successful academically and professionally – especially those descending from my great grandfather, James Simmons, who had worked in a coal mine at the age of 12 but had gone on to become one of the wealthiest and most successful people in our home town of Hemsworth. Also, the children of my great uncle Harold (Simmons), Barbara and Meg, had been educated in London universities - Barbara was a magistrate and Meg a high ranking civil servant in the Home Office. Like my great grandfather, James Simmons, therefore, I would be working my way up the professional and social ladder and doing most of it under my own efforts, as he had, rather than being born into a privileged position.

There were also social reasons for me considering a commission seriously. For one thing I was not a 'drinker' and had sometimes attracted criticism from various people who expected everyone to comply, and I had occasionally come into conflict over this issue, as related in this and previous chapters. As a commissioned officer I knew the likelihood of this attitude being present would be minimal, although there might well be some social situations I would be uncomfortable in – including making small talk at cocktail parties, after-dinner speeches and dealing with snobbery to one degree or another. I knew SD officers sometimes felt uncomfortable in their new Wardroom environment so it would be no different for me even though I would be taking a deviation into the Instructor Officer branch.

My AIB interview was an interesting experience as it taught me that tactics were important in becoming selected. This is because among my seven or eight fellow candidates, one or two were hatching various 'plots' or using strategies to increase their chances of success, which could clearly minimise the chances of other candidates. This first manifested itself in our accommodation the night before the formal assessments. As we were sitting around discussing how we had prepared I happened to mention that I had been memorising all the names of Secretaries of State in the present government. One colleague immediately recognised that this type of knowledge could be useful for the formal interview on the second day and he systematically went through the government's Cabinet asking the names of all the

Secretaries of State. It was difficult to avoid answering and therefore giving up my hard-won knowledge, but I quickly realised that it would be better to keep the further cards I had prepared closer to my chest.

On the second day the main test came from the leadership tasks we were set. The basic idea was that we took turns to take charge of the remainder of our group to get everyone from one side of an imaginary river to the other using various items such as ropes, planks of wood and barrels. Each scenario was slightly different and as leaders we were required to put a plan together, explain it to our teams, listen to any advice and either accept or reject it, and then execute the plan. This would reveal some aspects of our aptitude as leaders. These exercises naturally relied on people doing what had been asked of them but, as I witnessed, some people took the opportunity to spoil the chosen leader's plan. Fortunately this happened early in my round of tasks, when I wasn't the chosen leader, so I could work out who to trust and who not to trust in allocating tasks among the team. The exercise I learned this strategy from involved ropes hanging down from the ceiling with a triangle of planks formed above 'the river.' The duty leader allocated one individual to swing across to the triangle, establish and stabilise his position on that platform, and then receive further planks from the team so he could form a complete bridge. However, the person nominated to swing across accidently (or otherwise) collapsed the triangle into the 'water' by knocking the planks forming the triangle out of their securing ropes. The staff shouted, "Planks lost," which meant a new plan had to be quickly hatched by the leader and, needless to say, the mission failed and that duty leader received a 'fail.'

Therefore, when it came to my turn I allocated only a minor task to the person who had knocked the planks over so as not to destroy my mission. In fact I did not fully complete my task in the allotted time but it was considered a pass as it was very close to completion, and would have worked. As explained to us, it was power of command that was being tested and not the successful completion of getting a team from one side of the river to the other. However, this experience taught me some key lessons as I realised that individuals with the aspiration of reaching the officer fraternity were competitive and tactically aware. I therefore had to take these factors into consideration in my own strategies if I was going to be selected.

The final interview with the Admiral, a civilian school teacher and some other senior officers went quite smoothly. I think that out of perhaps eight of us, three passed and I was fortunate enough to be among them. My career was therefore set for a major change and in due course I would attend college in London. However, I was right to think 'things were going too smoothly' as my plans were badly affected by events unfolding 8,000 miles away when, on the 2nd April, 1982, Argentinian forces invaded the Falkland Islands. After some brief skirmishes involving a small garrison of British marines, Governor Sir Rex Hunt ordered them to lay down their arms. Other British South Atlantic territories, including South Georgia, were also seized and the prospect of a war with Argentina became an increasing reality.

Like my friends and colleagues, we started watching every news bulletin to see how the British government would respond.

****

During the late Sunday afternoon of the 18th April, 1982, I was working alone on my Rover in the garage when my daughter, Lisa, came running out of the house and called to me, "Daddy, you are wanted on the phone." I returned to the house and quickly washed my hands before picking up the phone. At the other end of the line, someone from the drafting section of HMS *Centurion* said, "Chief Nixon, as you know the Falklands conflict has developed and because of the Task Force deployment earlier this month we are bringing ships out of reserve. We are therefore drafting you immediately to your former ship, HMS *Falmouth*, which is in Chatham dockyard being brought out of moth balls. Other former crew members will be joining you or are already on board. You will be doing the same job of 903 radar maintainer as you did before being drafted to *Kent*. You are required to report for duty by 08.00 on Tuesday morning at Chatham and a signal has been sent to relieve you of your duties on HMS *Kent*."

Carol and I had been watching developments, as everyone else in the country had, following the invasion and the task force that had left for the South Atlantic on the 5th April under the directive of the Thatcher Government. It was clear that the Royal Navy was now in the forefront of the impending conflict, but we both felt a degree of shock as well as anticipation at such a sudden intervention to send me back to sea, and to my old nemesis, HMS *Falmouth*. At the very beginning of the Falklands War HMS *Kent* had been surveyed for possible re-commissioning as her large size, helicopter deck and four 4.5" guns would have made her a good Command and shore bombardment ship, and we all discussed our likely fate aboard *Kent*. However, her two years of unmaintained status meant a substantial amount of refit would have been required to make her sea worthy, and the decision was made to keep her at Whale Island.

I made a quick trip to the ship in the car to collect my belongings and say goodbye to colleagues in my department and other friends on the Monday morning, and once back home again Carol and I went about the task of putting my uniform and personal belongings together for the trip to Chatham, which I would do by car in the first instance, that very evening. A new episode was ahead of me with a great deal of uncertainty and potential risk. Whatever lay ahead, it was going to be hard work and my future plans regarding transfer to the Instructor Officer branch were well and truly 'on the back burner.'

When I arrived at Chatham I was accommodated in the Chief's Mess in the dockyard while the ship was brought back to operational standard. Every day a hive of activity was going on with windy hammers beating on the metal decks and equipment being repaired by the crew and dockyard workers. My equipment required repairs and I spent time in the dockyard acquiring spare parts and working with my new colleagues. I was pleasantly surprised to see that the new WEO of *Falmouth* was my fellow football team mate and Watch Supervisor in Mauritius - now Lt Cdr - Brian Welch. We quickly sprung up a good working relationship, as we had done in Mauritius, and he was pleased to see I had finally applied for and passed the process for being promoted to commissioned rank. He had been the first one to push me in this direction, and so it gave me some gratification to explain the rationale behind my choice of Instructor Officer. I was pleased to be working under him as WEO because he always put his confidence in my advice or explanations to him. Nevertheless, he wasn't slow in giving looks of disapproval or doubt when he needed more assurance – looking over his pipe as he did so. At this stage, our main concern was getting the ship operational once more and the matter of my future was largely irrelevant at that point in time.

Every evening in the Mess we would be looking on at the developments in the South Atlantic. The topic of conversation among my colleagues and I was often centred on the avoidability of the conflict. Britain was seemingly taken by surprise by the Argentine attack on the Falklands, despite repeated warnings by senior officers. Captain Nicholas Barker, for example, believed that the intention expressed in Defence Secretary John Nott's 1981 review and future plan to withdraw the ship he commanded, HMS *Endurance* - Britain's only naval presence in the South Atlantic - sent a signal to Argentina that Britain was unwilling, and would soon be unable, to defend its territories and subjects in the Falklands (Barker, 1997). We all knew that the invasion could have been avoided with a modest military presence. HMS *Endurance* was essentially an unarmed intelligence-gathering vessel but she could have been supported by perhaps only one submarine, one destroyer and a small number of fighter jets. Because of this lapse in cover, within the context of military rule and economic difficulties in Argentina, we knew a lot of people were going to have to give up their lives or suffer to correct this error of judgement on behalf of the British Government. However, as service personnel we knew that we had no choice other than to do our duty, and our personal views about political decisions were immaterial. Similar oversights throughout British naval history have had similar consequences, as exemplified by the potentially avoidable losses of merchant ships and seamen due to insecure naval telecommunications during World War II (Howson & Nixon, 2006).

In less than a month the ship was doing sea trials and workup at Portland was ahead of us – after that our orders would be issued. In between time I had been able to get home for week-ends but there was naturally a degree of concern among discussions with Carol and other family members. HMS *Falmouth* was featured in a BBC news bulletin one evening as we took on board ammunition in Portsmouth harbour, and my mother had seen this and expressed her worries to me about my safety. This was because, by now, a shooting war had developed with the early sinking of the Argentine cruiser, *Belgrano*, and daily attacks on British warships and task force vessels by the Argentinian air force. Probably the event that brought home to me just how vulnerable our ships were was the sinking of the Type 42 Destroyer, HMS *Sheffield*. She was fatally damaged south of the Falklands by an Exocet missile fired from a Super Etendard aircraft on the 4th May, 1982, and 20 of her crew were killed. She was a forlorn sight to all of us watching the news, seeing images of her burnt-out shell and her sinking on Monday the 10th May. The Task Force ship, *Atlantic Conveyor,* was also struck by two Exocet anti-ship missiles on the 25th May and later sunk.

We certainly knew of the low likelihood of our ships, despite having modern missile and gunnery systems, being able to defend themselves from a missile such as the French-built Exocet. This is because it was usually fired from an aircraft 30 or 40 miles away and it had its own navigation and radar guidance systems; the latter being turned on only in the last phase of its attack, thus making detection problematic. At that point, it flies at only 1-2 metres above the waves and travels at over 1,000 feet (383 metres) per second. In such a scenario, locking onto such a missile and firing either a missile or a shell to destroy it would be very challenging, not least because radar signals that might detect the incoming missile are hindered by 'line-of-sight' limitations and 'grass' (reflections) caused by waves. Firing off something to intercept such a missile was, at that time, almost impossible as Exocet missiles could not be detected by a ship's radar until it was about 6,000 metres away, leaving only about 20 seconds to respond. This made such a 'competition' highly biased in favour of the attacking aircraft, which could simply fly away once it had released its missile.

Warships in the Falklands were therefore heavily reliant on protective screens provided by Harrier jump jets from the two aircraft carriers, *Hermes* and *Invincible,* and other anti-missile strategies such as the jamming of Exocet radar signals, electronic decoy techniques and – as a last resort - small arms fire. This experience would stimulate the future development of close-in weapon systems (CIWS), such as 'Goalkeeper,' which consists of an auto-cannon and advanced radar which can detect incoming missiles within six seconds and respond automatically without human interaction (Ministry of Defence, 2013). But at the time of the Falklands War, if the Argentine Air Force had been able to source more Exocets and suitable aircraft to deliver them, many more ships would have been lost and those of us with some knowledge of missile and gunnery systems knew this all too well. The Argentine Navy had been effectively blockaded and never engaged itself in the conflict after the early invasion, but the impact of air attacks was putting the conflict on a knife edge as many other ships were being sunk or damaged.

After we had completed our workup period at Portland, which involved the usual long-hours of maintenance and repair of equipment and simulated air and sea-borne attacks, *Falmouth* became fully operational and we duly sailed out into the English Channel and down through the Bay of Biscay towards what we all anticipated would be the Falklands. However, although I do not recall the exact timing, the Captain made an announcement over the main broadcast. This sort of pre-arranged announcement was always prefixed by a click and the statement, "Do you hear there, Captain speaking." Sitting in the Chief's Mess with colleagues as the ship steamed south, the Captain went on, "*Falmouth* has been tasked with Gibraltar guard ship to relieve another frigate to go south and join the task force. What happens after this stage will depend on how long the conflict lasts, but our aim in Gibraltar will be to maintain the operational readiness of the ship to meet whatever role we are given in the future."

I suppose there was a sigh of relief in many ways as we would not immediately be in harm's way, but our time as 'Gib' guard ship could be anything from a few weeks to a few months depending on how many more ships were either sunk or damaged.

****

Although I was anxious about the future and my family's welfare at home, it was pleasant to once more look over the side of the ship and see dolphins racing and jumping through the blue and calm seas of the Mediterranean as we approached Gibraltar. Now that the 903 radar system was fully operational along with the other equipment I was responsible for, much of my time was spent on the upper deck servicing the spare radar and joining in with the painting of our areas of responsibility. Painting ship involved several trips to and from the paint shop, which was always at the very front of the ship and easily identifiable because of the strong smells of paint and white spirits. We would return our brushes and paint pots at the end of the working day and admire our handiwork - which made a pleasant change from the highly technical maintenance and repair tasks in our various offices around the ship. Once the ship was alongside in Gibraltar this upper-deck work was a pleasant way to pass the day as the view up the 'Rock' was spectacular and I once again enjoyed many a walk around the island.

While we awaited any development that might transpire as the war went on I played cricket regularly for the ship. By now my footballing days were largely at an end and I was good enough, because of my school days playing cricket, to open the batting with one of the officers who ran the team, and we usually put up a reasonable score. When I informed Carol of this recreation she suggested I 'wouldn't need another holiday' when I got home, and it was true that I was having a better experience than most people in active ships at that time. However, the uncertainty, perpetual bad news – including the IRA bombings and NHS strikes that were going on at the same time – separation and the doubts about my planned promotion and release to attend teacher training college, were all forms of stress and were having an impact. Indeed, I knew that I would not be released to attend college in the September unless the war came to a rather abrupt ending. In either event I would also need the permission of the WEO and Captain to be relieved, so my future was hinging on developments in the South Atlantic.

It would be possible for me to now summarise all the key events that unfolded during the Falklands war but there are many accounts in the public domain that surpass any contribution I could offer. Therefore I will limit my account to a few iconic moments and some personal accounts from two of my friends who were directly engaged in the conflict.

The Falklands were retaken following an amphibious landing of 3,000 British marines and troops on the East of the island on the 21st of May. The 'yomp' across the island by these forces and the overcoming of much higher numbers was a monumental achievement. On the 14th June, white flags were flying over Port Stanley, and very quickly British forces had advanced to the outskirts of Stanley, the capital city. General Mario Menendez surrendered to Major General Jeremy Moore, and 9,800 Argentine troops put down their arms. British troops then marched into Stanley. In due course all hostilities ended and major units of the task force started returning to the UK to tumultuous receptions – none more poignant for me than the return of HMS *Hermes*. Her experience perhaps best captured how most of us in the Royal Navy felt about the whole episode as she had spent an incredible 108 days at sea during her deployment. The photograph below shows just how much this ordeal had taken out of her superstructure and paintwork.

Photo 76 - HMS *Hermes* returning from the Falklands on 21st July 1982

Source: MaritimeQuest, by kind permission of Michael Peacock: www.marinequest.com/warships

The conflict at sea had been a difficult one for the Royal Navy – the whole war had been fought on a knife edge. Just after the return of *Hermes* I received a letter in Gibraltar from Carol, dated the 22nd July, which puts the relief we all felt into sharp perspective.

What a welcome the Hermes got on Wednesday. The men on board had tears streaming down their faces as they were so overcome with the welcome they received. There were helicopters and aeroplanes flying over with streams of coloured smoke coming from them. Dozens of small boats came out to meet her and thousands of flag waving people were lining the docks.

For me in Gibraltar, it was a case of waiting until *Falmouth* received orders to return to the UK, and once more the question of my future emerged as reflected in some correspondence back home and discussions on the phone with Carol. I was clearly in a quandary over what to do but matters were largely out of my hands for now. We received orders to return to the UK in August and duly departed from Gibraltar to pass through some very inclement weather and rough sea conditions in the Bay of Biscay. As I looked out onto the bows of the ship, toiling through grey and rough waters with sea spray being thrown towards the bridge and those dreaded seasick feelings inside me once more, I thought my misery, although relative would have no end. However, we eventually reached calmer waters as we entered the Channel. It was a relief to return home after being away for more than three months on and off, to see all my family were well and to visit some of my colleagues who had been directly involved in the fighting. I was naturally concerned for their welfare on hearing in the previous weeks and months that their ships were among those that had either been sunk or damaged. These included my close friend from *Mauritius*, Chris Sluman, and my good friend from HMS *Kent*, Henry Thorne.

We visited Chris Sluman and his wife, Elizabeth, in their home in Gosport in late August. Chris had been serving aboard HMS *Coventry*, a Type 42 destroyer, which went down in the South Atlantic on the 25th May, 1982. He explained his harrowing experience, which I could see had badly affected him. The ship had been hit on the port side just above the water line by three bombs from Skyhawk aircraft and although they did not all explode, they damaged critical parts of the ship and this resulted in uncontrolled flooding. The order to abandon ship was given very quickly and within 20 minutes she had completely capsized. Chris explained, "We were in the freezing cold water with the ship on its side and I was trying to swim away from it, but I kept being sucked back towards her as she was rolling over. After being in the water for a while we started singing 'Always look on the bright side of life' to keep up our spirits but it got worse. A rescue helicopter eventually started hoisting me out of the water, but as I was going up I started oscillating around and around, so the helicopter crew dropped me back into the sea and repeated this until I eventually got all the way up into the helicopter without rotating. The problem was that I didn't know why they were dropping me back into the sea." *Coventry* sank within half an hour of being hit and 19 of her crew were lost, and a further 30 injured (Parsons, 2000). *Coventry* had been working closely with HMS *Broadsword* that day, and the gallant efforts of her crew rescued a total of 170 people, including my good friend, Chris.

In the case of Henry Thorne, he, like me, had been drafted from *Kent* to an operational ship but his had become part of the Task Force after leaving Gibraltar – in this case the ship was the County Class Destroyer, HMS *Glamorgan*. I don't recall exactly when and where I met Henry again after the end of the war, but he had thankfully survived unscathed (at least physically) the attacks on his ship – the main one being an Exocet missile launch that came from land rather than from an aircraft. Henry explained that, "Before we were hit, the ship was steaming at high speed so it managed to turn in time to avoid a broadside strike (as had happened with HMS *Sheffield*). We were hit on the port side next to the hangar. Luckily the missile skidded along the deck, exploded and made a large hole in the hangar deck, knocked out the helicopter and started a fire. I wasn't near the explosion itself but it was serious as 14 people died." I didn't see Henry long enough to know if he suffered any long-term effects, but as we know all too well many people involved in these incidents went on to suffer from Post-Traumatic Stress Disorder (PTSD). His ship was also at sea a massive 104 days before returning to Portsmouth on the 10th July.

In terms of statistics, Britain suffered 258 killed and 777 wounded. In addition, two destroyers, two frigates, and two auxiliary vessels were sunk. For Argentina, the Falklands War cost 649 killed, 1,068 wounded, and 11,313 captured. In addition, the Argentine Navy lost a submarine, a cruiser, and 75 fixed-wing aircraft. In Argentina, the defeat led to the removal of President Galtieri and his downfall spelled the end for the military junta that had been ruling the country, and paved the way for the restoration of democracy. (Hickman, 2013). In some ways, therefore, there were unexpected benefits to this avoidable war and, rightly or wrongly, increased nationalism in Britain led to the re-election of Margaret Thatcher's government in 1983.

In closing this chapter, which would mark the end of my career in the Navy as a rating, I have to acknowledge at this point the help I was given by Brian Welch, my WEO on board *Falmouth* and boss from Mauritius. It was now August, and I was due to join Garnett College in London on the 14th September but Brian used his influence with the drafting authorities to obtain a replacement for me so I could take what was going to be a major shift in my career in the Navy. Indeed, I think that anyone with aspirations to improve themselves or the experience of their family members needs to have someone who 'believes in them' – they need a 'Brian Welch' behind them. However, I suspect Brian had seen my potential in Mauritius as a young Petty Officer, and later as his '903 maintainer.' In that respect, my potential in his eyes was clearly focussed on my work as an 'engineer' as well as my character and background. But now I would be moving into teaching and this subtle difference, coupled with some unanticipated developments ahead of me, may have had more significance than I realised at this time. I had been in the Navy for almost 14 years now and risen as fast as I possibly could have since joining at the age of 15, motivated by my family in many ways, and now I was going to face some major changes – not only for me but for Carol and our children. After a total of six years at sea, it was time to 'move on.'

VIII - Commissioned Officer [1983-92]

In September, 1982, I duly went to commence teacher training to gain a Cert Ed at Garnett College in Roehampton, London. I initially experienced some vivid contrasts with my highly-disciplined life in the Navy. One of these was the fact that my class mates and colleagues were not overly concerned about issues such as time keeping or turning up for lectures they were programmed to attend – the key point, as I soon worked out, was that they attended those events that they considered 'beneficial to them.' In contrast, and to the amusement of my new associates, I always arrived five minutes early and never missed a lecture – at least in the early stages. My experience of naval discipline had conditioned me to have a strong sense of duty at any personal cost to me – or even, in some instances, my family. I recall that I was once two minutes late arriving on board HMS *Falmouth* when I was a 25-year old Petty Officer with three children, and had never been late arriving at work for at least nine years. The other two occasions, as related in earlier chapters, were travesties of justice for which I was punished without any consideration of mitigating circumstances. I had to go before the Commander and then the Captain to explain my late arrival – my alarm clock had in fact failed to go off and I had driven as fast as possible to make up the time – and had had to remove my cap in front of several people and then be questioned. I was given a fairly considerable fine (about £50 in current values) and had to work extra hours to make up for the whole morning that these processes had taken up. It was therefore somewhat of a culture shock to see that people in the 'real world' faced few or no consequences for absence from work, seminars, lectures and other 'duties.' They could exercise their right to freedom of movement, speech and association. I had enjoyed these freedoms only to a minimal extent and within rigid structures.

The other experience that highlighted the enormous contrast of 'value systems' and conventions between me and my new peers, who had either just completed Bachelor's degrees or had worked for some time in industry before coming to teacher training (studying for a Post-graduate Certificate in Education – PGCE), emerged later in the year during 'Rag Week.' This is a tradition that was practiced by students at university when more or less any 'prank' or collective activity by students was acceptable as it had some beneficial aspects. The way it manifested itself for me was during a lecture, given by one of the female lecturers, when in the middle of her talk in front of 200 people a group of four or five students ran onto the stage from behind the curtains and threw fake paint all over her, and then ran off feeling pleased with their work. This left her absolutely distraught and quickly in tears, so she could not continue. The experience had actually frightened her and shocked many of us as these students could have been anyone. The lecture was abandoned and after learning more details about Rag Week I couldn't help contrasting the consequences of this event – i.e. no consequences for the perpetrators – with what would have happened to people in the Navy if they had done this kind of thing. In fact, I recall saying to one of my class mates on the road to our next lesson that if they had done that to me I would have "punched their lights out" – and I would have! The point I perhaps missed at this juncture, was that Rag Week usually involved raising money for charity through these 'imaginative deeds.'

However, I soon felt a degree of liberation and made some excellent friends – I became a regular contributor to the amateur dramatics society with my guitar playing, and accompanied some very accomplished singers or other musicians on many occasions in plays or musical evenings. I also became a member of a group of Christians that met regularly as I had become a committed Christian by then and was confirmed, with Carol, in Portsmouth Cathedral a few years previous. In my room in the halls of residence I recall arriving from home in the early hours of the morning and listening to a favourite song of mine at that time over the radio – 'Moonlight Shadow' by the multi-talented musician, Mike Oldfield (Oldfield, 1983):

Four A.M. in the morning, carried away by a moonlight shadow
I watched your vision forming, carried away by a moonlight shadow
A star was glowing in the silvery night, far away on the other side
Will you come to talk to me this night, but she couldn't find how to push through

One of my closest friends became Richard Tear; a highly intelligent and considerate person who, with his curly 'mop' of blonde hair, looked very much like Art Garfunkel of 'Simon and Garfunkel' fame. He was a leading member of both of the groups I was attached to and always keen to see me being involved with the community of students I associated with. He also asked me to compose one or two songs to support his theatrical productions, which I was happy to do. Richard was a keen jogger, as I was, and we often went jogging around the wide open spaces of Richmond Park adjacent to the college at the end of the day. It was on one of these jogs that probably the most fateful event of my life was agreed, when Richard said, "Hey, John, do you fancy running the London Marathon in April – I'm part of a Church Army group planning to register so you could always join us. We are all running for various charities and you can choose your own of course." Without any hesitation, I agreed to join in as I had watched the London Marathon on television and thought it would be a 'once in a lifetime' thing to experience. In due course, I decided to raise sponsorship money for the Leprosy Mission as I couldn't think of a worse disease to contract, and that victims of it must have had to endure an unbelievably miserable existence. In the training that I undertook over the coming months I consoled myself, in the face of considerable effort and discomfort, with the knowledge that I could help those less fortunate than myself.

My course presented me with many opportunities to extend my interests and I particularly enjoyed writing essays on the sociology and psychology of teaching. I especially found it inspirational and fascinating to learn about personality types in the context of the *introvert-extrovert* and *stable-unstable* spectrums. These were invaluable in what to recognise in our students and therefore how to get the best out of them – and not unduly pressurise, for example, the more sensitive and introverted among our classes, and how to capitalise on those with a more extroverted or forthcoming personality. As the academic year progressed I was doing well although I did recognise that teaching could be psychologically stressful and required a great deal of thorough preparation if it was to be successful. One of the most popular lecturers among my peers was a man called Pepi Cavilla. His lectures, in front of 200 people each week, were always fully attended and watched on recorded media by absent students. It was with some surprise, therefore, I discovered that in spite of his undoubted ability to prepare and deliver exceptional lectures, he had admitted – quite openly – to feeling physically sick on many occasions before coming to the lectern to speak.

In April, 1983, the time was approaching when I would run the marathon with Richard, his friends, plus one of my neighbours – John Thomlinson. By now I had achieved runs of about 16 miles but had never actually attempted the full distance because of work and other commitments at home. However, having observed the thousands of 'fun runners' on television successfully completing the marathon each year – often wearing some fancy (and heavy) attire – I thought I would be able to manage to finish without difficulty.

On the day of the event we all stayed in a boarding house in Blackheath, near to where the London Marathon started. I left my car there and would return after the event to collect it. Carol and the children came up by train to wait at the finish – over Westminster

Bridge next to the river Thames. It was an enormous event and all my family had pledged to look out for me on television and an army of well-wishers called me to say 'good luck' and offer to contribute to my pot for the Leprosy Mission. Richard and I had bought the same running gear from a sports shop in London – maroon shorts and a black and claret vest – and joined the enormous throng of runners about half a mile from the official starting line. It was more like a carnival than a sporting occasion and everyone around me looked fully pumped up and determined to do well. The marathon started at 9.00 am on a fairly cool morning, when a river of runners started to snake along the roads of London - with 26 miles and 385 yards ahead of them and about one million spectators spread across the route to the finish.

****

Initially we all ran together as a group but by the time we arrived at the Cutty Sark – about seven miles into the course – the others had managed to move ahead of me and so I was running 'alone.' I felt reasonably comfortable and marvelled at all the observers, who cheered, clapped enthusiastically and offered pieces of fruit and drinks. We knew that some of our friends were among the crowd and I remember seeing a group of students with a 'Garnett College' banner waving in our direction. They had been helped in identifying us due to the fact that our college name was inscribed on the front of our vests.

As the race wore on, I remember seeing so many groups of musicians playing outside pubs, marching bands and any number of other people engaged in celebratory activities. Along the roads were regular watering stations to keep the runners' hydration levels up. We had been told to drink regularly so I took liquids as we went past the watering posts – this usually involved a 'grabbing act' from someone holding out a plastic cup of water or squash, with cups being thrown untidily onto the ground a few metres beyond each post. As we reached about 15 miles I remember things started to feel quite uncomfortable as I pounded along a pebbled road next to the Thames. I had spotted Big Ben at about this point, which was adjacent to our ultimate destination, but the distance between me and the famous land mark seemed to shorten at a depressingly slow rate. Moving down a hill a few minutes later I was taken aback when two participants in wheel chairs came hurtling past me, and in general I was being overtaken by more participants than I was overtaking. It was becoming an endurance race by this stage and I could feel my legs becoming heavier. However, I knew there were only about six miles to go by now and I was committed to finishing in a reasonable time. My target was three hours and 30 minutes or thereabouts.

I realise that at this point I was facing what marathon runners refer to as 'the wall.' This is when the body's ready-use energy source of glucose runs out and the metabolic system looks to glycogen, stored in the liver and muscle tissue, to provide the blood with energy to nourish the internal organs – in this scenario, principally the heart. The inevitable onset of some dehydration in the body also adds to the impact of the wall, when people start to run on an 'empty tank.' This phenomenon could be seen clearly in the runners that were around me now as many were either walking or holding various parts of their bodies before resuming, clearly under strain. Several runners were sitting on the side of the road or being helped off to see the St John's Ambulance Brigade volunteers. Indeed, it was beginning to look like a war zone – and to feel like one too. However, the urge to stop running was dampened by all the smiling and cheering faces that lined the route, as well as the expectations of our supporters and the sponsorship money I would win, which was based on 'miles completed.' I also knew that Carol and the children were among the throng of people waiting on the banks of the Thames, by now about four miles ahead, and not being able to reach them would have caused some difficulties as we would be 'lost.'

The length of well-known roads seemed to be much longer than I could recall – running down the Mall towards Buckingham Palace seemed to take forever, and by now I was in some considerable pain and discomfort. My legs were definitely saying 'it's time to rest,' but the pressure of the occasion made me continue with the 'slog.' After what seemed like an age I could see the enormous arms of Big Ben and it was about 1.00 pm by now – four hours into the run. I finally reached Westminster Bridge, saw the sign on the road below me saying '385 yards to go,' and dragged myself at a slow canter to the finishing line. I was then filtered through some reception channels by stewards to receive my much sought-after London Marathon medal. The clock said 4 hours, 5 minutes and 19 seconds – which meant I had run the official distance in about 3 hours and 50 minutes because of the time delay to reach the start line in Blackheath. In the caption below, 'CA' across my vest stands for 'Church Army.'

Photo 77 - London Marathon completion & medal

Source: author

However, once I stopped, my body immediately felt like a ton weight and I walked slowly and painfully to the reception area sucking in the air with some difficulty. Like all the runners, I had had a silver-foiled cape thrown over me to keep warm and all I saw ahead of me was an army of people wearing the same cape, which had the sponsor's name printed in bright letters across it. I thought it would be impossible to find Carol and the children in such a vast crowd, but after about 10 minutes they found me as I gingerly moved among the crowd looking for them. After a short greeting and some "Well done, Daddy" comments, Carol said, "You look grey, John, are you feeling okay?" I replied that I wasn't feeling great – in fact I felt absolutely dreadful – and said to her, "I want to go straight home by train and I'll collect the car when I come back to college." Carol and the children rallied round with sweets, food and drink, and finally got me to Waterloo Station. I flopped around in my seat on the train feeling tight in the chest and uncomfortable as we journeyed south to our home in Hampshire. Carol explained that those who had finished within three hours looked absolutely fine, but as the time went by people looked more and more 'distressed.' I needed time to recover. I had finished in about 12,000th place (out of 18,000); I had my medal to prove it; but at what cost?

****

Three days after the marathon I was back at college but some symptoms remained such as tightness in the chest and difficulty in settling at night time. I didn't want to exert myself and just didn't feel right, so I decided to visit a local GP. She was a rather pleasant and straight-talking German lady who listened to my account and then took my blood pressure and said it was high - it was, in fact, 170/90. She then examined my chest with her stethoscope. After moving it around above my heart and lungs, and asking me to breathe in and out, she said, without any offence in her voice, "You silly boy, you should have stopped when you started feeling uncomfortable." She then called in her husband, who was also a GP, and said to him, "Can you hear anything unusual?" He listened to my heart and said he could hear a "systolic murmur." I was therefore referred back to the doctors in the Navy who also found some minor problems with an ECG they took (biphasic T waves), and confirmed the presence of a slight murmur. It could be that I had simply strained my heart on the marathon and I needed some time to recover, or it could mean that something had been uncovered during the marathon that I was not aware of, such as a congenital condition. Either way, this placed me on a long journey of future medical investigations – the results of which would often be equivocal - and complicated the experience of becoming an officer and changing my profession to that of a teacher rather than an engineer.

However, whatever had happened, I continued to study and work as normally as possible, although jogging and playing football stopped very soon after making some attempts to resume and becoming symptomatic. After doing my teaching practice for about two months at Eastleigh College of Further Education, which was close to home so I could avoid being in halls of residence in London, I graduated and awaited my first appointment as a Sub Lieutenant Instructor Officer. Before this happened, I attended the Royal Naval College at Greenwich to complete the Special Duties Officers' course.

I recall receiving my uniform grant and duly visited the famous naval officer tailors, Gieves and Hawkes. One sunny morning in Portsmouth I was carefully and meticulously measured up; the tailor taking an enormous effort in ensuring all measurements were as precise as possible and in helping me choose all elements of my new uniforms. The main uniforms were 'Number Fives' for daily formal duties and 'Mess Undress' for functions in the Wardroom, such as Mess dinners. Normal daily duties such as teaching were usually carried out in working clothes, namely black trousers, a navy blue jumper with lapels for our gold stripes, a white shirt and black tie. There was the option of purchasing a naval officer's sword, but I didn't think this was quite my style.

Before going to Greenwich College in early September, 1983, I purchased a new car – a red Renault 19 – as the literature I had received from Greenwich had included a warning that 'all cars parked in the college premises should be of good standard,' or words to that effect. I wasn't sure if our Morris 1100 Estate quite matched the Navy's expectations for a 'typical officer,' and convinced Carol this would be a step in the right direction – which she was eventually happy to agree with. Having done this, on my arrival at the college I couldn't help noticing all the 'old bangers' that were scattered across the car parks! In fact, as I would soon discover, driving a 'classic' car – banger or otherwise - was possibly more in keeping with what was expected of a typical British naval officer. However, I was happy with the Renault, as were Carol and the children, so it was progress of one sort or another. I suppose this highlights the fact that I was acutely aware of some social changes ahead and my reactions might be more dramatic than others who joined directly as officers.

[181]

Soon after arriving at Greenwich I met my new classmates. Our course would cover many aspects of naval history, international affairs and other interesting topics in addition to learning how to perform the many tasks of an officer both officially and, perhaps more importantly, socially. I was pleased to see that my friend, Mike Jones, was in my class as we were on exactly the same path as new Instructor Officers with similar backgrounds and were able to share accounts of what to do and how to behave in the many scenarios that lay ahead of us while at Greenwich. Much of our discussion with the teaching staff and course Director centred on our ability to communicate effectively in relation to 'service writing,' and we operated a 'pack' system with our group tutors.

We were given numerous scenarios in which we would be required to write letters to various officials, dignitaries, VIPs or contacts in the Ministry of Defence (MoD). We often received the instruction to re-submit due to poor or inappropriate English, or a lack of clarity. We were also required to draft detailed descriptions to an (imaginary) Captain concerning mishaps that occurred while we were 'Officer of the Day.' At the top of this list of priorities was our ability to write a 'thank you letter.' The typical situation we were given was that, during an official visit to a port we had been entertained by a local dignitary and we were required to draft something that not only expressed our thanks but showed some appreciation and recollection of their circumstances, actions and any gifts that had been passed on to us.

Photo 78 - Royal Naval College Greenwich as a Sub Lieutenant, 1983

JN back row, fourth from left, next to my fellow 'Schooly' Michael Jones, 3rd from left. **Source:** *author*

The term 'good enough is not good enough' was engrained into us, and we were encouraged to cultivate constructive criticism in those we were responsible for. Conducting Officer of the Day punishment trials were also commonly practised to determine our ability to manage these procedures in strict accordance with naval discipline, to accurately extract the facts of a case and to pass appropriate judgement. This could be case dismissed, a warning, punishment or referral to a higher authority.

We also went into great detail regarding social etiquette and took all our meals in the magnificent 'Painted Hall' in Greenwich College – the room that Nelson's body was returned to after his death at the Battle of Trafalgar in 1805. We often faced numerous combinations of knives, forks and spoons and had to learn to use the correct choice for each course of a meal – which was all provided through stewards and table service. The morning always started with a 'wash up' of the previous evening's meal, as all staff members and the Director, who was a Commander, joined us for meals to observe and coach us. Although this was often quite amusing – examples being corrected for cutting a bread roll rather than breaking it to avoid spraying a VIP guest with bread crumbs, and loudly tapping a coffee cup at the end of a meal with a spoon. I was fairly comfortable with these sessions but I think my main concern was the enormous amount of time it took to get through a meal and the necessary - and sometimes tedious - small talk that went on while waiting for the next course to arrive. In contrast to this, I was more used to being in a short queue with my colleagues as a rating, choosing my meal from a counter having looked at all choices (including dessert) and then sitting down to discuss the technical problem I was working on or something fairly innocuous. Guests in the Wardroom were inclined to ask personal questions about the backgrounds or interests of people around them, and I was perhaps reluctant, or had a disapproving attitude, when it looked like people were engaging in a process to establish the social hierarchy among those at the dinner table.

It was during one of these sessions that I said something that partly led to my final report classifying me as 'enigmatic and reticent.' The point was related to our use of language as this, not only in the Royal Navy but among wider society, is used as a 'social construct.' We had been invited to say something about our backgrounds and I had said, 'When I was *on* the *Bulwark*.' The key point being that I had used the preposition 'on' which, as I was very quickly told, should now be replaced with 'in.' It was explained to us that officers always said 'in *Bulwark*' rather than 'on (the) *Bulwark*.' It was elaborated further in that if we used such terms - including, for example, 'dinner' for the midday meal instead of 'lunch' - people would immediately "know our background." I received some disapproving looks when I candidly replied that "I had nothing to be ashamed about or wished to hide concerning my background." Perhaps in contrast to some of my colleagues, I was not afraid to challenge such 'conditioning' but it probably came with a cost, although I naturally appreciated that if I had chosen to become an officer I had to learn, and comply. Perhaps my time at Garnett College was also influencing my more liberal attitudes, which, coupled with my 'Yorkshire pride,' did not sit too comfortably with at least some conventions in the Royal Navy.

Carol also joined me at Greenwich to sample official occasions such as cocktail parties and meals in the Painted Hall as she would be much more active in my social life as an officer. Social events in the Chief's mess were always much more informal and there were fewer rules and conventions to be aware of or comply with. Carol also had to increase her range of clothing for social events in the Wardroom to include cocktail and long dresses. I must confess she took to this challenge with much enthusiasm and made choices that were consistent with what was expected. As our lives had been progressing she had been increasing her academic qualifications and so could always find something interesting to discuss with others and was not, as far as I could see, 'phased' by the social changes that had developed. I think that fear was more intensely focussed on me because I was going through a major social 'metamorphosis,' which could potentially be uncomfortable at times.

In due course I completed my initial training at Greenwich and was given my first appointment at the Royal Navy's Engineering School, HMS *Sultan*, where I would be part of the Academic Training group responsible for teaching electronics and electro-technology to Artificer Apprentices and Mechanicians.

My new life in Brunel Block at HMS *Sultan*, as an officer and teaching full time, brought a mixed bag of positive and negative experiences. The academic teaching staff comprised about 30 officers and the vast majority of my colleagues had joined the Instructor

Officer branch as graduates with degrees in a wide variety of subjects. They were a highly intelligent and talented group of individuals and engaged themselves in all manner of extra-curricular activities. This, as I quickly learned, was a key element of being an officer and I was expected to comply like everyone else. This was not such a problem in itself as I soon became involved in Wardroom music, and supported the amateur dramatics society as 'front of house' manager and musician. Consistent with my experiences at Garnett College, the range of gifted individuals ready and willing to engage in plays, sketches, music evenings and similar events was impressive. The complicating factor for me, was how to quickly learn the associated conventions attached to these events that related to 'being an officer.' It was always easy to forget, or not know, some etiquette that was usually required.

I soon acquired a number of close friends, although the backgrounds of some of them perhaps made me feel a little inadequate or at least 'different' to one degree or another. However, in other ways I had an enormous advantage as I had worked my way up through the ranks and had, in some respects, more affinity with my students. I remember being made to feel discouraged after a conversation with one of my new colleagues over lunch as he asked me what my qualifications were. When I said I had a HNC and a Cert Ed he retorted rather indifferently that he also had a HNC but that he "did not count it anymore" as he now had a degree. In fact, my qualifications were much more suited to our teaching roles as he knew very little about the Navy in terms of serving in ships and associated equipment, and did not have a teaching qualification. However, these and similar 'off the cuff remarks' left an impression on me, although they had a productive aspect to them as they encouraged me to keep developing myself.

In terms of teaching, although I was well organised and prepared, and always got good reports from my excellent and very talented boss, Lt Cdr Alan Jones (who would proceed to reach the rank of Captain in a very short space of time), I felt rather tired and bored quite often. Electronics can be a very dry subject to teach as it requires an enormous amount of information to be passed on without much opportunity to discuss concepts or express opinions. This was in contrast to my previous role as a diagnostician of highly complicated radar and radio systems. My symptoms since the marathon were often present but the programmes we ran had very demanding contact times to add to this influence. It was not unusual, for example, to teach a five-week module at more or less full-time classroom contact. Therefore, a class could report at 8.15 am for instruction and I may be teaching them until 4.15 in the afternoon. This was more demanding when I had been duty officer the night before as it was common not to finish my duties, which may include locking up drunken sailors or handling bomb scares, until 2.00 or 3.00 in the morning.

However, as usual in my career, a number of 'like-minded' individuals became allies and friends, and there were many from Brunel Block that I could mention. I also played cricket for the Wardroom - a more sedate affair compared with marathons or football - with my colleagues Lieutenants Ian Searginson, Kevin Grimsley and Andy Robinson. Andy, as a fellow Yorkshire man, became a close friend and was probably one of the most confident people at his job I had ever come across. I worked closely with Ian in my teaching duties and Kevin, who was incredibly intelligent, witty and sharp, was always happy to give advice. My closest friend, however, at this time was Lt Maurice Moore. He had a calm demeanour, was quite tall with brown hair and a reddish beard, and I often conversed with him in the coffee room during the morning and afternoon breaks. I think Maurice was aware of my vulnerabilities at being promoted from the 'lower deck' and therefore someone who had become educated largely through my own efforts and time. There were times when I had to teach topics that were, at least for me, intellectually challenging - such as 'j-notation,' which encompasses some abstract concepts as the topic includes 'imaginary numbers.' While some

[184]

of my colleagues would have found this to be in their comfort zone and may make a remark or two to suggest the topic was 'elementary,' Maurice always seemed to come to the rescue by saying something like, "Ah, j-notation, I'm sure I've seen a really good explanation in a book in the library (which was attached to the coffee room) – just a minute, John, I'll see if I can find it." Maurice would then return in a few minutes, or seconds, with a book and find the appropriate section and read through it aloud. Having such support made an enormous difference as I went through various trials and tribulations that came along with my new role in the Navy.

Maurice also had some similar personality traits to me – he was more reserved by nature and liked 'fixing things,' for example. He was a good teacher and clearly concerned for the welfare and sensitivities of his students and others. He also had a similar hobby to my 'Rover 75' renovation project; he lived just down the road from me in Hill Head but his house was immediately recognisable as it had a yacht perched proudly in the back garden. However, the vessel in question was being built from scratch by Maurice, and he was spending most of his spare time – and money – on his hobby. We were therefore both fairly obsessive by nature as we relished these challenges, even though our wives couldn't see what all the fuss was about. In time, we would both share a similar fate with these enterprises as my Rover would eventually, and sadly, have to be towed away for a nominal fee from a scrap merchant, and Maurice's yacht would be sold, incomplete, to another enthusiast.

I think one of the greatest challenges that came along with my new role was the ethos and traditions to be found at Mess dinners in the Wardroom. This was because the Royal Navy has a very long and rich history that reflects class structures in British society, and life in the Wardroom was predominantly based on 'public school' conventions and etiquette. This is not surprising as naval officers had, for centuries, come from the aristocracy or upper echelons of society. As well as dressing formally at Mess dinners there were a plethora of rules that had to be strictly complied with. For example, 'passing the Port' at the end of the meal had to carried out in the correct direction and the removal and replacement of the stops for the Port and Madeira decanters had to be completed by officers according to a long-established tradition – and woe betide anyone who made a mistake. The Mess president, who was the senior Executive Officer of the ship or establishment, sat at the top table and orchestrated the whole evening using a gavel and block in conjunction with formal instructions. This included a toast to the Queen before the meal commenced and, more to the point concerning my 'fears,' after dinner speeches. There was clearly some psychology going on in my mind during the early days of my promotion, and it wasn't difficult to work out what it was from my own perspective.

The first source of anxiety was the fact that I was in the company of people with many different ranks. It was quite normal to have senior officers as guests and, in any event, there were people much more senior to me in abundance and these had often been my bosses or even 'punishers' in the past. Moreover, from the age of 15 I had been taught to jump and salute in their presence. Even though they were now my 'peers' within the Wardroom, I couldn't help but feeling great apprehension at being asked to give a speech in front of them as there was always the possibility that the President would strike his gavel and randomly call out an officer's name, who would then be required to give an impromptu speech to 'entertain' the gathered company. In fact the President usually nominated people in advance of the requirement to give a speech, so those given this task usually had some notes prepared and had practised their speeches.

The other piece of relevant psychology related to the fact that so many (but certainly not all) of the speeches I heard were both articulate and genuinely humorous, and I felt sure I could not match their performances as I was a poor story teller and could not tell jokes.

However, it was the ever-present risk of being asked to get up and say something witty and entertaining that filled me with dread – any natural humour I possessed mostly came from spontaneity in every-day life situations. Many of my friends, on the other hand, seemed to relish such an opportunity – but I definitely did not and this created certain anxieties for me. I did learn, quite quickly, that the key to making a good speech was the choice and delivery of the first line. One of the best starts I recall was given by a Lt Cdr from my department who, at a Ladies' Night Mess dinner, after the gavel had come down and his name announced, stood up opposite to me and Carol and said:

Mr President, thank you for giving me this rare opportunity of speaking uninterrupted in the company of my wife.

Sadly I have forgotten his name even though I knew him well. More interestingly, as well as receiving a great deal of laughter and table banging – another convention and tradition of naval officers – his wife (and the other ladies present) took it in good spirit. It clearly created the necessary atmosphere for my colleague's speech to move forward and be well received. It was also clever because the period of laughter he had created gave him the opportunity to pause and move forward having scanned his notes for the next phase of the speech.

The legacy of 'anxiety-related' cardiac symptoms since running the London marathon continued in the background, and I was duly referred to see one of the top consultant cardiologists to the Royal Navy in London during December, 1983 – his name was Alistair McDonald and he practiced at the London Hospital in Whitechapel.

****

Following an early-morning train ride from Fareham station to London, and a transfer across town on the underground, I arrived at my destination. The London Hospital was an impressive and imposing Victorian building and I was, understandably, a little apprehensive about what lay ahead. I was given an x-ray and ECGs before going in to see Dr McDonald in his office. He warmly shook my hand and I soon observed that he was Scottish, with a re-assuring, efficient and friendly manner about him. After reviewing my notes and results he came over to me and listened to my heart while giving me some discerning looks and making some brief comments – he was an instantly likeable person and I was sure that all his patients would have readily trusted him. After the customary deep breaths while he listened intently to his stethoscope, he looked at me with a wry smile on his face and said, "I can hear a wee squeak but you are of no interest to me." He meant this in a positive way, of course, as a means of perhaps saying, 'your cardio-vascular system isn't perfect but let's not push this one too much.'

He asked me questions concerning my work and how I personally felt about my new promotion and teaching. After our discussions his view seemed to be that I was experiencing some worries and concerns about major changes in my life, and that my symptoms would subside with time. Indeed this would be a common response over the coming years, which I had to at least acknowledge as a reasonable hypothesis in the absence of anything conclusive from my test results. Nevertheless, I wasn't able to dismiss the sudden change in my physical 'fitness' that had occurred after the marathon – I had stopped jogging seriously and couldn't play field sports without getting flutters and bumps in my chest – and this had all happened before I had been promoted and faced my new social and professional challenges. Therefore, although I received assurances that I did not have, for example, ischaemic heart disease, I was stubbornly of the opinion that I had damaged myself by over-exertion and that I had some newly-acquired limitations to my health. However, I couldn't have seen a more reassuring and competent cardiologist than Alastair McDonald and I became more determined to overcome my difficulties.

At this point it is perhaps worth discussing a phenomenon in medical statistics known as a 'confounding variable.' I was not aware of such analytical techniques at the time, but a brief overview here may help with the understanding of such situations. Simply put, a confounder is something that appears to be linked (correlated) with an outcome of interest (such as health) but there is no 'causal' relationship between them. In my case, the change in health I was experiencing may have been caused by the marathon or my promotion and new profession, but either or both of them could be significant or a confounder. There could also be other un-recognised or non-declared variables that were affecting my health. A good example in medicine is the often-discovered link between heart attacks and high coffee drinking, but the more appropriate link is with smoking, which many coffee drinkers engage in. Therefore coffee drinking is the confounding variable (Hennekens & Buring, 1987) and the true etiology is between smoking and heart attacks, although caffeine is present in coffee or tea and can induce heart palpitations as I was to discover in due course.

Usually in such scenarios, it is necessary to control the effect of confounders to see if health status changes under the sole influence of the variable of interest. In my case, I naturally had responsibilities as a provider for my family and therefore felt I had limited room for changing what I now did for a living. However, over the coming year, despite the contradiction of being able to play squash well enough to be runner-up in a squash competition among Brunel officers, I continued to experience problems and was again referred back to London in December, 1984; this time as an in-patient for more in-depth tests. Whilst in my hospital bed I was visited by numerous doctors who were under the wing of Dr McDonald and he probably wanted to see what their verdict was as part of their training. They all listened to my heart and wrote fairly copious notes without giving away their opinions to me personally. On the second day of my admission I underwent an ultrasound scan and then a stress ECG, which was supervised by Dr McDonald's Senior House officer, a pleasant doctor called Danny McCrea.

Although I simply followed instructions at the time and walked or ran on the treadmill, it is worth explaining that the stress test relies on something called the 'Bruce Scale' to determine cardiovascular risk and fitness, and has up to 12 levels that gradually increase in speed and inclination. The test therefore gets progressively more difficult for the patient and stops when the patient is too fatigued or develops pain. I was wired up with various ECG leads and my blood pressure was taken as I progressed in my running gear. I reached and completed level seven before stopping due to tired legs. The results were 'consistent with those of a very fit young man' and Dr McDonald once again reassured me that I had no evidence of heart disease. He stated that I would not undergo the final test of angiography because of the risks involved with such a procedure, which is an invasive test that involves radio-opaque dye being injected into the arteries of the heart and imaging them. Dr McDonald possibly knew that this final test may give me a more definitive diagnosis but as he said to me, "Some people do in fact die having angiograms – even though they are mostly elderly and frail patients – and I'm not happy about exposing you to such a risk and believe me, not many of my patients get past level 1 on the stress test let alone level 7." With that, he shook my hand, smiled in his usual manner, and wished me a safe journey back to Hampshire.

In his report back to the Navy he did, however, point to another potential cause of my health problems that I must have mentioned to him – difficulties in my marriage.

Indeed, it was an occupational risk of Service people, as I had witnessed many times for myself and recounted in earlier chapters, to have problems in their family life because of the stresses Service life places on them. Following my promotion, we had moved to a larger house at Osborne View Road, Hill Head, as we needed more space as a family, and although we were all extremely happy there it was more financially challenging for us and it wasn't long before Carol went out to work part-time for Social Services at Fareham to help with our income. Luckily, as she had been progressing with her general education and had taken several GCE O' and A' levels since our time in Mauritius, she had little difficulty in finding a job. We also studied both French and German together at Fareham Technical College. It is true that my new health issues and promotion had generated stress that was felt within the family, and there were various legacies of my long periods at sea that emerged once we were in a more stable situation. Other internal and external factors were also clearly colluding with each other to put our marriage under stress. However, we all proceeded with our various duties and lives and anticipated that things would improve with time.

Back at work there was some welcome respite from the conveyor belt of teaching and marking exams. I spent some time re-writing course books in electronics and electro-technology with Maurice Moore and other colleagues, but the most enjoyable project I got involved with, as part of my role of CCTV officer of the establishment, was the making of a training film, entitled 'Sultan – The Movie' (SMOPS, Royal Navy, 1985). I had already undertaken some training in the production of videos at HMS *Nelson* and knew the Navy's film production team at HMS *Mercury*. I also had the services of a CPO to look after the maintenance of the establishment's video equipment – mostly used in classrooms – and so I turned my attention to the making of a film on the history and daily life of HMS *Sultan*. My co-producer and script writer was Lt Newman – a young and talented officer with a love of classic sports cars who owned an open-topped racing green Austin-Healey. I recall in the early days of researching and writing the script I knocked on the door of his classroom and went in to tell him I had planned some recording that afternoon. His class, sitting there in their usual orderly rows in Number 8 uniform, immediately burst into laughter and started nodding to each other as I had said, "Morning, Paul," before starting my conversation with him. Our students never usually knew our first names as a matter of protocol so they must have been speculating that he might be 'Paul Newman,' but my interjection confirmed that for them. With Paul Newman as my co-producer, co-director, co-script writer and bit-part actor, how could we go wrong? We also asked Ian Searginson to narrate the film as he had a polished 'BBC' voice.

To make the film we spent a considerable amount of time researching the history of HMS *Sultan*, which went back to 1917 when it was the home of the Royal Flying Corps, and recording with Ian, sometimes during the evening. The filming, however, was done by the unit from HMS *Mercury*. It was always an enjoyable afternoon for Paul and I to drive up through the South Downs on a sunny summer's day in uniform to *Mercury* in Paul's Austen-Healey. It was like being on a motorbike because of the breeze and fresh air, but we could also discuss the film as we drove along the quiet roads that led to the establishment. As in the case of the famous British film director, Alfred Hitchcock, we wrote in small cameos for ourselves. Paul played the part of an officer on a selection panel for a rating being recommended for advancement, and I played the role of an Instructor Officer teaching quadratic equations in one of our classrooms – with lots of formulae and diagrams chalked up on the board. Making this film was incredibly enjoyable for me as it allowed us some 'artistic license,' and orchestrating so many shots and participants around the establishment and aboard Sultan's training ships was highly rewarding. The star of this film, undoubtedly, was the Captain, who played his role completely naturally in promoting an artificer to 'Acting LMEA' at Captain's Table.

Looking back now I can see that, possibly, the reason I felt little less stress when doing these things was that they were more appropriate for my personality and interests. The film was a big success and formed a template for other similar films to be made about the life and times of personnel in other Royal Navy establishments or branches. Our use of trainees to provide voice-overs regarding their training and career paths was a novel approach that added a great deal of interest to the film as it was 'their story.'

As well as producing this film I often got up at Mess dinners to accompany someone singing after the meal had finished. I especially remember accompanying a WREN officer as she sang the Jean-Paul-Égide Martini song (1784), 'Plaisir d'amour,' an Irish officer who sang the traditional Irish song (composer unknown), 'Old woman from Wexford,' and two officers, one of whom was Lt Cdr Herb Edwards (who had performed at the Royal Albert Hall), who sang the John Denver (1982) song 'Perhaps Love.' I felt no stress in these situations in comparison with the thought of standing up in front of the gathered company to make an impromptu speech.

****

On the 1st October, 1985, I was appointed to HMS *Mercury* as a full lieutenant. The Royal Navy's Telecommunications training establishment was situated at *Mercury*, nestled in the rolling South Downs at East Meon and close to Petersfield.

Photo 79 - Carol and John (Instructor Lieutenant)

Source: *author*

I joined a very small and exclusive section that contained only me and my new boss, Lt Cdr 'Rob' Linton. Rob, I quickly discovered, was an astute person by nature with a critical but sympathetic eye for detail. He was clearly very intelligent and had some refined hobbies and interests. He gave me a warm welcome on my arrival in the office and explained that he had inherited the section from someone who could only be described as a 'leading academic authority' in his field – Lt Cdr Peter Evershed. Peter, who I met briefly before his retirement from the Navy, had worked as the Navy's principal expert in telecommunications at *Mercury* for many years. He was certainly a difficult act to follow and most of the material we used in teaching derived its content from Peter's long history and publications.

My principal instructional duty was to teach the theoretical aspects of radio communications to naval ratings that were completing qualifying courses for RS, LRO and

RO. Opposite our office was the laboratory we usually taught in, which was full of spectrum analysers, radio equipment and various progressive teaching aids. Rob, in contrast to me, taught various officers' courses comprising mainly Principal War Officers (PWOs). I was very pleased to be given this job as it was well within my comfort zone in terms of the material I would teach, and the establishment was small with extensive green areas and gardens and a rich and important history. The 'Signals School,' as it was more formally known, was established at Leydene House – which was now the Wardroom - on the 16th August, 1941. Leydene House was where Rob and I would spend lunch times over a drink discussing our work and generally socialising with colleagues.

As my time at *Mercury* continued, it is accurate to say my health difficulties at work and problems at home began to escalate quite badly. I found myself, on too many occasions, finishing my teaching for the morning and going to see the Principal Medical Officer (PMO), Commander Howard. He could probably be described as a straight-talking, no nonsense doctor in his mid-50s. In my consultations with him I kept coming back to the marathon as the source of my symptoms and I knew that when he took my blood pressure it was always of concern to him, although he was quite guarded in coming to any conclusions in view of my previous tests and results in London with Dr McDonald. My constant complaints and discussions with Carol at home were also clearly taking their toll and most of my colleagues and family were at a loss as to how they could help. Carol had noticed me at Mess dinners holding my wrist to check my pulse, making my apologies to those around us and leaving her to take some fresh air. This naturally left her more exposed and rather embarrassed in such social occasions. Considerable anxiety.

Perhaps at this point it is timely to mention the stresses that came from the common practice in the Navy of requiring people to teach subjects that they had very little knowledge of to audiences that were either formidable, reluctant, challenging or all of those things. To illustrate, I recall one morning being informed that I would need to stand in for Rob with a class of PWOs and to teach them about a particular radio transceiver, used in helicopters, that I had absolutely no knowledge or experience of. Quite naturally, my assembled audience expected me to be somewhat of an expert and to discuss the finer points of that equipment and show evidence of relevant theory and practical experience. I believe the session lasted for 1-2 hours although I cannot imagine what I found to speak about for such a long period of time. The fear in these scenarios was that of being 'found out' and 'exposed' in the role of 'pretender.' It wouldn't have mattered if my audience had been my more familiar classes of ratings, but attempting this in front of senior officers who often put the fear of God into people at sea, as I had witnessed myself in my previous experience as an engineer, caused me a great deal of grief and discomfort to the point of being unwell.

My situation at *Mercury* came to a head on the 6th June, 1986, when I was admitted to Haslar hospital in an ambulance for more tests as I was not able to go on with my work. This again resulted in some equivocal E.C.G. results being found but they were thought to be broadly within the 'normal' range. I was connected to a heart monitor and it often alarmed when, for example, I got out of bed – I was experiencing 'tachycardia' (fast heart rate) and, in contrast, bradycardia (slow heart rate) when asleep on the ward. Indeed, my resting heart rate had always been lower than normal due to the amount of sport I had done from a very young age – I had what is commonly termed an 'athletic heart.' I recall reading that many international swimmers had resting heart rates of about 40 beats per minute as their heart muscles were so well developed, and mine, when at rest and relaxed, was in the mid-50s range. I also had a series of panic attacks on the ward and had to be sedated with intravenous valium, so things were getting very difficult for me, my colleagues and my family. I recall my father came down to see me just after this episode and had to drive me around town – he was rather shocked to see me having such health problems at a relatively young age as he was thirty years older than me and 'as fit as a fiddle.'

The doctors at Haslar understandably decided it was necessary for me to have the 'gold standard' test of angiography and I was duly referred to Southampton General Hospital, and underwent the test on the 15th July. The procedure itself was not particularly pleasant but I could see many patients on the ward – some of whom were scheduled to undergo major heart surgery – were in a much worse state than me. The radiologist's report back to the Navy stated: 'I am pleased to say that the left ventricle showed normal contraction, the mitral and aortic valves were normal and the coronary arteries were all normal. Obviously these findings were very reassuring for him.' Although this latest barrage of tests again suggested very strongly that I did not have a heart problem, and Rob Linton supported me as much as he could under the circumstances, my appointer in the Ministry of Defence decided it would be of benefit to all concerned if I were appointed to a non-teaching job for a reasonable period while my future was considered. Although I was very sad and disappointed in many ways to leave HMS *Mercury*, I was pleased to be given some respite and to be appointed back to HMS *Sultan* to work with my good friend and colleague, Maurice Moore. I arrived back there on the 14th October, 1986.

****

My new section was in its infancy and Maurice, along with two Chief Petty Officer Artificers, had been busy purchasing a whole range of test equipment and microprocessor modules from a company in Norwich that could be connected in various combinations to serve as a hands-on teaching vehicle for our students – who were Artificer Apprentices and Mechanicians. Naturally there was also a considerable amount of academic input to our teaching as we had to cover computer fundamentals from first principles. I duly attended some courses to extend my knowledge of the equipment and microprocessor theory. In the early days at *Sultan*, all four of us were accommodated in a portacabin next to what was known as 'Parsons Block,' which is where we initially taught our students. It was a new and refreshing start and I immensely enjoyed the many discussions and plans Maurice and I went through in our shared office in the portacabin.

There were two Chiefs in the section although I only recall Chief Palmer by name. He was extremely bright and amiable by nature, with a novel method of preparing coffee for everyone as he pre-prepared cups with whipped-up cold milk, coffee and sugar, ready for the hot milk to be poured in when needed. Unfortunately I recall that I threw some of it away assuming the cups were in need of washing – much to his surprise as he had explained his method to me before, but I clearly didn't register properly what he had explained. Chief Palmer and our other Chief were excellent people to work with and the arrangement we had as a team perhaps felt a little more familiar to me. I therefore settled down to some degree and enjoyed a period of 'symptom-free' research in the context of a low teaching load.

After about six months we moved to a brand new building with state-of-the-art classrooms, teaching facilities, and regular flows of classes to teach. Much of the ingenuity in our teaching aids, such as software-driven explanations about how a computer works, came from the flare of Maurice but we all worked well together as a team. At this time I also became the Public Relations Officer for the wider department, which involved writing stories for local press outlets around the country on the achievements of people who worked in the department. This was something I particularly enjoyed as I could interview candidates for stories and learn something of their backgrounds. Many were CPOs that instructed in the wider department and I got to know many of them well as I organised the cricket team and even had the odd game of football for the department. Parsons Block was headed by a very

[191]

amiable and popular Lt Cdr called Colin Podmore. He was easy to get on with as he was an SD Engineering Officer who had a calm and considered way of interacting with us in his moderate Birmingham accent. It was always a pleasure to attend Mess dinners with my colleagues and boss (we did actually call him 'Boss' as a sign of respect) from Parsons Block.

In 1988 Maurice left the department and my section was then headed by Lt Michael (Mike) Rose. Mike and Maurice had an affinity with each other in some ways as they were both very bright and knowledgeable about computing and writing software programs. Mike and I immediately got on well together, partly because he was a gifted musician and played the piano and keyboard. It wasn't long before we would be spending lunch times playing music together and learning a reasonable repertoire of tunes, which we eventually played at lunch times in the Wardroom to provide background music in the bar area.

Photo 80 - Teaching microprocessors to artificer apprentices

Source: author

Although the Commander approved of this venture, I do recall him asking Mike and me to turn down the volume on one or two occasions when we put too much 'gusto' into our playing. We also went to each other's homes to practise and Mike became a close friend of my family and probably, between us, we encouraged all of my children to expand their interests in music or learn to play, or continue playing, various instruments. Lisa, by now, was an accomplished violinist and played in a local school's orchestra and was selected for Hampshire Youth Orchestra as a viola player. Philip took up piano and keyboard and would go on to compose and record many songs as a young adult, and Christopher took up the Oboe and could, like me, 'bash out' various tunes on the piano using my 'playing piano by ear' approach. Like me, he would learn to play guitar well in his teens and young adulthood.

In 1989 a third officer, Lt John Gunn, joined our section. He was a very likeable Scot who was also an accomplished lead guitarist and expanded our group to what we Christened 'NRG' – the initials of our surnames – and even did some social work in the local area by playing music at a retirement home, although I'm not sure they fully appreciated some of our 'best' performances like 'You look wonderful tonight' (Eric Clapton, 1976). However, we did include many more traditional songs that they were familiar with but the lack of a singer among the three of us was something that Carol, Julie (Mike's girlfriend) and Audrey

(John's wife) noted from the back of the room while gesturing to one or more of us to 'produce some vocals.'

It is interesting for me to recall that Mike and Julie chose me as their best man when they married in 1989. I say 'interesting' as the reception was held at the Wardroom with more than 100 guests, and I therefore had to make a speech as part of my best man duties. However, this did not cause me any particular stress or worry as it might have done on other more formal occasions. This tended to confirm my perceptions, as mentioned previously in this chapter, that it wasn't making speeches *per se* that was the difficulty, it was the social (or military) context in which they had to be delivered and the absence, or otherwise, of preparation time.

Photo 81 - Teaching staff at Parsons Block, HMS *Sultan*, 1988

JN front row left, Lt Gunn 3rd from left, Lt Rose 4th from left, Lt Cdr Colin Podmore 5th from right One section chief is behind me and Chief Highland is 3rd row 4th from left. **Source:** *author*

In terms of developments at home, it was true that the lives of Carol and I, and perhaps our children – who were all well into their teenage years by now – were developing in such a way as to make living together difficult. As if to give some respite, I was appointed to a three-month position within the International Military Staff (IMS) at NATO Headquarters in Brussels. Following a very enjoyable holiday as a family in Alsace, France, which we got to by driving across the country on an epic journey in a new Renault 25 we had bought, I moved to a flat in Brussels to undertake my temporary job to help expand and formalise the Information Technology systems in the Secretariat of the IMS.

My boss there was a senior WREN Officer but I actually worked more closely with a senior Belgian Air Force Officer called Colonel Coupez. He was of medium height with a shaved head and was extremely articulate in English as well as his native French. He was clearly well respected and seemed to know almost anyone of any significance in NATO HQ, and we immediately got on well together. I was rather taken aback when attending my first high-level meeting with any number of very senior officers in attendance, when Colonel Coupez – who was chairing the meeting – announced that the "IMS is pleased to welcome Lieutenant John Nixon, Royal Navy, who is going to be our computer expert and improve computer security in the Secretariat."

When I heard the word 'expert' I felt this was an ambitious title for me as my teaching in *Sultan* had not been on Personal Computer (PC) systems so I was on a very steep learning curve in my new position. NATO HQ itself was set in a large, plush and impressive building that I loved walking around because of its wide open spaces, internal shops and banks, and relaxing restaurants. I also shared my office with an American Air Force Colonel called Dennis Chya (although I fear I may not have recalled his surname correctly – it was of Polish origin). Dennis and Colonel Coupez, despite being of much higher rank to me, soon became close associates and took me under their wings to one degree or another. I recall that we often went to the restaurant together for coffee, where we shared stories, opinions and jokes in a convivial manner gathered around a table. Both took me to their homes and showed me around Brussels, and I often visited Dennis and his lovely wife in the large and luxurious flat they had a few stops away on the city's metro system. I remember Dennis being highly amused one day when I rang the transport section to book a car to the airport, and the person at the other end said, "Who is calling, please?" When I answered, "Mister Nixon," Dennis burst into a wide smile and chucked to himself. This was because he had served for many years in the military with Richard Nixon as president of the United States, so my name meant something to him. It was even more amusing for me when I went to be picked up by the car the following day and the drivers said he and his colleagues in the car pool couldn't remember who had ordered the car, but that the person had an American president's name. They were speculating if it was Mr Kennedy or Mr Eisenhower and so on, through a long list of U.S. presidents' names. These little things made me feel 'at home' to one degree or another and I found working with officers and people from other nationalities a refreshing change from that to be found in the Royal Navy and British society in general.

Some characteristics that always struck me about Brussels were the constant smell of chocolate waffles and the large numbers of well-dressed commuters that I encountered when I went through the metro stations there. My flat was in the same street as the European Parliament buildings, which explained the higher numbers of professional people passing through the streets and metro stations, and sitting outside cafés and restaurants. I was also very comfortable with the life-style of Brussels and the fact that it was not unusual to sit in the impressive and cultured Grand Place and drink coffee or hot chocolate outside a restaurant in the evening. I have to confess that I could not help but contrast it with the over-indulgence in alcohol and anti-social behaviour I had often witnessed at home, and any rowdy behaviour on the streets invariably turned out to be from British visitors. Because I was fairly competent in French, I could also communicate well enough to do my shopping and exchange some conversation with Colonel Coupez, or other colleagues, over coffee.

I flew home regularly for week-ends and I was very keen for Carol and the children to come and spend time in the city as there was a realistic possibility that my appointment could be extended to two years. I especially wanted this to happen as I was beginning to feel some comfort and sustainability in my new work and surroundings, and my only visit to a doctor there was for a minor physical ailment. About half way through my appointment Carol and Christopher did fly over to spend the week-end with me and we even went on the tram to see the British school in Brussels, as the children would have attended that school if everyone moved to join me. As it transpired I was offered the chance to extend as a married-accompanied appointment but it was clear that the children were all at important stages in their education in Hampshire and the opportunity I had was declined. I suppose it confirmed to me that, unlike our time in Mauritius when we were very much younger, the workings within my family were no longer centred on my career.

When I came to leave Brussels I had a jolt to my emotions one morning as Colonel Coupez, who was a man I liked, admired and respected, came into my office and said,

"Lieutenant Nixon, please come into my office." I duly complied and after joining him there he said, "Sit down, John, as I need to send a report to the British Ambassador about you and I always show people what I have written on these occasions. I picked up the manuscript he had placed on the desk and read first a description of my work contributions, which I had personally felt were not as significant as they could have been due to my steep learning curve, but the final line told me that my personal contribution as a British Royal Navy officer in NATO was more relevant to him. It said, 'During his time in the IMS, Lieutenant Nixon has been a pleasure to work with and he has been a credit to his country, the United Kingdom.' I wasn't expecting such an endorsement and perhaps because it came from Colonel Coupez I suddenly found it difficult to stop an emotional response, so it was with some humility that I briefly expressed my thanks to him and returned to my office. Although this event may appear of minor importance, it taught me a very important lesson – it is not 'what' is said about us by others that is important, but 'who' says it.

Photo 82 - With Carol, Lisa & Lt. John Cockcroft, HMS *Collingwood*, 1991

Source: author

I arrived home for Christmas and in the New Year joined an advanced computing course at Blanford in Dorset. In general my difficulties due to the impact of Service life both as a rating and an officer, my health challenges, and the impact on my marriage came to a head and I took the decision to resign my commission and leave the Navy at the earliest opportunity. This was reluctantly accepted by my appointer, Cdr Alan Prosser – a man I had enormous respect for as he had always been very supportive in my career as an Instructor Officer. I was informed, in due course, that I could retire in September, 1992. My next planned appointment was therefore changed to HMS *Collingwood*, where I would work on the development of a Management Information System (MIS) for the establishment.

Very soon after joining *Collingwood*, life at home for Carol and I was becoming ever more strained and this made me particularly unwell. Eventually I simply had to leave home and live as a single officer at *Collingwood* and also, for a time, in the Wardroom at Whale Island to make my separation less visible to my colleagues. The Commander of *Collingwood* was particularly understanding and helpful to me as he, along with many colleagues around us, had been through similar difficulties in his own marriage. Mike and Julie Rose were also very supportive in accommodating me for short periods and being 'agony aunts' as Carol and I tried several times to resume our married life because we both had in mind the welfare of our children. However, every avenue we went down to re-build our home life came to a juddering halt and we had no option other than to seek permanent separation, and ultimately, divorce.

As my time at *Collingwood* drew to a close, I considered what would be my best option. The stresses and strains of life and my patchy poor health meant I needed to do something that would give me a long period of respite, during which I could hopefully recover. I always remained in regular contact with my children but naturally I did not have a home where I could accommodate them, so my decision was to attend university and study for a degree in the social sciences as I felt my interest in the welfare of others was where my natural instincts lay. I therefore applied to do a three-year BA Honours degree at the University of York and was successful in my application.

Just after my 40th birthday I said farewell (but not goodbye) to my three children and two dogs at the gates of HMS *Collingwood*. Arrangements had been made between Carol and me for the family home to be guaranteed financially until everyone was ready to move at a natural point in time. The situation was, of course, surreal, and one which I think wise not to expand on for obvious reasons, but I headed off in my car towards Yorkshire where I would stay for a time with my parents, my sister Barbara, and in halls of residence until circumstances allowed me to purchase a small flat in York the following year. My son, Christopher, was already studying at Bath University and graduated successfully with a BSc in Mechanical Engineering in 1994.

Carol also took this opportunity to study for a B.Ed at King Alfred's College in Winchester. She would eventually become a successful English primary school teacher in both the state and public sectors. It seemed that academia was the place Carol and I sought refuge and an opportunity to find our bearings in life once more, and perhaps seek the sense of fulfilment in our lives that may have been denied us in our youth. However, our changes of direction did not diminish the importance of our children's welfare and progress in life, and although we now both have settled new family lives, we remain on good terms and recognise that the Navy was both a good provider as well as a great burden to endure at times.

****

My 24-year career in the Royal Navy had started as a 15-year old school boy at HMS *Ganges* and had involved the climbing of two ladders of promotion from a starting point of no formal educational qualifications. Each phase of my career in the Navy had its calm as well as its rough times – both literally and metaphorically – but there had always been numerous inspirational friendships and experiences along the way. However, as I have recounted in the chapters of this book, there were many trials and tribulations related to Service life, and especially those that involved service-family conflicts. Some of these were damaging to friends and colleagues as well as for me personally, and it is undoubtedly the case that the end of my career was more challenging than the beginning; it certainly felt like I had lost all that I had strived for over so many years. However, I knew that some aspects of my predicament were down to poor decision-making by me and the onset of many health challenges half way through my career – even if they arose out of seemingly good intentions.

There were therefore many lessons and situations for me to consider over the coming years as I began to study and work in a more liberated environment. One of the first impressions that struck me as I walked around the leafy campus of York University was the fact that I could be anonymous – no-one was looking out for me to salute and I was not looking for those I would have been required to salute. Students and staff wore what they felt comfortable in, and believed matched them as individuals. It was also clearly the case that freedom of expression on any subject that arose in conversations or study was neither restricted nor judged in the same way that it had sometimes been in the Navy. I also acquired the time and space to reconcile and manage my health problems and re-establish proper links with my children as they continued with their own lives. My studies at York would eventually lead to a doctorate and a fruitful career as a research fellow in health economics.

Photo 83 - Graduation of Christopher from Bath University, 1994

Philip, Lisa, Carol, John, Michael Lingard (son-in-law) and Christopher. ***Source:*** *author*

IX - Lessons and Reflections

Having completed this book and read it for the first time from start to finish, I considered how my story might be classified. Perhaps, first and foremost, it is an autobiography within the genre of military history. However, it has some elements that might make it an adventure story, a tragedy, a disaster, a drama, a family history, a love story, a sociological account of every-day life in the Services, or even a medical case study. I suppose it is my hope that this ubiquitous characteristic will broaden its appeal to a wider audience of readers.

I quickly focussed my attention, also, on the differences in size between each chapter, the result of which sheds some light on the relative weight I have placed on different phases of my time in the Royal Navy. The most obvious distinction is seen when comparing the volume of pages covering my service as a junior rating and then senior rating, from 1968 to 1983, and my subsequent career as a commissioned officer between 1983 and 1992. The former represents more than 80 per cent of the book so it might be possible to deduce that the early stages of my career, when life in the Royal Navy was new, have attracted much of my attention and thus dominate the content of this book.

In this respect, Chapter IV appears to stand out as it covers my first sea-going ship, HMS *Bulwark*, which encompasses many events and experiences that went on to shape my future life. These included a steep but enjoyable learning curve regarding my profession, a tour of the Far East and other parts of the world with many exotic and interesting places to visit, sporting events played against a wide variety of opponents across the globe, marriage at a relatively young age, fatherhood, my first significant promotion, high quality and influential friendships, numerous operational exercises, and encounters with potential danger in the evacuation of British Service personnel from Malta in 1972. The imagery associated with this two-and-a-half year period has clearly left an indelible impression on me, as recorded in the many photos I have included for that period. I also suspect that my time on board a large commando carrier, with its associated military hardware and programme, suited me personally and was also a faithful manifestation of what I expected life to be like in the Royal Navy before joining. It is also significant that much of my sea-time aboard *Bulwark* was spent in the warm, blue and relatively calm oceans of the world, with one or two exceptions.

The troubled waters of my time as a rating came later when serving aboard HMS *Falmouth* before, during, and after the time of the Falklands War. In between time, the idyllic life on the island of Mauritius, in particular, was the pinnacle of my career in more ways than one, although undergoing training at HMS *Collingwood* was also an enriching experience. However, my first year as a boy trainee at HMS *Ganges* clearly left, by far, the most enduring impression on me as it was a truly unique and inspirational phase of my life.

The 20-page chapter covering my transition to, and life as a commissioned officer, however, probably has a more qualitative and analytical feel to it as I was facing a significantly different life in terms of my work, family and social life. I exercised much more power over my whereabouts at that time, and enjoyed a stable home life in many ways. However, my decision to run the London Marathon just before facing some significant challenges was clearly a move that weakened my capacity to fully embrace this change of direction.

Therefore in this final chapter I attempt to draw some key lessons from the experiences I went through over a long and eventful career. In doing so, I introduce some evidence from the wider sociological and psychological literature that might help to explain, and expand upon, some of the points I have focussed on in order to place them within a wider context.

My experiences relating to the first two chapters of this book strongly tell me there are many potential sociological and psychological issues that arise from leaving home as an adolescent. As is often the case for 'boy entrants' who eagerly join the armed services, there is frequently an underlying reason other than a wish to 'see the world, get a career and seek their fortunes.' I would not seek to place any criticisms on any of our parents or guardians as everything is relative and some of my young colleagues did not come from stable family environments. In my case I was fortunate to come from a strong and loving 'working class' family which owned its own, albeit modest, property and had a colonial – possibly privileged - past in Africa. I certainly was not short of support from my parents and siblings at any time whilst serving in the Navy.

However, it is important to be cognisant of the fact that adolescents do not have developed decision-making powers, and thus have a tendency to do 'the wrong thing for the right reasons,' or the 'right thing for the wrong reasons' – or even worse, the 'wrong things for the wrong reasons.' Supportive evidence indicates this is because adolescents' decision making is 'biased more by motivational factors than by cognitively-driven calculations of outcome probabilities' (Luciana & Collins, 2012). Put in simple terms, this means that many of us who joined the Navy so young were motivated by, for example, images of ships at sea, navy blue uniforms with light blue and white-striped collars that flap in the wind, (sanitised) war films we had seen, the sound and sights of marching bands, long-established traditions that looked 'solid,' and exotic places to visit, among many more. We did not usually consider things like our long-term living arrangements, the fact that we may be injured or killed in future conflicts that we may or may not feel are justified, the potential for severe punishment for behaving 'naturally,' our loss of liberty and the impacts this would have on our future family life. There are therefore differences in the rates of development in motivational and regulatory-control systems of the brain and, in an ideal world these should be allowed to reach similar levels of development before making any major decisions.

It is also important to remember that whenever large numbers of (especially all-male) teenagers live together, as we did at HMS *Ganges*, it is inevitable that some degree of bullying or intimidation will be present. Although I was not personally bullied in a physical way, I did occasionally witness this being inflicted on those close to me and I was physically threatened because I was put in a position of authority among my peer group at an early stage of my training. This meant that my circumstances may have resulted in an abrupt distancing from close friendships that I actually needed to sustain me through my experiences. I think this is why Chief Jones became so important at that stage of my life as he was a father figure with a capacity for compassion and understanding over and above his role of instilling discipline in us. I believe the regime at *Ganges* was based on practices and traditions that went back to Nelson's time and were deliberately meant to test us as well as develop us in a positive way. The arrangements we went on to at HMS *Collingwood* were much better in this regard because Killicks lived in our mess decks and supervised us, and as such there was a significant difference in age as well as experience between us.

In summarising this point, therefore, I feel it is important, whenever feasible within any individual's life, to be fully grown and sufficiently mature before leaving home or making major life-changing decisions. If this has to happen for various reasons, there could be some long-term psychological impacts that may have to be dealt with depending on their severity. In some people there may be few consequences, but in my case there were clearly some that shaped or influenced me in many ways.

Matching personality type with work or profession

This particular issue is of vital importance, in my opinion and experience, if we are to be fulfilled in life and reach our true potential. I think everyone would be wise, as early as feasible in their lives, to discover their personality type. This ought to be done before choosing a job or profession as personality type and careers should, as far as possible, be complementary. The basic principle to know is that 'there are horses for courses' and making inappropriate choices can seriously limit the potential achievements of any individual. Fortunately, finding out one's personality type is relatively straight forward and can be done simply by completing a questionnaire.

Perhaps the best known example is based on the work on 'psychological types' by the Swiss psycho-analyst and author, Carl Gustav Jung (Jung, 1971) within the Myers-Briggs typological approach. Katharine Cook Briggs and her daughter, Isabel Briggs Myers, began developing their methods during World War II as they believed that knowledge of personality preferences would help women who were entering the industrial workforce for the first time to discover the sort of work that they would be most comfortable and effective in (Myers & Myers, 1995).

Depending on the answers to about 70 questions, an individual's personality type can be classified into one of four dichotomies. These are:

Extraversion **(E)** – **(I)** Introversion
Sensing **(S)** – **(N)** Intuition
Thinking **(T)** – **(F)** Feeling
Judging **(J)** – **(P)** Perception

For each sub-classification, a percentage is attached; for example **I** (86%), **E** (14%) would indicate a highly introverted personality. Interestingly for me is that my result placed me in a minority classification of 'INFJ.' Whilst it would not be productive to give a detailed analysis of this classification, the first point of interest is that introverts are basically happy *doing their own thing* and 'expend energy' in social gatherings, and re-charge themselves when working or being alone. Extroverts, in contrast, 'gain' energy in social gatherings and lose it when alone. This probably explains a great deal as to why I was much more comfortable as a diagnostician and engineer - which involves many hours of working alone or in small groups solving problems - than as a teacher with long days in front of a class passing on knowledge and facts. There are, as I was to find later in life as a student and researcher at university, subjects and scenarios in teaching that introverts do thrive in.

In my case it was the teaching of English and also the social sciences as they afford many opportunities for techniques such as role play and discussions through an exchange of opinions about philosophies or concepts, so students themselves become much more pro-active and contribute to the teaching/learning experience.

The remainder of my own classifications briefly mean that I am more intuitive **(N)** about assessing situations and other people, I am influenced more by my feelings **(F)** than my senses, and I am more judgemental **(J)** - about others, but also myself. The most important concept to focus on is that of being *true to yourself*, and you cannot do this unless you *know yourself*. Anyone undertaking this test can be given a detailed report and a list of the kinds of jobs that would be suitable for them. This information can help us to study appropriate subjects and pursue particular jobs or professions before jumping into something that is unsuitable for us.

The cost of 'life, liberty and the pursuit of happiness'

Although the sub-title I have selected for this issue comes from the American Constitution, it arguably has relevance for all political democracies. One of the key lessons that my service life taught me relates to the importance of liberty and the consequences of belonging to an organisation that clearly controls this facet of its members' lives. Indeed, the term used for those permitted to go on leave was 'liberty men.' This means the Navy controlled when and under what circumstances its members would be free to visit, stay with, and look after their friends and relatives. In my experiences and discussions with former members of the armed services in general, this is more often than not the non-combat factor that causes the most psychological damage among service personnel.

One needs to consider that for the vast majority of the population in countries like the UK, it is possible to return home or visit a sick relative without suffering punishments such as fines, confinement or even imprisonment. Although the Navy did accommodate this aspect of life to one degree or another through the granting of 'compassionate leave,' this was sometimes a lottery and decisions depended heavily on operational circumstances and the perceived importance of the individual's role within the ship he or she was serving in.

As I experienced myself, and saw in many of my closest friends and colleagues, there were many negative consequences of not being at home when we were needed. In some cases, as I have recounted, some of them refused to comply with the rules or harmed themselves. However, it is perhaps necessary to acknowledge that the loss of freedom is not restricted to those who serve in the armed forces. As the Swiss philosopher, Jean Jacques Rousseau, correctly stated more than 250 years ago (Rousseau, 1762):

Man is born free, yet he is everywhere in chains

It is also important to consider the conflicts that service people are sent into because they may be expected to pay with their lives for the oversights or incompetence of political leaders. The Falklands War is arguably an example in which more than 250 UK servicemen and many more Argentineans died when the conflict could have been avoided simply by recognising the threat and then stationing a relatively small force there before the invasion of the Falkland Islands took place. As recounted in chapter VII, the British government had not taken heed of intelligence concerning the Military Junta's hostile intentions in Argentina and had publicised its intention to remove HMS *Endurance*, the only Royal Navy vessel in the area, from its role of overseeing security for the Falkland Islands. These were, effectively, green lights for a dictatorship with severe economic and political difficulties to do something to increase its popularity and national cohesion. What should be borne in mind, therefore, is that service personnel will invariably have no say in the wisdom or legitimacy of any future conflict, but may have to pay the price of the chosen response of the government.

This is perhaps more important when considered in the context of 'voluntary participation' in the armed services as the sacrifices people may have to make in armed conflicts can simply be avoided by others under freedom of choice. Many would see this as a 'disconnect' between the 'benefits of freedom and democracy' and the 'costs of winning and maintaining them.' Life in the armed services can be an enriching and enjoyable experience, as I often found, but many people may focus on peace-time service and not what may lie ahead in terms of future decisions for the country to go to war. Ex-servicemen and women should also be aware of the fact that they will enter civilian life and compete with others without credit being given to their sacrifices and the risks they have taken. In my own case, to cite two examples on this issue, I was refused the opportunity to be placed on a council house waiting list after 24 years' service as I was a 'single 40 year-old male.' Similarly, I was not selected for my first major job application in academia as the position was offered to a person outside the European Union and, in order to justify this, a declaration was made that 'no suitable British candidates could be found,' even though I had the required master's degree and relevant experience. The Royal British legion, in a review of homelessness in ex-Armed Service personnel states: 'There is some evidence that, for a minority, military life, through factors such as trauma of combat, mobility of the job or the drinking culture, had reduced their ability to cope post-Service.' (The Royal British Legion, 2013)

If, in full knowledge of these considerations people decide to join the Services, at least they will be fully informed of the potential consequences. Anyone seeking to join the Navy, without wishing to appear flippant, should check if they are prone to sea sickness. If not, they could be in for a miserable experience at times as my former instructor in the ATC had, indeed, warned me back in 1967. I think this also reflects the importance of knowing who you are and what is best for you and your family.

Recognising one's limits

Probably the most important lesson I have learned in compiling this book is that it is not wise to push yourself beyond what nature has intended for you. In my case I would state it even more strongly: **don't run a marathon unless your life depends on it.** As recounted in chapter VIII, my health suddenly became a major concern after I completed the London Marathon. Its after-effects became entangled in the pressures of my work and family life as I immediately embarked on very significant challenges in moving to commissioned rank, with all the sociological and psychological challenges that entailed as an officer and a full-time teacher. It is important to note, also, that I began to experience symptoms six months before I was promoted, but the psychological challenges associated with promotion and teaching were presented as the major contributors in the context of equivocal medical test results. I think the points made above about personality type and choice of profession are also relevant as I do acknowledge that the major driver behind my decision to apply for Instructor Officer was that of avoiding separation from my wife and children. This clearly means I may have been guilty of 'doing the wrong thing for the right reasons' and then being faced with the consequences.

However, in the course of writing this chapter I have naturally thought long and hard about what may have happened to me during the marathon. Clearly I should have stopped before I began to feel distressed, but like all human beings I was able to disregard the signals I was receiving and press on regardless. It should be borne in mind that marathon running as a mass participation event was in its infancy back in 1983 and there had only been two previous London Marathons. So what evidence is there today about the detrimental effects of running for long periods without a break?

One study of interest to me, reported in the British Medical Journal, confirms that 'eleven runners have died while running the London Marathon since it began in 1981, and every year a handful of runners die while competing in such events.' The risk of sudden cardiac deaths during a marathon is now quantifiable at about a rate of 0.8 per 100,000 participants (Redelmeier & Greenwald, 2007). Whilst it is universally recognised that regular and sustained exercise is beneficial for health and fitness in most individuals, some experts describe the level of exercise derived from a marathon as 'the reverse effect' – where too much of something that is normally good for us can have the opposite impact. Researchers at Harvard's McLean Hospital also found that during a marathon 'more than half of the segments in the heart lose function due to an increase in inflammation and a decrease in blood flow' (therefore ischaemia), and this temporary heart damage may play a role in marathon deaths (Siegel & colleagues, 2001).

Whilst it is not my intention to discourage marathon running *per se*, as most of the negative impacts on individuals are among the 'non-elite' category of runners, as witnessed by family members on the day I ran, I can say in my case it was not a wise decision. Although the doctors I saw did rule out disease as the source of my symptoms, I see now there is a good body of research that can at least partly explain why I felt so unwell and why my blood pressure was so high three days after the event. I probably needed a very long period of rest – some accounts on this issue say this should be ten days or more – before resuming my work. Because of my busy life at that time, I perhaps did not train sufficiently to prepare for the full event. Therefore, I strongly subscribe to the view that our exercise patterns, when we are young, should broadly fall within what 'hunter gatherers' did for millennia to catch their prey; long and brisk walks, periods of rest, sustained high speed running for short bursts, and carrying fairly heavy objects to build up strength. Indeed, many sports such as football, hockey and rugby fall into these categories either by chance or design and I enjoyed them regularly before I ran the marathon – but in a very limited way after my marathon run. In view of what happened to me I keep to the position that it was one of the biggest mistakes of my life as it confounded most of the consultations I subsequently had, and planted seeds of doubt in my mind that could not be easily reconciled – especially in the context of some questionable outcomes of medical examinations and test results.

I would also extend this marathon running lesson to other pursuits of human activity, such as over-use of our mental faculties. Whilst we may feel a need to minimise our weaknesses, we should focus our attention on cultivating and using our strengths in the work we do and the hobbies we take up. We should naturally value our friendships but not bow to peer-pressure, however well-intentioned it may be. As I discovered many times during my career, I had to deal with disapproval and even rejection for not complying with the expectations of others – but I discovered that if you are not true to yourself you will suffer far more than if you give way and do something that would not be appropriate for you. In the early years of my time in the Navy I put myself in some danger by 'following the crowd' but quickly learned to stand up for my own principles. We should keep in mind the old adage here of 'act in haste and repent at leisure.'

Family formats and sociological issues

The final topic, which may in fact be the most important in many ways, relates to the various family formats that emerge as a result of Service life. As recounted in the chapters of this book, individuals and their partners are required to leave their **extended family** units, where they have the support of parents, siblings, grandparents and other important relatives who they can consult or visit as they choose. Their primary support network therefore comes from their blood relatives to whom they have immediate access as they often live close to one another. Clearly, in my case, the need to have the support of my extended family was a crucial aspect of my life, and one that may have been overlooked by me and my parents in reaching the decision for me to leave home at the age of 15. The role of parents is therefore vital, although they may not always act in the best interests of their children due to a lack of awareness, ignorance or shortcomings in their own education. This latter point was certainly the case of education for girls, which was often disregarded in the 1960s as in the case of Carol and many of those I attended school with.

In the armed services, and more widely in society, there arises the next family format, which I would describe as the ***independent nuclear family*** – namely two parents living with any children they have, away from their extended families. This arrangement involves living primarily under the support of respective partners, close friends and children once they become sufficiently mature. While this arrangement can strengthen the bond between family members, as it did in my case while living in Mauritius, there is no immediate help from extended family members. This arrangement is susceptible to conflicts caused by temporary re-unifications brought about by visits to extended family units 'back home' or by extended family members visiting the separated family. The issues of insufficient accommodation and re-constituted alliances between one partner and his or her extended family members often become sources of disagreement that are difficult to reconcile. The reliance on particular friends to provide support may have mixed blessings as I also discovered in my career.

The next format that emerges is the *separated independent nuclear family.* This happens when the serving partner leaves the family home to undertake service, as I often did, in a ship or another operational area for either short or long periods of time. In this scenario the remaining partner and children have to learn to get by without the separated partner and they naturally develop their own decision-making strategies, coping mechanisms and cultivate support networks with trusted friends. Because the bulk of the financial commitments falls on the family home, the partner at home usually takes up the principal role of 'accountant and financial manager' while the separated partner often utilises what is needed for essential costs and entertainment. As such, both partners tend to develop their own independent means of surviving and may even grow to prefer the independence this arrangement affords.

The final format I would like to describe is the *reconstituted independent nuclear family.* This is what most married people in the Services are seeking to achieve, and certainly occupied many of my thoughts and plans in achieving it. However, this format is fraught with danger as the re-adjustments in the way decisions are made about any number of issues and how finances are allocated can be problematic. These issues can reach a point when it seems logical and even desirable to revert to the previous format when independence can once more be re-established.

In bringing this issue into a wider context it cannot be ignored that my marriage ended in divorce but certainly this outcome cannot be attributed in a negative sense only to life in the Royal Navy. Examined from a wider sociological perspective, the factors that influenced divorce are fairly well established, and include 1) changes in the law to remove legal and financial barriers to divorce; 2) changes in expectations of marriage; 3) changes in the social position of women [and, possibly to a lesser extent, men] in society; 4) changes in social values and the elimination of stigma associated with divorce; 5) demographic changes that include increases in life expectancy and teenage marriages. As such, my experiences, while exacerbated by my career in the Royal Navy, reflect the social trends that we all lived through and statistics show that divorces in 1968, when I joined the Navy, were 40,000 at a rate of about 12%, and this rose to 160,000 or 22% in 1990 (The Education Forum, 2013).

****

When considering how to find a closing message for my story, I began searching for a suitable quote as I usually do. Pondering this point I walked around my home and after a while stopped to gaze at a small wooden plaque with small, silver hands on it.

Although I had not read the words engraved on it for quite some time, I quickly recognised that it had been in my mother's bedroom until she died in 2001. After a few moments I realised that the words on it capture the essence of this book in many respects in considering how we might all manage our lives, and to know what to do and when. This is something that often becomes difficult for many of us in our busy and demanding lives, no matter what we choose to do in them, although the unpredictable hand of fate can always overpower us when we least expect it. Perhaps my mother had been watching over my work during the three years I have spent compiling this book, as she had throughout my highly rewarding, if challenging, career in the Royal Navy:

God, grant me the serenity to accept the things I cannot change;
The strength to change the things I can change;
And wisdom to know the difference

(Attributed to Karl Paul Reinhold Niebuhr, 1937)

Bibliography

Andersson, B., & Ulvaeus, B. (Composers). (1977). Eagle. [ABBA, Performer] Sweden.

Andersson, B., & Ulvaeus, B. (Composers). (1978). Move on. [ABBA, Performer] Sweden.

Andersson, B., & Ulvaeus, B. (Composers). (1979). Chiquitita (from the Album 'Voulez-vous'). [ABBA, Performer] Sweden.

Barker, N. (1997). *Beyond Endurance*. Barnsley: Pen and Sword.

BBC. (2008). *Local History*. Retrieved February 2013, from 'Hampshire & Isle of Wight': http://www.bbc.co.uk/hampshire/content/articles/2007/03/26/haslar_march_feature.shtml

Bible. (1995). *Exodus 20:17 (New Revised Standard Version)*. Oxford: Oxford University Press.

Burns, K. a. (1986). *HMS Bulwark 1948-1984*. Liskeard, Cormwall: Maritime Books.

Cooksey, J. (2006). *Barnsley Pals: The 13th and 14th Battalions York & Lancaster Regiment*. Barnsley: Pen & Sword.

Daily Telegraph. (2012). *Jenny*. London: The Daily Telegraph.

Denver, J. (Composer). (1966). Leaving on a jet plane. [Peter, Paul, & Mary, Performers] United States.

Durham, J., & Reilly, D. (Composers). (1967). Colours of my life. [T. Seekers, Performer] Australia.

Greenbaum, N. (Composer). (1969). Spirit in the Sky. [N. Greenbaum, Performer] Reprise, United States.

Hennekens, C., & Buring, J. (1987). *Epidemiology in Medicine*. Toronto: Little, Brown and Company.

Hickman, K. (2013). *The Falklands War: An Overview*. Retrieved March 22nd, 2013, from: http://militaryhistory.about.com/od/battleswars1900s/p/falklands.htm

HMS Bulwark. (1971). *HMS Bulwark - 1969-71*. Plymouth: Clarke, Doble & Brendon Ltd.

Howson, L., & Nixon, J. (2006). *Intercepted at Sea: The human cost of insecure naval communications during two world wars*. Bognor Regis: Woodfield Publishing.

Jung, C. G. (1971). *Collected Works of C.G. Jung, Volume 6: Psychological Types*. Princeton: Princeton University Press.

Lennon, J., & MCartney, P. (Composers). (1968). Hey Jude. [T. Beatles, Performer] UK.

Luciana, M., & Collins, P. (2012). Incentive Motivation, Cognitive Control, and the Adolescent Brain: Is It Time for a Paradigm Shift? *Child Development Perspectives*, 1;6(4):392-399.

Mauritius Meteorological Office. (2012). *List of historical cyclones*. Retrieved October 2012, from Mauritius Meteorological Office: http://metservice.intnet.mu/?cat=28

Ministry of Defence. (2013). *Protecting our Nation's Interests*. Retrieved March 21st, 2013, from: http://www.royalnavy.mod.uk/The-Fleet/Ships/Weapons-Systems/Goalkeeper

Myers, I. B., & Myers, P. B. (1995). *Gifts Differing: Understanding Personality Type:* Mountain View, CA: Davies-Black Publishing.

Nixon, J., & Smith, B. A. (2006). *Mother's Apple Pie: The true story of Japanese POW Alan Nixon, 196 Field Ambulance, Royal Army Medical Corps (RAMC)*. Stockport: A. Lane Publications.

Oldfield, M. (Composer). (1983). Moonlight Shadow. [M. Oldfield, & M. Reilly, Performers] Denham, UK.

Parish, M., Edwards, M., & Spaeth, S. (Composers). (1971). Tell me why. [M. Salfka, Performer] United States.

Parkinson, B. (Composer). (1971). Mother of mine. [N. Reid, Performer] UK.

Parsons, M. (2000). *The Falklands War*. Sutton Publishing Ltd.

Phillips, J. (Composer). (1967). Sanfrancisco (Be sure to wear some flowers in your hair). [S. McKenzie, Performer] USA (MCA Music Publishing).

Redelmeier, D., & Greenwald, J. (2007). Competing risks of mortality with marathons: retrospective analysis. *British Medical Journal*, 22;335(7633):1275-1277.

Rousseau, J. J. (1762). *The Social Contract*. Public domain: Translated in 1782 by G. D. H. Cole .

Shakespeare, W. (1596). *Henry IV*.

Shakespeare, W. (1599). *Julius Caesar*. Oxford: Oxford University Press (2002).

Siegel, A. J., & colleagues, &. (2001). Effect of marathon running on inflammatory and hemostatic markers. *American Journal of Cardiology*, 88(8):918-920.

SMOPS, Royal Navy. (1985). Sultan - The Movie. Gosport, UK: Royal Navy (Wessex film & sound archive, Hampshire Recods Office). Written and produced by Sub-Lieutenant J. Nixon, R.N. and Lieutenant P. Newman, R.N.

Stevens, C. (Composer). (1971). Moonshadow. [C. Stevens, Performer] UK.

The Education Forum. (2013). *Divorce*. Retrieved April 2013, from The Education Forum: www.educationforum.co.uk

The Royal British Legion. (2013). *Literature review: UK veterans and homelessness*. Retrieved May 2013, from www.britishlegion.org.uk

Union Castle Line. (1975). *Extracts from the Ship's Official Log of R.M.S. "Windsor Castle" Voyage 108 Cape Town to Southampton via Las Palmas and Madeira, by Commodore H. Charnley*. Mccorquondale & Co. Ltd., England.

Abbreviations of RN Letters

A/CCWEMN - Acting Charge Chief Weapons Electrical Mechanician
AIB - Admiralty Interview Board
A/LREM - Acting Leading Radio Electrical Mechanic
A/POREL - Acting Petty Officer Radio Electrical Mechanic
AWOL - Absent Without Leave
BOAC - British Oversees Airways Corporation
BR - Book of Reference
BTEC - Business and Technical Education Council
C&G - City & Guilds
Cdr - Commander
CEM - Control Electrical Mechanic
CMG - Central Mess Galley
Comcen - Communications Centre
Col - Colonel
CPO - Chief Petty Officer
CREL - Chief Radio Electrician
DCN - Defence Communications Network
DO - Divisional Officer
DQs - Detention Quarters
DWEO - Deputy Weapons Electrical Officer
EMR - Electronic Maintenance Room
FAA - Fleet Air Arm
FLYCO - Flying Control Officer
FTC - Full Technological Certificate
G.C.E. - General Certificate of Education
GI - Gunnery Instructor
HF - High Frequency
HMS - Her Majesty's Ship
HNC - Higher National Certificate
IMS - International Military Staff
IO - Instructor Officer
JEM - Junior Electrical Mechanic
JI - Junior Instructor
JOEM - Junior Ordinance Electrical Mechanic
JREM - Junior Radio Electrical Mechanic
L/A - Local Acting
LCEM - Leading Control Electrical Mechanic
LEP - Local Employees
LMA - Leading Medical Assistant
LOEM - Leading Ordinance Electrical Mechanic
LREM - Leading Radio Electrical Mechanic
LSAOP - Long Service Advance of Pay
LRO - Leading Radio Operator
Lt - Lieutenant
Lt Cdr - Lieutenant Commander
LUF - Lowest Usable Frequency
LWEM (R) - Leading Weapons Electrical Mechanic (Radio)

MA - Medical Assistant
MAA - Master at Arms
Mech - Mechanician
MoD - Ministry of Defence
MUF - Maximum Usable Frequency
N.A.A.F.I. - Navy, Army and Air Force Institution
NATO - North Atlantic Treaty Organisation
OEM - Ordinance Electrical Mechanic
OIC - Officer in Charge
ONC - Ordinary National Certificate
PMO - Principal Medical Officer
PO - Petty Officer
POMEA - Petty Officer Marine Engineering Artificer
POREL – PO Radio Electrician
POREA – Petty Officer Radio Electrical Artificer
POMEM – Petty Officer Marine Engineering Mechanic
P.P.E. – Preliminary Professional Examination
P.Q.E. – Professional Qualifying Examination
PTI – Physical Training Instructor
PWO – Principal War Officer
QARNNS - Queen Alexandra's Royal Navy Nursing Service
R.A.F. - Royal Air Force
REA - Radio Electrical Artificer
REM - Radio Electrical Mechanic
RMECH - Radio Mechanician
RN - Royal Navy
RNC - Royal Naval College
RNH - Royal Naval Hospital
RO - Radio Operator
RPO - Regulating Petty Officer
RS - Radio Supervisor
SD - Special Duties (officer category)
SL - Supplementary List (officer category)
S/Lt - Sub Lieutenant
SRE - Ship's Radio Equipment
TS - Transmitter Station
UHF - Ultra High Frequency
WEA - Weapons Electrical Artificer
WEMN - Weapons Electrical Mechanician
WEM (R) Weapons Electrical Mechanic (Radio)
WEO - Weapons Electrical Officer
WRNS - Women's Royal Naval Service ('WRENS')